# Body Image

This text provides a comprehensive review of research on body image from psychology, sociology, and gender studies in men, women, and children.

There has been a significant increase in research on body image since the first edition of *Body Image* was published. This second edition is thoroughly revised and updated, and includes new empirical data. In addition to reviewing evidence for sociocultural influences on body image, the book reviews recent literature and includes new data on body-modification practices (cosmetic surgery, piercing, tattooing, and bodybuilding), and takes a critical look at interventions designed to promote positive body image. It also attempts to link body image to physical health, looking in particular at motivations for potentially health-damaging practices such as anabolic steroid use and cosmetic surgery.

The only text to date that provides a comprehensive view of body image research focusing on men and children as well as women, it will be invaluable to students and researchers in the area as well as those with an interest in body image and how to promote a positive body image.

**Sarah Grogan** has been involved in research into body image since 1990. She is particularly interested in promoting positive body images in men, women, and children, with a particular focus on the impact of body image and related behaviors on physical health.

# Body Image

Understanding body
dissatisfaction in men, women,
and children

Second edition

WITHDRAWN

**Sarah Grogan**

 Routledge
Taylor & Francis Group

LONDON AND NEW YORK

First published 2008
by Routledge
27 Church Road, Hove, East Sussex BN3 2FA

Simultaneously published in the USA and Canada
by Routledge
711 Third Avenue, New York NY 10017 (8th Floor)

*Routledge is an imprint of the Taylor & Francis Group,
an Informa business*

Copyright © 2008 Psychology Press

Typeset in Times by
RefineCatch Limited, Bungay, Suffolk

Paperback cover by Hannah Armstrong

*British Library Cataloguing in Publication Data*
A catalogue record for this book is available from the British Library

*Library of Congress Cataloging in Publication Data*
Grogan, Sarah, 1959–
    Body image : understanding body dissatisfaction in men, women,
and children / Sarah Grogan. – 2nd ed.
        p. cm.
    Includes bibliographical references and indexes.
    ISBN 978-0-415-35822-4 (hardcover) – ISBN 978-0-415-35821-7
(pbk.) 1. Body image—Social aspects—United States. 2. Body
image—Social aspects—Great Britain. I. Title
    BF697.5B63G76 2007
    306.4'613—dc22
                        2007008369

ISBN: 978-0-415-35822-4 (hbk)
ISBN: 978-0-415-35821-7 (pbk)

In memory of Edward Grogan

# Contents

# List of illustrations

## Plates

## Figures

# Preface to the second edition

This second edition of *Body Image: Understanding Body Dissatisfaction in Men, Women, and Children* updates literature reviewed in the first edition, and presents fresh data investigating factors influencing body image in men, women, and children. Data from qualitative and quantitative research in psychology, sociology, cultural studies, women's studies, and media studies are integrated, to provide a comprehensive summary of what we know about body image today.

Until the 1990s, most psychological investigations of body image were conducted with young women, largely because body image research in psychology has its roots in clinical psychology and psychiatric work focusing on eating disorders. Unfortunately, this has reinforced the idea that the psychology of body image is only relevant to young women, and that the construct only encompasses weight and shape concern. Although these are important, body image and its consequences are of relevance to men and women of all ages, and the concept incorporates more than just concern about shape and weight. The 1990s and the present decade have seen a significant shift in focus in favor of broadening the participant population in body image studies in psychology to incorporate boys, men, girls, older women and men, and "body image" into a multifaceted construct that includes more than weight and shape concern. Body image is defined in different ways depending on the specific areas of interest and aims of particular researchers, and there has been an exponential increase in the number of new and revised psychology measures that have been developed to assess dimensions of body image in the last ten years. An increasing interest in desire to be more muscular in both women and men has also produced a marked change in the ways that body image has been conceptualized by researchers from a variety of disciplines. This text reflects these changes and reviews work on body image in men and women of all ages, including consideration of cultural pressures to be slender and muscular and the effects of sociocultural factors on experiences of embodiment.

This text is intended for students of psychology, sociology, women's studies, men's studies, and media studies. It will hopefully be useful to anyone with an interest in body image.

Sarah Grogan
January 2007

# Acknowledgments

I would like to thank all the people who have given their expertise and their time to make this book possible. Thanks to all those who agreed to be interviewed or to complete questionnaires and who shared their experiences of body (dis)satisfaction.

Thanks to Jo Ann Campbell for her help and support with some of the literature searches conducted for this text. Thanks also to ex-students at Manchester Metropolitan University, Manchester, UK (Penny Cortvriend, Lisa Bradley, Helen Richards, Debbie Mee-Perone, Clare Donaldson, Wendy Hodkinson, and Nicola Wainwright), and at Santa Fe Community College, Florida, USA (Jacqueline Gardner, Renee Schert, Melissa Warren, Harry Hatcher, Damien Lavalee, Timothy Ford, and Rhonda Blackwell), for collecting data for the last edition of this book, some of which appear again in this version. Thank you to MSc students at Staffordshire University (Vivienne Hopkins, Jo Ann Campbell, and Beth Rhodes) for enabling me to include excerpts from your dissertations. I am also indebted to Paul Husband, Sarah Shepherd, and Ruth Evans for running interviews with steroid users; to Geoff Hunter for advice on anabolic steroids; and to Sam Wright for her work on all aspects of the steroid project. Thanks also to the late Precilla Choi for encouraging me to produce a second draft of this text and for helpful discussions on bodybuilding with women. Thank you to Lina Ricciardelli for invaluable conversations and support on boys' body image and work on ethnicity and body image, and to Marika Tiggemann and Tom Cash for inspiration at crucial periods. Also, many thanks to Caroline Haywood at Kobal and Kirsty Arkell at Retna for advice and help when choosing images for this book, to Pat Evans for help with French translations and contact for permissions, and special thanks to Tara Stebnicky at Routledge for all your help.

Thanks to all colleagues who have read various drafts and provided invaluable suggestions and support. In particular, thanks to Angie

Burns, Mark Forshaw, Lina Ricciardelli, Helen Fawkner, Brendan Gough, and Mark Conner. Thanks to the following for permission to include plates, figures, and tables: Musée du Louvre for Plates 1 (*Bathsheba*), 7 (*Study of Two Nude Figures*), and 11 (*The Turkish Bath*); Sterling and Francine Clark Art Institute for Plate 2 (*Blonde Bather*); Mary Evans Picture Library for Plate 3 (Flapper fashion); Kobal for Plates 4 (Marilyn Monroe), 8 (Marlon Brando), 9 (Dolph Lundgren), and 13 (Arnold Schwarzenegger); Retna Pictures Ltd for Plates 5 (Twiggy), 6 (Kate Moss), 10 (Robbie Williams), and 12 (Claudia Schiffer); Select Press for Figures 3.2 (Female body shapes), 6.2 (Female stimulus figures varying in breast size), and 6.4 (Male stimulus figures varying in chest size); Raven Publishers for Figures 3.1 (Figural rating scale for women) and 4.1 (Figural rating scale for men); Simon and Schuster for Figure 4.2 (Computerized body image test); and the American Psychological Association for Figure 6.1 (Female stimulus figures varying in WHR) and Figure 6.3 (Male stimulus figures varying in WHR).

Thank you to all friends, colleagues, and family who have provided encouragement and support, and especially Io Evans, Will Waldron, Simon Stanley, Rachel Davey, Linda Hammersley-Fletcher, Rachel Povey, Rosie Clements, Emily Buckley, and Sheila Ford.

Most of all, thanks to Mark Conner for consistent encouragement and support while I was writing and researching this book.

# 1  Introduction

In recent years, there has been a noticeable increase in academic and popular interest in body image. Researchers from a number of disciplines have become interested in factors that affect people's experiences of embodiment, and in the impact of body image on behavior. The significant rise in referral for cosmetic surgery operations, concerns about unhealthy eating, and an increase in the use of drugs designed to make men and women more muscular have inspired researchers to try to understand the motivations behind these behaviors and more general experiences of embodiment.

There has been a significant increase in interest in the psychology of body image in the last 30 years. Thomas Cash (2004) notes that there was an impressive escalation of body image and body (dis)satisfaction citations in the PsychINFO database from 726 in the 1970s, to 1,428 in the 1980s, to 2,477 in the 1990s; and the success of the dedicated journal *Body Image: An International Journal of Research*, which was first published in 2004, attests to the importance of this area of research within psychology in the 2000s, that is, the first decade of the twenty-first century. Psychological models of body image have also shown significant development in the last 10 years. In 2002, Thomas Cash presented a cognitive-behavioral model of body image development and experiences that emphasized the importance of cultural socialization, interpersonal characteristics, physical characteristics, and personality attributes in body image evaluation and investment (Cash, 2002, 2004). This model recognizes the reciprocal relationship between environmental events; cognitive, affective, and physical processes; and the individual's behaviors in determining body image, and has been influential in the ways that psychologists have talked about and researched body image in the last few years. There have also been significant developments in social psychology and feminist approaches to body image in the last 10 years that will be reviewed later in this book.

The sociology of the body became an established discipline in the 1990s, Bryan Turner (1992) coining the term "somatic society" to describe the newfound importance of the body in contemporary sociology. The success of the journal *Body and Society*, set up in Britain in the mid-1990s, demonstrates the high level of interest in the role of the body in social theory work. There has also been a significant increase in the popular interest in body image since the 1990s. In the 2000s, newspapers and magazines in Britain, Australia, Canada, and the USA have been replete with stories about cosmetic surgery and reducing diets (and the dangers of dieting), and critiques of the use of skinny models to advertise products (often placed adjacent to pictures of skinny models in advertisements), and there has been a recent trend of television "makeover" programs that include cosmetic surgery as part of the package to reduce body dissatisfaction in willing participants (*Ten Years Younger* in the UK and *The Swan* in the USA), communicating the message that cosmetic surgery is a legitimate way to reduce body image concerns.

Since the previous edition of this text (Grogan, 1999), one of the most notable changes has been an increased academic interest in factors influencing the desire for muscularity in both men and women. Researchers based in the USA, Canada, Australia, and Britain have developed an understanding of the motivations for, and experiences of, increased muscularity (Thompson and Cafri, 2007). This work has involved the development of psychology measurement scales that can be used to assess drive for muscularity in adults and children. Researchers in psychology, sociology, and gender studies have also investigated the experience of muscularity in men and women, including bodybuilders. The drive for muscularity in women is an area largely ignored in the psychology research literature until quite recently. Research on body image in children, especially boys, has also been an area of significant growth in the 2000s, along with a focus on developing ways of trying to help children become resistant to internalization of the thin/muscular cultural ideal. Various researchers have also engaged in some interesting debate around the potential positive and negative effects of sport and exercise on body image, and particularly gender differences in these effects. This text will review all these areas and will present an account of what we know about body image in the early 2000s.

Interest in the psychology and sociology of body image originated in the work of Paul Schilder in the 1920s. Prior to Schilder's work, body image research was almost exclusively limited to the study of distorted body perceptions caused by brain damage. Schilder developed this work to consider the wider psychological and sociological frameworks within which perceptions and experiences of body image take place. In *The Image and Appearance of the Human Body* (1950), he argued that body image is not just a perceptual construct, but also a reflection of attitudes and interactions with others. He was interested in the "elasticity" of body image, the reasons for fluctuations in perceived body size, feelings of lightness and heaviness, and the effects of body image on interactions with others. He defined body image as:

> the picture of our own body which we form in our mind, that is to say, the way in which the body appears to ourselves.
>
> (Schilder, 1950: 11)

Since 1950, researchers have taken "body image" to mean many different things, and have moved beyond Schilder's primarily perceptual definition. Kevin Thompson and colleagues in 1999 noted 16 different definitions of "body image" used by researchers and clinicians. These included weight satisfaction, size perception accuracy, appearance satisfaction, body satisfaction, appearance evaluation, appearance orientation, body concern, body esteem, body schema, and body percept. In an attempt to incorporate the key elements, the definition of body image that will be taken for this book is:

> a person's perceptions, thoughts, and feelings about his or her body.

This definition can be taken to include psychological concepts, such as perception and attitudes toward the body, as well as experiences of embodiment. Perceptual body image is usually measured by investigating the accuracy of body size estimation relative to actual size. Attitudinal body image is assessed by measures of four components: global subjective satisfaction (evaluation of the body), affect (feelings associated with the body), cognitions (investment in appearance, beliefs about the body), and behaviors (such as avoidance of situations where the body will be exposed). Psychological measures of body image assess one or more of these components (Thompson and Van Den Berg, 2002).

Although all aspects of body image will be discussed in this text, there is a focus on trying to understand the factors that influence body dissatisfaction in men, women, and children. Body dissatisfaction is defined here as:

a person's negative thoughts and feelings about his or her body.

Body dissatisfaction relates to negative evaluations of body size, shape, muscularity/muscle tone, and weight, and it usually involves a perceived discrepancy between a person's evaluation of his or her body and his or her ideal body (Cash and Szymanski, 1995).

In this book, body image will be investigated from both psychological and sociological viewpoints, because body image is a psychological phenomenon that is significantly affected by social factors. To understand it fully, we need to look not only at the experiences of individuals in relation to their bodies, but also at the cultural milieu in which the individual operates. Only by investigating the psychology and sociology of the body will it be possible to produce an explanation of body image that recognizes the interaction between individual and societal factors.

Body image is conceptualized here as subjective. There is no simple link between people's subjective experience of their bodies and what is perceived by the outside observer. This is obvious in distortion of body size (e.g., many young women who experience anorexia nervosa believe they are much heavier than they appear, and some highly muscled bodybuilders believe that they are less muscular than they are in reality), and in cases of "phantom limb" phenomena (in which people who have had limbs amputated report still feeling the missing limb). It is also relevant (though less obvious) to the large number of women and girls who "feel fat" although they are objectively of average (or below average) weight for their height, and to men who feel too thin or too fat although they are objectively of average size.

The image that an individual has of his or her body is largely determined by social experience. Body image is elastic and open to change through new information. Media imagery may be particularly important in producing changes in the ways that the body is experienced and evaluated, depending on the viewer's perception of the importance of those cues (Tiggemann, 2002). It is likely that some viewers are more sensitive to such cues than others. For instance, it has been suggested that adolescents are especially vulnerable because body image is particularly salient while they undergo the significant physical and psychological changes of puberty. Other groups who attach particular importance to body-related imagery (e.g., people with eating disorders, bodybuilders) may also be sensitized to media cues. Research has suggested that most people have key reference groups that furnish social information relevant to body image (friends, family, media). Since body image is socially constructed, it must be investigated and analyzed within its cultural context.

Promotion of positive body image is important in improving people's quality of life and physical health, and body image is implicated in a number of health-related behaviors. Although being dissatisfied with the way that we look and "feeling fat" can motivate us to exercise, it may also prevent us from engaging in organized sports activities such as joining a gym or exercising due to concern about whether we have the right kind of body to fit in with a sports culture that promotes a slender ideal. Body dissatisfaction and size underestimation may also lead to the use of anabolic steroids and other drugs to try to increase muscularity, with associated risks of blood-borne diseases if these are injected, as well as liver, kidney, and other health problems associated with their use. Body image factors may also influence whether we eat healthily and whether we restrain our eating. Positive body evaluation has been linked with healthy eating, and we are less likely to binge eat and engage in restrictive dieting and self-induced vomiting if we feel satisfied with the way that we look. Body concern can also affect our decision to quit smoking if we fear that we will gain weight as a result, and can lead us to undertake unnecessary cosmetic surgery, putting our health at risk.

This book investigates men's and women's body image, focusing in particular on cultural influences, and on the degree of body dissatisfaction in men and women of different ages and backgrounds. Theory and data from psychology, sociology, women's studies, and media studies are integrated to address the question of how men and women experience body shape, size, and weight. It will be argued that some body dissatisfaction is normative in women in the Western world from 8 years of age upward, and that this has a significant impact on behavior such that many women try to change their shape and weight and avoid activities that would involve exposing their bodies. Body image in men and boys will also be investigated. Data show that boys from as young as 8 years also show concern over being acceptably V-shaped with a well-developed upper body and slim hips, and that adult men's self-esteem is related to how good they feel about their body shape and weight. There is an emphasis in this text on understanding factors that promote satisfaction in women and men, and in using these to promote body satisfaction. Understanding how some people manage to resist social pressure to conform to the cultural ideal may be helpful in promoting positive body image in those less satisfied.

Chapter 2 reviews current research on culture and body image. It is argued that Western cultures prescribe a narrow range of body shapes as acceptable for men and women, and that those whose body shape and size fall outside this range may encounter prejudice, especially if they are heavier than is culturally acceptable. The debate as to the basis for current Western cultural ideals is reviewed. Arguments from the biological determinist perspective (suggesting a biological basis for body shape preferences), and from social psychology and sociology (stressing cultural relativity), are evaluated. An historical review of trends during the twentieth century shows how cultural ideas of acceptable body shape have changed radically over the years, particularly for women. Myths about weight and health are questioned, and the impact of the dieting industry on the lives of men and women is examined. New trends relating to body image (including resistance to idealized imagery and the diet industry and cultural shifts in favor of body-modification practices) are reviewed. Chapter 2 provides a backdrop for the data on body dissatisfaction presented in subsequent chapters, demonstrating the extent of sociocultural pressures in Western societies.

Chapter 3 looks specifically at body dissatisfaction in women. Different techniques that have been used to assess body image are evaluated, along with findings based on each technique, to determine the extent of body dissatisfaction and the reasons why women are dissatisfied. Women's attempts to modify their bodies through cosmetic surgery, dieting, exercise, bodybuilding, and anabolic steroid use are investigated, reflecting data from psychology, sociology, and women's studies. New data are presented from women who have had cosmetic surgery, who engage in bodybuilding, and who use anabolic steroids. The chapter ends with a review of cultural pressures on women to conform to the socially acceptable "slim but shapely" body shape, drawing mostly on work from contemporary feminist writers on the social construction of femininity.

Chapter 4 focuses on body satisfaction in men. Work conducted prior to the late 1980s tended to focus on body image in women. A review of men's body satisfaction is timely in the light of recent arguments that there has been a cultural shift in the 1990s and 2000s such that men are under increased social pressure to be slender and muscular, and because more and more research on body image and the experience of embodiment is being conducted on men. Men's satisfaction is evaluated, using work from sociology and psychology and introducing new data from interviews with young men, to determine whether men seem to be aware of societal pressures, and whether these pressures affect their body satisfaction. Recent work on bodybuilding and anabolic steroid use is reviewed, including new data from interviews with male bodybuilders, some of whom use anabolic steroids, to understand the psychological and social effects of becoming more muscular, and the motivations behind taking anabolic steroids in spite of negative side effects. Work on the social construction of masculinity is also reviewed, to produce a picture of social pressures on men, and to evaluate the extent of recent cultural changes on men's acceptance of their body shape and size. Chapter 5 looks directly at studies of the effects of media pressure. Theory and data from psychology, sociology, and media studies are discussed in relation to effects of exposure to idealized media images of attractive photographic models. Content analyses of media portrayal of the male and female body are reviewed. Empirical evidence from studies linking media exposure to body dissatisfaction is reviewed and evaluated. Theories of media influence are reviewed, along with their implications for observing body-related media imagery. Data from surveys and laboratory experiments are complemented by data from interviews to evaluate the mechanisms through which media role models may affect body satisfaction in men and women. The trend in the 2000s for mainstream magazine and newspaper journalists to critique the use of extremely thin models in the media is discussed, along with ideas for reducing the effects of media imagery based on current psychological and sociological theories.

Chapter 6 investigates the effects of age, ethnicity, social class, and sexuality on body satisfaction. Questionnaire studies that have charted changes in satisfaction throughout the life span are discussed, along with relevant data from interviews of children and adolescents. Dissatisfaction is identified in the accounts provided by children as young as 8 years, and the reasons for this dissatisfaction are discussed. There is discussion of ethnicity and body dissatisfaction, evaluating claims that black women and men are more satisfied with their body shape and size in the context of a subculture where plumpness may be perceived as attractive and erotic. Social class differences in body satisfaction are discussed within a social context that associates slenderness with the middle and upper socioeconomic classes, especially for women. Finally, differences in body satisfaction in heterosexual men and women, gay men, and lesbians is investigated, including an evaluation of evidence suggesting that lesbian subculture protects against body dissatisfaction and that gay male subculture promotes dissatisfaction.

In the concluding chapter, arguments presented in the earlier chapters are summarized, with an exploration of their implications for men's and women's health. This chapter summarizes factors that seem to predict body satisfaction, to identify ways to counter social pressures and develop positive body image in men, women, and children.

This book presents a comprehensive review of the variety of influences on men's and women's body image and the behavioral effects of these influences. It also presents original data relating to body image in men, women, and children. It provides an evaluation of what we know about body image in the 2000s, and makes concrete suggestions for how we might go about trying to promote body satisfaction at individual and societal levels.

# 2 Culture and body image

This chapter explores the effects of cultural influences on body image. Cultural prejudice in favor of slenderness and against overweight is placed in its psychological and sociological context, with a critical evaluation of the roles of biology and culture in promoting the slim ideal.

## The idealization of slenderness

In affluent Western societies, slenderness is generally associated with happiness, success, youthfulness, and social acceptability. Being overweight is linked to laziness, lack of willpower, and being out of control. For women, the ideal body is slim. For men, the ideal is slenderness and moderate muscularity. Nonconformity to this ideal has a variety of negative social consequences. Overweight (for both men and women) is seen as physically unattractive and is also associated with other negative characteristics.

Tracing the social meanings attached to slimness over the years, Susan Bordo (2003) shows how, starting at the end of the last century, excess flesh (for men and women) came to be linked with low morality, reflecting personal inadequacy or lack of will. This has continued into the 2000s, where the outward appearance of the body is seen as a symbol of personal order or disorder. Slenderness symbolizes being in control. The muscled body has recently lost its associations with manual labor and has become another symbol of willpower, energy, and control. The firm, toned body is seen as representing success. Most people do not have slim, toned bodies naturally, so they have to be constantly vigilant (through exercise and diet) so as to conform to current ideals. Bordo argues that the key issue in the current idealization of slenderness is that the body is kept under control:

The ideal here is of a body that is absolutely tight, contained, bolted down, firm.

(Bordo, 2003: 190)

This links the spare, thin, feminine ideal with the solid, muscular, masculine ideal, since both require the eradication of loose flesh and both emphasize firmness. In the preface to the 2003 edition of *Unbearable Weight*, and reflecting on the lack of significant change since the 1990s, Bordo notes that the pressure to have a spare, hard body is still intense in the 2000s despite cultural discourses suggesting that variety in body shapes is a positive thing. Noting that Beyoncé Knowles and Jennifer Lopez dwell on how happy they are with their "bodacious bottoms," she suggests that having a body that is not thin is acceptable only if it is worked out and hard:

Sexy booty is OK, apparently, only if it's high and hard, and if other body-parts are kept firmly in check. Beyoncé is comfortable with her body because she works on it constantly. On the road she does five hundred sit-ups a night.

(Bordo, 2003: xxii)

People who do not conform to the slender ideal face prejudice throughout their life span. Thomas Cash argues that overweight people are treated differently from childhood. Children prefer not to play with their overweight peers, and assign negative adjectives to drawings of overweight people. This prejudice continues into adulthood, when overweight people tend to be rated as less active, intelligent, hardworking, successful, athletic, and popular than slim people. People who are overweight are likely to find more difficulty in renting property, being accepted by "good" US colleges, and getting jobs than their slimmer peers (Cash, 1990).

In an early study of stereotypes assigned to different body types, Marika Tiggemann and Esther Rothblum (1988) asked large groups of American and Australian college students about their stereotypes of fat and thin men and women. They were asked to rate the extent to which eight qualities were typical of thin men and women and fat men and women. Men and women in both cultures reported negative stereotypes of fat people. Although fat people were seen as warmer and friendlier, confirming the traditional stereotype of the fat and jolly person, they were also viewed as less happy, more self-indulgent, less self-confident, less self-disciplined, lazier, and less attractive than thin people. These differences were more marked for judgments of fat women than fat men. The results indicate negative stereotyping of plumper people, especially women, in these college students (Tiggemann and Rothblum, 1988). What was particularly interesting was that there were no differences in stereotyping between students who were fat and those who were thin. Even those who were overweight had negative stereotypes of fat people. This finding has been replicated by other studies showing that individuals perceived to be overweight are rated as lazy, unhealthy, and deserving of teasing and ridicule (Lewis *et al.*, 1997; Teachman and Brownell, 2001; Grogan and Richards, 2002; Greenleaf *et al.*, 2004). Christy Greenleaf and colleagues (2004) found that their participants associated terms describing the heavier weight body (such as "fat" and "obese") with negative personal characteristics such as "lazy," "gross," slow," and "disgusting."

The tendency to link physical attractiveness with positive personal qualities has been documented since the 1970s, when Dion and colleagues coined the saying "What is beautiful is good" (Dion *et al.*, 1972: 285). They suggested that people tend to assign more favorable personality traits and life outcomes to those they perceive as attractive. In an updated review of evidence in this area, Alice Eagley and colleagues (1991) suggested that the effects of the physical attractiveness stereotype are strongest for perceptions of social competence (sociability and popularity). Negative stereotyping of overweight people may be a specific aspect of the physical attractiveness stereotype that refers specifically to assignment of negative traits to those who have a body size and shape that is not considered attractive by dominant groups in Western culture.

It is likely that causal attributions also affect responses to overweight people. If overweight is seen as being caused by factors within the individual's control (through overeating and lack of exercise), then overweight people are more likely to be stigmatized. For many people in the USA and other Western countries, being perceived as overweight is the ultimate failure and represents a public demonstration of weakness of will (Lewis *et al.*, 1997). Christian Crandall and Rebecca Martinez (1996) compared attitudes to being overweight among students from the USA and Mexico. The USA was chosen because it has been considered to be the most individualistic culture in the world (Hofstede, 1980). That is, US culture (in general) values independence, and tends to perceive individuals as responsible for their own fates. Mexico, on the other hand, was thirty-second out of the 53 countries ranked for individualism by Hofstede, and is generally perceived to be a culture that emphasizes interdependence and connection, with more focus on external, cultural influences on behavior. Crandall and Martinez predicted that Mexican students would be less likely to see being over-weight as within an individual's control, and less likely to stigmatize someone for being overweight. They supported both these hypotheses, finding that antifat attitudes were less prevalent among Mexican students and that Mexican students were less likely to believe that weight gain is under personal control. US participants were more likely to agree that fat people have little willpower and that being fat is their own fault. Crandall and Martinez argue that antifat attitudes are part of an individualistic Western ideology that holds individuals responsible for their life outcomes. The Crandall and Martinez study is typical of others in the literature, since it stresses that prejudice against overweight is culturally bound and depends on attribution of blame. Within Western ideology, being overweight is perceived to violate the cultural ideal of self-denial and self-control. In fact, there is a growing body of evidence that overweight results, at least in part, from genetic factors (Monaghan, 2005a). However, people still tend to hold the erroneous belief that the individual is "to blame" for increased body weight, because it fits ideological beliefs of personal responsibility. This results in prejudice against people who do not conform to the slender cultural ideal.

## The basis of body shape ideals

The debate continues on why Western culture, in particular, shows a preference for slenderness. On the one hand, biologists and some psychologists have suggested that these body shape preferences derive from biology. They argue that these ideals are based on the fact that slenderness is more healthy than overweight. On the other hand, theorists who have looked at cultural differences in body shape preferences at different times and in different cultures have tended to suggest that biology plays only a minor role in the idealization of slenderness, and that it is largely learned. These two views will be evaluated here.

### Body weight and health

Biological arguments stress the importance of slenderness for health (and the unhealthiness of overweight). Slenderness has not always been linked with health. At the start of the twentieth century, thinness was associated with illness in the USA and in Britain, because of its link with tuberculosis (Bennett and Gurin, 1982). More recently, extreme thinness has come to be associated with AIDS. Indeed, AIDS is known as "slim" in some African countries. The cultural effects of this association between thinness and illness in Western industrialized countries may become apparent over the next decade, but, at present, thinness does not generally produce the negative stereotypes that are found in much poorer nations. Instead, there is a general belief that to be plump is unhealthy, and that thinness is an indicator of good health. However, this is a matter of significant debate in the literature on weight and health.

In order to determine the health risks of overweight, it is first of all necessary to draw a distinction between mild to moderate overweight and obesity. Overweight is usually defined as having a body-mass index (BMI) (see below) of 25–29.9 kg/m$^2$, and obesity as having a BMI of 30 or more. Obesity has generally been seen as harmful to health and has been associated with heart disease, hypertension, and diabetes. According to Kelly Brownell and Judith Rodin,

> Obesity is a major cause of morbidity and mortality. To argue that greater levels of excess weight are not associated with increased risk is to dismiss an abundant and consistent literature.
>
> (Brownell and Rodin, 1994: 783)

However, overweight has generally not been linked with excess mortality (Flegal *et al.*, 2005), and many authors have argued that overweight represents no significant health risk. This sounds straightforward, but in fact there is very little agreement as to the cutoff point between these two categories. Although it is generally believed that obesity is an objectively defined medical condition, definitions vary, so that the same person may be considered overweight, obese, or within the normal range, depending upon which measure is used, and when the measure is taken. In the UK, the most widely used measure is BMI, also known as Quetelet's index. BMI is obtained by dividing weight in kilograms by squared height in meters. The normal range of BMI is 20–25. Those with BMI of 25–30 may be classified as overweight, and those over 30 as obese (British Heart Foundation, 1994). The advantage of BMI is that it controls for a person's height. However, the scale is only valid if it is assumed that adults should not gain weight during adulthood. Moderate weight gain with increasing age is healthy (Andres *et al.*, 1993). This means that classifications of older people as obese need to be interpreted with caution. BMI also does not take into account body composition, and highly muscular people (such as bodybuilders and some other sports people) may fall into the overweight or obese category because their high levels of muscularity mean that they weigh heavily in spite of having very low levels of body fat (Bee, 2006).

A measure of body weight that is still widely used in the USA is based on people's weight relative to their frame size (small, medium, or large). Weight is compared with a standard weight table, and obesity is commonly defined as weight that is at least 20 percent above the ideal weight for a person's frame size. Different levels of obesity are sometimes defined: 21–30 percent above ideal weight—mild; 31–50 percent—moderate; 51–75 percent—severe; 76–100 percent—massive; and 101 percent or more—morbid (see Hanna *et al.*, 1981). As a standard, this has been extensively criticized. Norms are based on life insurance applicants in 1959 who were white, male, middle-class, and of northern European descent (Bennett and Gurin, 1982), and are not necessarily applicable to other groups. The norms assume no change in weight after age 25, and that people can be categorized by frame size, with little guidance as to how to do this. The norms were revised in 1979, and the results indicated that the ideal weights were now at least 10 lb heavier than they had been in 1959. This change meant that some people who had previously been labeled obese no longer fell into this category, emphasizing the cultural specificity of the classification scheme. This has caused some commentators to be highly critical of weight tables, which have been dismissed as "arbitrary, random and meaningless" (Gaesser, 2002: 106).

Yet another way of defining obesity is in terms of the extent of subcutaneous body fat rather than general body weight. Skin-fold thickness measures involve applying calipers to various target areas of the body to measure the thickness of the fold. This gives a direct measure of body fat, but assumes that people do not gain fat with age. This means that norms (derived from young adults) are not valid for older adults. This may be a particular problem when assessing women, who carry more subcutaneous fat than men. From birth, the thickness of subcutaneous fat is greater in females, and this increases through the life span. By age 55–9, women (on average) have skin-fold thickness between 42 percent (triceps) and 79 percent (subscapular) thicker than men (Greil, 1990). Estimates of obesity in older women may be inflated if norms based on younger women are used, because of the significant progressive increase in fat distribution in women that is normal through the life span. Moreover, the skin-fold thickness measure has low inter-rater reliability (i.e., different raters produce varying estimates), is uncomfortable for the person being assessed, and is time-consuming (Rothblum, 1990). Largely because of these problems, most researchers use either BMI or the Metropolitan Life Insurance Company Tables to decide whether a person should be categorized as obese. However, these measures are flawed, and recent evidence suggests that a measure that is more predictive of health problems is waist circumference, since most health problems correlate with fat collected in the abdominal region (Bee, 2006).

In addition to problems over definitions of obesity (and, by inference, the level at which overweight represents a health risk), there are important shortcomings in research design in this area. Evaluation of research is difficult because of reliance on correlational data. Most studies have looked at mortality and target health factors in a sample of people (usually men) of different weights. It is obvious that extraneous variables may operate to confound the relationship between weight and health, such as frequency of stringent dieting in the obese, which may itself be deleterious to health (Rothblum, 1990). It has also been suggested that body fat distribution may be as important as degree of overweight in predicting health risks (Taylor, 1995). Lee Monaghan (2005a) critiques the link between obesity and health, making a strong case that cardiorespiratory fitness, not fatness, is important in predicting mortality rates, and showing that obese men who were fit had similar mortality rates to lean men who were fit, and that active obese individuals had lower morbidity and mortality rates than normal-weight people who were sedentary. He argues that the case for a link between obesity and health is far from proven and suggests that:

> The highly publicised war against fat is about moral judgements and panic (manufactured fear and loathing). It is about social inequality (class, gender, generational and racial bias), political expediency and organisational and economic interests.
>
> (Monaghan, 2005a: 309)

Tom Sanders, a British nutritionist, argues that being slightly overweight can have positive effects on health, particularly for women. He argues that being plump means that the heart has to work harder during exercise, perhaps explaining why more overweight than thin people survive heart attacks. Plumper women are less likely to experience early menopause, heart disease, and osteoporosis than thin women. He argues that the health advantages of being slightly overweight have been largely ignored because of cultural prejudice against overweight (Sanders and Bazelgette, 1994). Esther Rothblum (1990) also argues that there is no conclusive evidence that being moderately overweight is bad for health. She suggests that medical concern with overweight is grounded on cultural prejudice against people who are overweight, rather than on realistic health risks. This has been supported more recently by other authors who have suggested that overweight has become a visible marker of poverty and inferior social status (Campos, 2004), and that "fat bigotry" in the medical profession may lead doctors to focus on weight loss and to ignore more important health risks, and so compromise patient health (Monaghan, 2005a). Clearly, this issue has generated controversy. The most parsimonious explanation of the data as they stand at present is that severe overweight may represent a health risk to some individuals, but moderate overweight (BMI 25–30) probably represents a minimal health risk or may even be advantageous, particularly to women. The belief that slenderness is healthier than moderate overweight is not borne out by medical research (Monaghan, 2005a; Rich, 2005). This suggests that social pressures to be slender are based more on cultural aesthetic preferences than health concerns.

## Culture and body shape preferences

Many authors have argued that cultural differences are primarily responsible for body shape ideals. Data mostly derive from studies of historical differences in body shape preferences, and from studies of differences between different cultural groups. Here evidence for historical changes in body shape fashions in the Western world will be reviewed, followed by some evidence of cultural variation in body shape preferences.

## Historical trends: portrayal of the female body

There is general agreement that the social pressure to conform to the slender ideal is greater on women than on men. The idealization of slenderness in women is often viewed as the product of an historical evolution that has occurred over the past century. Within Western industrialized cultures, there have been many changes over the years in the body shape and size that is considered attractive and healthy, especially for women. It is possible to trace a cultural change in the ideal body from the voluptuous figures favored from the Middle Ages to the turn of the twentieth century, to the thin body types favored by the fashion magazines of today.

Plumpness was considered fashionable and erotic until relatively recently. From the Middle Ages, the "reproductive figure" was idealized by artists. Fleshiness and a full, rounded stomach were emphasized as a symbol of fertility (Fallon, 1990). The female body was frequently represented with full, rounded hips and breasts. This trend is represented in the fleshy bodies painted by Rubens in the 1600s, and in Rembrandt van

Rijn's *Bathsheba* (1654), which portrays a woman with a plump body, and which represented the aesthetic ideal of its time (Plate 1).

This trend is also evident in the fleshy bodies painted by Rubens in the 1600s and by Renoir in the 1880s. Renoir's *Blonde Bather* (1881) (Plate 2) portrays a healthy-looking, plump figure, idealized as the antithesis to the taut male body portrayed around this time.

Slender figures were not seen as attractive until the twentieth century. In fact, Manet's *Olympia* (1863) (which he considered his masterpiece) was denounced when it was shown in 1865, because the subject was not considered sufficiently plump to be erotic (Myers and Copplestone, 1985). Various authors have dated the origin of the idealization of slimness in Western culture to the 1920s, and it is argued that the thin

*Plate 1* Rembrandt van Rijn, *Bathsheba* (1654).

*Source*: Musée du Louvre © Photo RMN, Jean Schormans

*Plate 2* Pierre-Auguste Renoir, *Blonde Bather* (1881).

ideal is the outcome of successful marketing by the fashion industry, which became the standard of cultural beauty in the industrialized affluent societies of the twentieth century (Gordon, 1990). Clothes fashions were represented by hand-drawn illustrations until the 1920s, when they started to be photographed and widely distributed in mass-market fashion magazines. These magazines presented a fantasy image of how women should look. The fashions themselves demanded a molding of the female body, because each look suited a particular body shape (Orbach, 1993). Flapper fashion, which originated after the First World War, demanded a boy-like, flat-chested figure to show off the straight, low-waisted dresses to advantage (Plate 3).

At this stage middle- and upper-class women began binding their breasts with foundation garments to flatten their silhouettes (Caldwell, 1981). They used starvation diets and vigorous exercise to try to get their bodies to the preadolescent, breast-less, hip-less ideal (Silverstein *et al.*, 1986; LaFrance *et al.*, 2000), and in 1920 a conference of the New York Academy of Science was convened to study the new phenomena of eating disorders. Winners of the "Miss America" beauty contest at this time had average bust–waist–hip measurements of 32–25–35. In the 1930s and 1940s, ideals moved toward a more shapely figure, epitomized by Jean Harlow and Mae West in the 1930s and Jane Russell in the 1940s. The mean measurements of Miss America winners changed to 34–25–35 (an increase of 2 inches in bust size from the previous decade) in the 1930s, and to 35–25–35 in the 1940s. Breasts became fashionable, along with the clothes that emphasized them. Lana Turner and Jane Russell became famous as "sweater girls." In the 1950s, this trend continued, when the Hollywood movie industry and the fashion industries promoted large breasts (along with tiny waists and slim legs). Marilyn Monroe personified this trend (Plate 4), and was the first *Playboy* centerfold.

Miss America winners increased in bust and hip measurements in the 1950s, and reduced in waist measurement, so that the body was (on average) an exaggerated hourglass shape of 36–23–36.

In the 1950s there was also a significant move toward slimness. Grace Kelly and Audrey Hepburn were slim (rather than buxom) and were portrayed to movie-goers as symbolizing sophistication (rather than sensuality). They became role models for some young women, and slimness became associated with the upper classes (Mazur, 1986). The trend for slimness became particularly acute in the 1960s, when the fashion model Twiggy became the role model for a generation of young women (Plate 5). She had a flat-chested, boyish figure, and weighed 96 lb (Freedman, 1986).

*Plate 3* Flapper fashion.

*Source*: Mary Evans Picture Library

*Plate 4*  Marilyn Monroe.

*Source*: United Artists (courtesy Kobal)

Slimness came to exemplify unconventionality, freedom, youthfulness, and a ticket to the "Jet-Set" life in 1960s Britain, and was adopted as the ideal by women of all social classes (Orbach, 1993). Miss America winners also were slimmer and taller in the 1960s than in the previous

*Plate 5* Twiggy.
*Source*: © King Collection/Retna UK

decade, with an increase of about an inch in height and a weight loss of about 5 lb by 1969 (Mazur, 1986). This trend occurred across Europe and the USA. Studies of the portrayal of the female body in the media have reliably found that models became thinner and thinner between the 1960s and 1980s. For example, models in *Vogue* magazine became gradually thinner, and even *Playboy* centerfolds became taller and leaner so that, although their breasts remained large, Playmates became slim and nearly hipless in the 1980s (Fallon, 1990). This trend for thinness as a standard of beauty became even more marked in the 1990s than it had been in the 1980s. In the 1980s, models were slim and looked physically fit, with lithe, toned bodies. *Time* magazine, in August 1982, argued that the new ideal of beauty was slim and strong, citing Jane Fonda and Victoria Principal as examples of the new ideal of beauty. In Britain and the USA, the slim, toned figure of Jerry Hall epitomized this ideal. The 1990s saw a departure from this trend with the emergence of "waif" models with very thin body types, perhaps the most famous of these being Kate Moss (Plate 6), who has a similar body shape to Twiggy from the 1960s.

Although the three most highly paid supermodels of the mid-1990s were not "waifs" (Cindy Crawford, Claudia Schiffer, and Christy Turlington), designers and magazine editors often chose to use extremely thin models such as Kate Moss to advertise their clothes and beauty products. The late 1990s saw the rise of "heroin chic"; that is, fashion houses made very thin models up to look like stereotypical heroin users, with black eye make-up, blue lips, and matted hair. In a *Newsweek* article of August 1996, Zoe Fleischauer, a model who was recovering from heroin addiction, told the interviewer that models are encouraged to look thin and exhausted:

> They [the fashion industry] wanted models that looked like junkies. The more skinny and f——ed up you look, the more everyone thinks you're fabulous.
>
> (Schoemer, 1996: 51)

In the late 1990s, the model Emma Balfour publicly condemned the fashion industry for encouraging young models to take stimulants to stay thin, and for ignoring signs of heroin addiction (Frankel, 1998), and US President Clinton denounced "heroin chic" in the wake of fashion photographer Davide Sorrenti's death from a heroin overdose. In 2000, the Women's Unit of the British Labour government were so concerned about the potential effects on young women's health of representations of magazine and other media images of "waif" models that they convened a meeting to discuss the potential links between eating problems and these media images. This Body Summit prompted a flurry of articles discussing the potential link between thin images and young women's body image and eating, most of which suggested that magazines and newspapers needed to review their practices (e.g., Reid, 2000). However, irrespective of this moral panic in the early 2000s, the extremely thin Western ideal has been maintained into the mid-decade

*Plate 6* Kate Moss.

*Source*: © Marineau/Starface/Retna UK

(Bordo, 2003; Wykes and Gunter, 2005). In addition, digital modification of images in magazines now means that virtually every fashion image is digitally modified. Susan Bordo (2003) notes that digital modification of images means that we are being educated to shift our perception of what a normal woman's body looks like, so that we see our own bodies as wanting because they do not match an unrealistic, polished, slimmed, and smoothed ideal:

> These images are teaching us how to see. Filtered, smoothed, polished, softened, sharpened, rearranged. And passing. Digital creations, visual cyborgs, teaching us what to expect from flesh and blood.
>
> (Bordo, 2003: xviii)

### Historical trends: portrayal of the male body

Representation of the male body also has an interesting history. Myers and Copplestone (1985) note that sculptors in ancient Greece were keenly interested in the problems of representing the anatomy of the human figure in a realistic form, and that it was at this stage that lifelike male nudes started to appear. Men were often presented nude, whereas women were represented clothed in cloaks and undergarments. The male body was revered and considered more attractive than the female body. In the seventh century BC, a trend developed for a broad-shouldered, narrow-hipped ideal that has become known as the "Daedalic" style, after the mythical Daedalus, who, according to legend, was the first Greek sculptor. At this stage, the male body was idealized and presented in a strictly stylized way, with emphasis on clearly defined muscles that were carved into a surface pattern on the marble.

Idealization of the male body can also be found in the art of the Roman Empire, where the epitome of physical beauty for the Romans, who hated obesity and idealized slenderness in their paintings and sculpture, was the slim, muscular warrior. In Renaissance art, too, the male body was traditionally presented nude, emulating the physique represented in classical Greek sculpture. The naked, muscular male body which represented this aesthetic ideal can be seen in Signorelli's *Study of Two Nude Figures* (1503) (Plate 7).

The male body continued to dominate art until the mid-nineteenth century, when artists such as Courbet shifted the erotic focus from the male body to the female body. From then until the 1980s, the male body was rarely idealized in art, except in paintings and photography aimed at a gay male audience. However, there were exceptions. Thomas Eakins

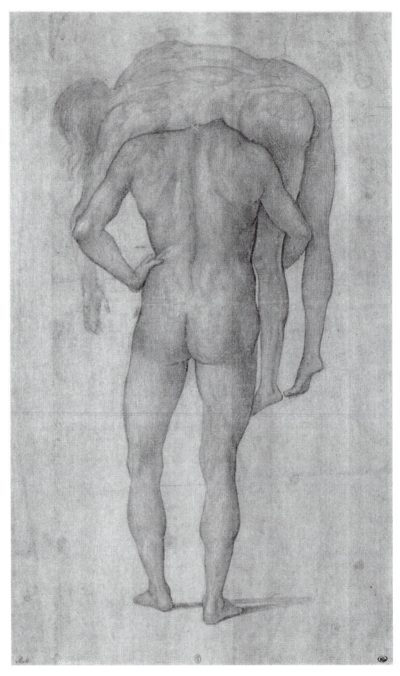

*Plate 7* Luca Signorelli, *Study of Two Nude Figures* (1503).

*Source*: Musée du Louvre © Photo RMN, Michèle Bellot

in the late nineteenth century (in the series *Thomas Eakins at 45 to 50*) photographed his own nude body, in defiance of the convention that male bodies should not be shown to a heterosexual audience. However, his body is not presented in an idealized form. On the contrary, it is seen as mature and fleshy, without the firm muscles usually portrayed in pictures of the male body. Another notable exception to this general trend was the idealization of the male body in Nazi propaganda. Leni Riefenstahl's photographs of the 1936 Olympic Games (*Schönheit im olympischen Kampf*) were modeled on classical Greek poses, and were used by the Nazi propaganda machine to represent the Teutonic ideal. This ideal (highly muscled and engaged in athletic pursuits) is echoed in images in the specialist bodybuilding magazines that emerged in Europe in the 1940s (Ewing, 1994). In publicity photographs explicitly aimed at a female audience, the Hollywood idols Rock Hudson, Kirk Douglas, Marlon Brando, and James Dean were also portrayed semiclothed, in poses designed to flatter their muscularity (Meyer, 1991) (see Plate 8).

However, it was not until the 1980s that idealized images of the naked (or seminaked) male body started to become common in mainstream Western media. The 1980s and 1990s saw an increase in the objectification of the nude male body in photographs that follow the conventions of photographing the female nude (eyes or face averted or not visible). Some of these photographs were specifically aimed at gay men, such as those by Robert Mapplethorpe, but entered the mainstream market (Pultz, 1995). The advent of the magazine *For Women* and the appearance of male strippers and dancers such as the Chippendales in the 1990s, blurred the traditional boundaries between men as viewers and women as the viewed. Muscular actors such as Dolph Lundgren exemplified the well-muscled male ideal as portrayed in the popular media in the 1990s (Plate 9).

The 1990s were an important turning point, as the male body lost its originally homoerotic connotations, and advertisers felt happy to use the naked male torso in mainstream advertising to sell everything from ice cream to perfume and orange juice. Lisa O'Kelly (1994) discusses the influence of gay culture in making men's bodies more visible, showing that the iconography of gay culture has moved into the mainstream, blurring the edges of men and women's sexual identities, and extending the range of images that are considered acceptable for men:

> Once advertisers would have been fearful of linking their products with images that might have been thought homoerotic. Now even Marks and Spencer advertises its socks with pictures of hunky men. . . . Mainstream women's publications such as *Marie Claire*

*Plate 8* Marlon Brando.

*Source*: Courtesy Kobal

> regularly feature articles on men and their bodies and have no
> qualms about including revealing pictures.
>
> (O'Kelly, 1994: 32)

The muscular physique was preferred by advertisers, although male
"waif" figures also made an appearance in the 1990s. Greg Buckle (head

*Plate 9* Dolph Lundgren.
*Source:* Courtesy Kobal

of the male division at the Storm model agency) confirms that their preferred look for men in the 1990s was

> slimmed down—the male waif is what everyone's after.
>
> (O'Kelly, 1994: 32)

Peter Baker (1994) argued that there were sound commercial reasons for this increase in the visual portrayal of the male body in the media. Cosmetics companies came to realize that there was a gap in the market for male cosmetics, and that men need to be persuaded to buy them.

They had to find a way of persuading men that it's actually macho to use a moisturiser and not fey to have a facial, hence the pictures of hunks splashing on the perfume.

(Baker, 1994: 132)

Baker argued that the portrayal of idealized images of men's bodies in the media is likely to lead to increasing problems with self-image and body satisfaction in men. This has been echoed in the 2000s by Karen Henwood and colleagues (2002), who have argued that men are increasingly defined by their bodies, and that media representations of male bodies present a slender and muscular ideal linked with aspirational consumer goods aimed at men:

> Media advertising routinely depicts in positive ways youthful toned muscular male bodies or focuses on style in men's clothing and physical appearance.
>
> (Henwood *et al.*, 2002: 183)

In fact, there has been a growing preoccupation with weight and body image in men, which parallels this increased "visibility" of the male body (Pope *et al.*, 2000). Harrison Pope and colleagues, in *The Adonis Complex*, note that contemporary actors dwarf Hollywood icons of the 1950s and 1960s, and cite evidence that the average *Playgirl* centerfold man lost 12 lb of fat while gaining approximately 27 lb of muscle in the 25 years leading up to the turn of the century, and Roberto Olivardia (2002) suggests that this is paralleled in men's dissatisfaction with the ways that they look, especially with their chests and muscle tone. Don McCreary and colleagues have carried out extensive work on men's drive for muscularity (see McCreary and Sasse, 2000, 2002; McCreary *et al.*, 2006), showing the importance of the muscular ideal for men, and demonstrating links between desire for muscles and low self-esteem, depression, and psychological distress (see also Thompson and Cafri, 2007). Clearly, social pressure on men is different and less extreme than that on women, since men still tend to be judged in terms of achievements rather than looks (Bordo, 2003). However, men are under increased social pressure to conform to the muscular, well-toned, mesomorphic (medium-sized) shape, and increases in anabolic steroid use and cosmetic surgery in men in the 2000s suggest that pressure on men to attain a slender but muscular physique should be a matter of concern.

## Cultural variations in body shape preferences

Few researchers have considered body image in non-Western cultures. Work that has been reported indicates significant cultural differences in the meanings associated with thinness and plumpness. In poorer cultures, thinness may be seen as a sign of malnutrition, poverty, and infectious disease, and increased weight may be viewed positively, as an indication of health, wealth, and prosperity. Research in Latin America, Puerto Rico, India, China, and the Philippines in the 1980s showed that in these cultures increased body weight was linked with wealth and health (Rothblum, 1990), and in a cross-cultural study in the 1970s, Iwawaki and Lerner (1974) found that Japanese college students tended to assign more negative stereotypes to thin bodies than to fatter body types. Various authors have reported that a large body size has been regarded positively among Pacific populations, such as on Fiji, as late as the 1990s, as reflecting agricultural expertise, community commitment, and high quality of care, and that, in women, big hips were associated with ability to bear children, and large size indicated health, nurturance, and attractiveness (Becker, 1995). Other work has shown that moving from a culture where plumpness is valued to one where slenderness is the cultural ideal may lead to a shift in body weight preference. In one cross-cultural study (Furnham and Alibhai, 1983), Asian women living in Kenya and Asian women who had emigrated from Kenya to Britain were asked to rate line drawings of women of different body weights. The Asian women who were living in Kenya gave more positive ratings to line drawings of heavy women than the women who had emigrated to Britain. Although not conclusive, these data suggest a cultural shift in body weight preferences where women who had moved to Britain had assimilated British cultural prejudice against overweight.

Recent work suggests that a desire to be slender is becoming more and more common across cultures, particularly in individuals who have much contact with Western media and culture. Research in South America (Negrao and Cordas, 1996), South Korea (Kim and Kim, 2001), and Japan (Nagami, 1997) has indicated that in cultures where extreme thinness previously signified disease and poverty, many women now aspire to the thin Western body shape ideal. In one recent British study, white and Asian women living in London and women living in Pakistan that were all recruited from slimming clubs and gyms scored similarly on body esteem and attitudes to eating (Bardwell and Choudury, 2000). Another recent study (Swami *et al.*, 2006) found that Japanese men prefer pictures of women with significantly lower BMI than British men, suggesting that the Japanese preference for larger

BMIs observed in the 1970s by Iwawaki and Lerner (1974) has undergone a significant change in favor of the Western ideal of thinness. Ye Luo and colleagues (2005) present evidence that urban Chinese women, who had been generally reported to have fewer body image concerns than Western women, now have significant body image concerns and desire to lose weight at modest BMI levels. They conclude:

> The findings suggest that China has joined the worldwide diffusion of the thin ideal, with negative consequences for women.
>
> (Luo *et al.*, 2005: 333)

Some authors have suggested that Western media are responsible for the development of body dissatisfaction and eating problems in cultures where such concerns had previously been rare. In a study reporting data from semistructured interviews with adolescent women in a rural community in western Fiji three years after Western television became available, Becker (2004) has shown that women reported explicit modeling of Western media models. They also reported developing weight and shape preoccupation, and purging behavior to control weight. A similar pattern of results was found by Lauren Williams *et al.* (2006) in interviews with 16 Fijian and European Australian 13–18-year-old girls. They found that both groups of girls experienced body concerns including body dissatisfaction and a preference for thinness.

There can be no doubt that the idealization of slenderness depends on cultural factors. Historically, poorer cultures (where thinness may signify negative factors such as poverty and/or disease) have been more likely to value plumpness, whereas affluent cultures (where thinness may be associated with self-control and self-denial in the face of plenty) have valued slenderness. However, promotion of the "culture of slenderness" through mass media may be reducing this gap.

## The diet industry

One of the most powerful social forces in the promotion of thinness in Western society is the diet industry. Books, slimming plans, and diet foods are all sold to a public that "feels fat." Of course, a proportion of that public is overweight to a degree that will affect their health. However, many more people diet than need to do so for health reasons, and most do so for aesthetic reasons. Recent statistics from surveys carried out in Britain in 2001 showed that 86 percent of women have dieted (Wykes and Gunter, 2005), supporting earlier British and US data (Ogden, 1992; Brownell and Rodin, 1994).

"Dieting" means different things to different people. It usually means a reduction in the intake of calories for the purpose of weight loss. However, approaches differ in numerous ways, from drastic weight-reduction programs such as the "slim fast" (low-calorie meal-replacement drinks) and "Beverly Hills" (fruit) diets to the relatively more gentle approaches such as the "hip and thigh" (low-fat diet with exercise) and F-plan (high-fiber, low-fat) diets. Jane Ogden (1992) argues that the dieting industry is the perfect industry, because it creates a problem (body dissatisfaction) and then offers to solve it:

> By creating a market for itself it ensures that women will continue to feel fat and will continue to support the dieting industry.
>
> (Ogden, 1992: 48)

She suggests that dieting is often a state of mind, whereby a person thinks about dieting and counts calories but does not eat significantly less than a nondieter. However, some dieters use more extreme strategies for weight loss. These include smoking (which suppresses appetite), vomiting, laxatives, exclusive use of very low-calorie drinks, diet pills, and fad diets such as all-fruit diets. All threaten health, and none work in the long term. She argues that all are particularly dangerous when used by normal-weight individuals who "just feel fat." There has been a well-publicized debate about the long-term efficacy of dieting. Prodieting lobbyists argue that dieting leads to long-term weight loss, and generally that weight loss improves health. When assessing the effectiveness of diets, it is important to distinguish between dieting in normal-weight individuals in order to reach an aesthetic ideal, and dieting in those whose degree of overweight may be injurious to their health. The latter group is likely to be better motivated and better supported (clinically and socially) than the former, and diets that work with obese people will not necessarily be effective (or appropriate) for those who are not obese.

Even the most positive outcome data suggest that diets lead to significant long-term weight loss in only about 25 percent of obese people (Brownell and Rodin, 1994). This has important implications for understanding the effects of diets on normal-weight people who are dieting to reach an aesthetic ideal. Researchers have generally found that dieting works in the long term for only around 5 percent of nonobese dieters (Brownell and Rodin, 1994). This means that the other 95 percent are likely to feel that they have failed. Nickie Charles and Marion Kerr (1986) interviewed over 200 women about their experiences of food and dieting, and found that most had tried and failed to keep to a diet, leaving them feeling guilty and dissatisfied with their willpower, and with their body shape and size. It is not surprising that these women felt like this, given the marketing of diets that emphasize that willpower is all that is needed to lose weight. Antidieting lobbyists argue that dieting may actually lead to an increase in weight. The tendency to gain weight after successful dieting is well established in the medical and psychological literature. It is suggested that the body interprets dieting as a period of starvation and slows the metabolic rate to make more efficient use of the calories that are eaten. When dieters come off the diet, the body sends signals to store extra fat that can be used in the next famine. So they put on the weight that they lost and some extra, because the body is now more efficient at storing calories. They then go on another diet and lose the weight that they put on, and the whole cycle starts again. Kelly Brownell and colleagues used the term "weight cycling" to describe this phenomenon (Brownell *et al.*, 1986), and it has become known colloquially as "yo-yo dieting." Weight cycling can lead to chronic weight increase due to decreased metabolic rate and more efficient utilization of calories.

Some antidieting lobbyists have argued that dieting presents more of a health risk than being overweight. Esther Rothblum (1990) presents evidence that it is weight-reducing diets, rather than being overweight, that result in health problems. She argues that weight-reducing diets lead to "dieter's hypertension" in which the stress of deprivation leads to raised blood pressure. This is supported by studies showing that weight-loss diets may lead to a variety of problems, including heart problems and hypertension (Polivy and Herman, 1983). Moreover, epidemiological studies have shown an increased mortality rate in obese individuals who lose weight (Wilcosky *et al.*, 1990), and some authors have argued that the link between weight loss practices and mortality and morbidity is too convincing to be ignored (Gaesser, 2002). Other authors have reported the opposite pattern of effects. For instance, Wannamethee and Shaper (1990) found that there was a 10 percent reduction in mortality caused by heart disease in a group of over 7,000 British men who lost at least 10 percent of their initial body weight. The reduction in mortality rose to 50 percent for obese men.

Kelly Brownell and Judith Rodin (1994) provide a useful summary of the data relating to weight loss and health. They conclude that it is not possible to evaluate the effects of weight loss on health on the basis of existing data because of problems in the ways that studies have been designed. Most studies have taken self-selecting (obese) groups of people, and compared mortality in those who lose weight with those who do not. Factors such as body fat distribution, dieting history, and disease-related factors may be confounded with weight loss. Only a study with random allocation of participants to weight-loss or non-weight-loss groups would enable a realistic evaluation. Brownell and Rodin also argue that the risk-to-benefit ratio must be assessed separately for individuals of different weights (and with different health risks), and that the decision to diet should be based on likely health outcomes (and not aesthetic ideals). Antidieting arguments are often based on the assumption that people are marginally overweight, or only overweight by some arbitrary aesthetic standard. Morbid obesity may lead to more severe health problems than dieting. However, for people who merely "feel fat" and are not significantly overweight, dieting may represent a health risk.

## Recent cultural trends

### *The antidieting movement*

The antidieting movement is helping to make people aware of the potential dangers of dieting, and is starting to reduce the power of the dieting industry. In the 1990s, campaigns by groups such as Diet Breakers in the UK (Evans-Young, 1995) worked to raise public awareness of the dangers of dieting and the importance of healthy eating; and the popular press carried articles warning of the dangers of crash dieting ("Breaking the Diet Habit" in the *Daily Mail*, May 1992; "Diet Addiction: Your Ten Point Recovery Plan" in *Options*, January 1993). Since 2000, however, the pressure to be slim is still apparent. Models are as thin as they were in the 1990s, and the cultural preoccupation with weight and body shape is as strong as ever, although the new cultural trend is to attain the perfect body through exercise rather than diet, and to achieve a slender, toned, hard-looking body (Bordo, 2003). For instance, *Eve* magazine in February 2006 carried the front-page headlines, "I jogged off 9 stone [126 lb]"; and "Become a 5K runner," alongside the traditional dieting message, "Exclusive Food Doctor Diet: Lose 7 lbs in 7 Days." Celebrities today promote exercise DVDs rather than diet books, selling the promise of a similarly slender body to the body-aware consumer (Freeman, 2007). Overweight is still linked to lack of willpower and laziness, but in the twenty-first century this relates to lack of exercise rather than diet-breaking. This may be a generally positive move in terms of encouraging a healthy lifestyle for people who are within the normal range of weight, by encouraging them to exercise, especially given the relatively low numbers of women and men in Western countries such as Britain who take regular exercise (Office of

National Statistics, 2005). Exercise has many benefits, including toning the body by strengthening muscle, and can lead to increased feelings of well-being, increased energy levels, and benefits for cardiovascular health, and may be particularly beneficial for women in terms of raising self-esteem and mood (Choi, 2000b). However, for people who are significantly overweight (and particularly those who are obese), exercise can be difficult because of social stigma in the sports/exercise culture against overweight (Monaghan, 2005b). So, although this trend may be generally positive for people who just "feel fat," it may be unlikely to benefit those who are obese.

## Body-modification practices

Since 2000, there has also been a huge increase in body-modification practices. These include the insertion of implants, branding, cutting, tattooing, and piercing (Featherstone, 1999). Tattooing and body piercing have become popular with people of all ages, occupations, and social classes, and have become mainstream and acceptable across the social spectrum, at least for the young (Armstrong and Fell, 2000). British government guidelines describe tattooing as "a procedure that involves the puncture of the skin so that a dye may be inserted into the dermal layer to achieve a permanent design," and piercing as "the perforation of the skin and underlying tissue, in order to create a tunnel in the skin through which jewellery is inserted" (Health and Safety Executive, 2001). Tattooing involves inserting pigment into the dermis (Long and Rickman, 1994). Modern tattooing is generally performed by machine whereby a cluster of rapidly oscillating needles deposits liquid pigment into the upper layer of the skin. Piercings are performed by one of two methods. In the first method, the target area to be pierced is held taut with forceps while a needle is inserted to create a passageway for the jewelry. Alternatively, a spring-loaded piercing gun may be used which creates an opening into which jewelry is introduced. Tattoo prevalence is estimated to range from 10 percent for adolescents to 25 percent for the general population (Mayers *et al.*, 2002). The numbers of physical locations of body art are also increasing. Piercings of the face (for example, nose, eyebrow, lip, tongue, and upper ear) and body (for example, nipple, navel, or genitals) have become increasingly popular in recent years (Koenig and Carnes, 1999).

Tattooing and piercing carry various health risks, such as bacterial infections, viral hepatitis, and HIV (Long and Rickman, 1994). Viral infections caused by tattooing are rare, and the most common noninfectious complication is that of acquired hypersensitivity to the pigment, leading to adverse skin reactions (Sperry, 1992). Risks associated with body piercing include allergic reactions, infection, transmission of blood-borne diseases, and medical complications such as bleeding, tissue trauma, scarring, and oral and dental injuries (Mayers *et al.*, 2002). In spite of these risks, recent studies have found that health concerns do not influence tattooing and piercing. One recent study (Huxley and Grogan, 2005) predicted that people who engage more frequently in healthy behaviors, and those who attach a higher value to health, would be likely to engage less frequently in body-modification practices such as tattooing and piercing. A total of 108 participants (28 percent of whom reported having at least one tattoo, and 83 percent at least one piercing) completed questionnaires assessing issues surrounding tattoos and piercings, levels of healthy behaviors, and health value. There was no significant relationship between healthy behaviors, health value, and numbers of tattoos or piercings. A significant proportion of pierced and tattooed participants had not considered possible health risks, and those that had were often unaware of potentially serious health problems associated with piercing and tattooing. It was concluded that the suggestion that people opting for tattoos or piercings attach a lower value to their health is erroneous in a climate of increasing popularity of body modification in people of all ages, occupations, and social classes.

The recent development of body modifications and their move into the cultural mainstream have led to significant changes in the cultural meanings attached to these forms of body modification. Tattoos have historically signaled membership of particular groups such as sailors, bikers, and prison inmates (DeMello, 2000), and piercings (other than conventional ear piercings), membership of punk and sadomasochistic subcultures (Pitts, 2003). However, various authors have suggested recently that both forms of body modification have entered the mainstream and are now just fashion accessories (Turner, 1999). Certainly, media imagery aimed at 18–25-year-olds, including that of the pop music industry, is replete with images of men and women with body modifications. Pop icon Robbie Williams sports several large tattoos (Plate 10), and David Beckham, who maintains a high public profile through his work in soccer and advertising, has several large and prominent tattoos.

The view that tattoos and piercings have become primarily fashion accessories has been contested by researchers who argue that body modifications still serve a communicative role (Stirn, 2003; Atkinson, 2004) and by those who note that the permanence of tattoos and the effort required for aftercare of both piercing and tattoos takes them out of the realm of fashion accessories (Sweetman, 1999). Marika

*Plate 10* Robbie Williams.

*Source*: © Els Deckers/Retna UK

Tiggemann and Fleur Golder (2006) found that the 50 tattooed individuals in their study scored higher than the nontattooed on "need for uniqueness," and that the most common reason for getting tattooed for both men and women was "to express myself." Certainly, recent work has suggested that people with piercings today present them as acts of rebellion and self-identity irrespective of how far they have now entered the cultural mainstream, although social support from peers and exposure to celebrities with piercings predict decisions about whether to have a piercing and its site.

Beth Rhodes at Staffordshire University interviewed British women and men about motivations for piercings (Rhodes, 2004). Nineteen pierced and nonpierced participants (7 men, 12 women) aged 18–28 years took part in focus groups discussing experiences of, and motivations for, body piercing. Peer pressure was the main influence on deciding to get a piercing in this young adult group. Participants argued that it was often the suggestion of a particular piercing by a friend that led them to make the final decision to get the piercing, and that friends often went together to get the piercing done. Participants suggested that knowing someone else had had a particular piercing done at a particular studio would often lead to the decision to have the same piercing done themselves, as they would feel confident that it was safe. Knowing that celebrities had had a particular piercing was a significant incentive to get the same part of the body pierced. People who were perceived to be authority figures (such as parents and GPs) were expected to hold negative views of piercing, and the decision to have it was represented as an act of rebellion by some participants. They reported that they would avoid approaching parents or health professionals before getting a piercing done, and would often feel reticent about approaching parents or health professionals when piercings became infected. Participants were aware of the potential health risks associated with body piercing, but these were not seen as significant disincentives and were minimized relative to other risks in their lives.

Clearly, motivations for body modifications are complex and person specific, but social support and exposure to media images of pierced and tattooed celebrities may be triggers to decide to have a body modification. It is also clear that cultural meanings attached to piercings and tattoos in the 2000s have yet to be fully understood. Although it has been argued that piercing and tattooing have entered the cultural mainstream in Western cultures, people who decide to get piercings and tattoos may still see the decision to engage in body modification as an act of rebellion. The cost involved, the permanence (in the case of tattoos), and potential health problems associated with both procedures distinguish them from temporary fashion accessories such as cosmetics and clothes, so, clearly, they should not be dismissed as "mere fashion accessories." The site of piercing and tattoos may be crucial in determining the cultural meanings associated with both. Tattoos and piercings that are more visible and difficult to hide may be less socially acceptable and more likely to represent resistance and individuality (lower arms, lower legs, and face and neck). Piercings may also be more likely to be perceived as fashion accessories than tattoos due to their reversibility. Future research should look separately at motivations for tattoos and piercings, and at ways in which piercing and tattooing are gendered, to understand more fully this significant cultural change in acceptability of body-modification practices.

## Summary

- Western society promotes slenderness for men and women. Women are expected to be slim and shapely; men to be slender and muscular.
- There is some disagreement among theorists as to the basis for these cultural ideals. Psychologists working within a biological framework have stressed the healthiness of the slender ideal. However, there is evidence that being slightly overweight may have health benefits for women, and that being very thin may impact negatively on health.
- Social psychologists have emphasized the importance of cultural factors in determining what is attractive, demonstrating that the slender ideal is relatively recent, and has become thinner over the last few years with the emergence of the (male and female) "waif" model in the 1990s and its continuation since 2000 in spite of some challenge to this ideal.
- The diet industry promotes a very thin ideal, although dieting may lead to health problems and is unlikely to lead to long-term weight loss.
- The antidieting lobby is actively involved in promoting the dangers of dieting and is reducing the power of the diet industry.
- The Western ideal remains slenderness in the 2000s, although pressure to exercise is replacing pressure to diet as the socially acceptable means to the ideal.
- Body-modification procedures such as body piercing and tattooing have become significantly more widespread in the 2000s than previously, and there is some suggestion that body modifications are losing their association with rebellion and membership of alternative subcultures.

# 3 Women and body image

Slimness is seen as a desirable attribute for women in prosperous Western cultures, and is associated with self-control, elegance, social attractiveness, and youth (Orbach, 1993; Bordo, 2003). The ideal female shape is epitomized in the slim but full-breasted figures of models such as Elle MacPherson and Claudia Schiffer, the body type that Gail Marchessault (2000) describes as "the physically impossible, tall, thin and busty Barbie-doll stereotype" (204). Muscle tone is also important, and the 2000s ideal is a firm-looking body for women as well as men (Bordo, 2003), although visible muscles are not usually considered gender appropriate for women (Choi, 2000b). Chapter 2 showed how body shape ideals for women changed in the twentieth century. Despite changes in the feminine ideal, one thing remains constant through the decades. Women have always been encouraged to change their shape and weight to conform to current trends. Through the ages, women have undergone pain to attempt to conform to the current ideal. This is clearest in relation to practices such as foot binding and the wearing of restrictive corsets, whereby women suffered discomfort and immobility in the name of particular fashions. In Western society today, we have replaced these practices with strict diets (which weaken and debilitate) and cosmetic surgery (in which women undergo painful and potentially dangerous procedures) to try to attain culturally defined, attractive, slender body shapes.

This chapter evaluates evidence from Britain, the USA, Canada, and Australia to investigate body image in women in these cultures. Body image is defined and measured in different ways depending on the specific backgrounds and aims of particular researchers, and there has been a huge increase in the number of new measures that have been developed in the last 10 years (Stewart and Williamson, 2004). Body image has been defined by some authors in terms of perceptual factors (estimated size of the body), and by others as attitude to the body.

Within attitudinal work, some authors have focused on satisfaction with, and evaluation of, the body (the affective-evaluative dimension) and others on rated importance of, and investment in, appearance (the cognitive-behavioral dimension). Researchers have used a variety of different techniques to study how women evaluate their bodies and have concluded that many women in Western culture are dissatisfied with some aspect of their body weight and shape, and are taking behavioral steps to try to change the look of their bodies. A variety of techniques will be discussed in this chapter to illustrate how body image has been investigated, and how such work helps us to understand body dissatisfaction in women. The second part of the chapter will look at ways in which psychologists and sociologists have tried to make sense of women's dissatisfaction with body shape and weight within a feminist framework.

## Assessment of body image

Psychologists and sociologists have used various measures to assess body image. Many of these techniques were originally produced to assess body dissatisfaction in women who have problematic relations with food. This text aims to look at body image in women who have "normal" relations with food rather than those who have been classified as anorexic or bulimic. Readers with a special interest in anorexia are referred to Helen Malson's excellent commentary (Malson, 2000). The studies discussed here are ones that have looked at body image in women picked at random, or on an opportunity basis, rather than those referred to professionals as a result of problematic relations with food. As such, these women's experiences constitute majority views, rather than those of a more specific group. However, this does not imply that the women whose experiences are discussed in this chapter have unproblematic relationships with their bodies. As will be demonstrated here, evidence shows that many women experience levels of dissatisfaction with weight and body shape, and overestimate the size of key areas of their bodies, suggesting a problematic relationship.

### *Figural rating scales*

Figural rating scales, or silhouette techniques, were developed in the 1950s and remain a widely used quantitative measure of degree and direction of body dissatisfaction. In this technique, silhouettes ranging from very thin to very fat are presented to the participant, who is usually asked to choose the silhouette closest to her own body size and that representing her ideal size. The discrepancy between the two figures is seen as an indication of (dis)satisfaction, and the figures chosen indicate whether her ideal is thinner or fatter than her current body type. Studies using this technique have found that women show a reliable tendency to pick a thinner ideal than their current figure. This effect has been replicated in the USA, Australia, and Britain (Cororve-Fingeret *et al.*, 2004).

In one of the earliest published studies using the figural rating scale, April Fallon and Paul Rozin (1985) asked 227 women studying psychology at the University of Pennsylvania to indicate their "ideal figure," their "current figure," and "the figure that most men would find attractive," using Stunckard *et al.*'s (1983) scale. This scale is a set of nine figure drawings arranged from very thin to very heavy figures (Figure 3.1). In general, women picked a heavier figure for their "current figure" than for "the figure that most men would find attractive," and an even thinner figure for their "ideal figure." Fallon and Rozin (1985) conclude that the pursuit of thinness is motivated by self-imposed pressure to be thin rather than the desire to be attractive to men.

Sue Lamb and her colleagues (1993) administered silhouette scales to 34 women enrolled on US degree courses who were studying psychology (average age 20), and to 42 older women (average age 47) who were US public (i.e., state) schoolteachers, or who were chosen from a middle-class preretirement village. They were each given the scale used by Fallon and Rozin (1985), and were asked a series of questions, including their perception of their current and ideal body sizes, and the figure they expected men to find most attractive. The older women were objectively heavier, and perceived themselves to be heavier, than the younger group. Both groups presented an ideal that was much thinner than their perceived size. The younger group had a significantly thinner ideal than the older group. Both groups believed that men favored an extremely thin ideal body size for women. One of the interesting things

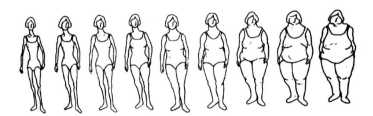

*Figure 3.1* Figural rating scale for women.

Source: Adapted from Stunckard *et al.*, 1983 with permission.

about this finding was that body shape dissatisfaction was not confined to young women. Women in the older group were aged between 40 and 60, and none were obese. Yet they wished to be slimmer. This effect has been replicated in Australian and British work. Marika Tiggemann and Barbara Pennington (1990) gave questionnaires to 52 undergraduate women (average age 23) that contained the Stunckard *et al.* silhouette drawings. Participants were asked to indicate the figure that most closely approximated their current figure, the one they would like to look like, and the one that they thought would be most attractive to the opposite sex. The women rated their current figure as significantly larger than both their ideal figure and the figure that they thought would be most attractive to men. These data show that discrepancy in size between how women perceive themselves and how they would ideally like to look is not a specifically American phenomenon.

Gail Huon and colleagues (1990), in another Australian study, used photographs of women varying in size from very thin to very fat instead of the silhouette pictures, and found very similar results to the silhouette work. Forty young women were asked to pick one photograph that represented their own size, one to represent their ideal, one that they thought most men would prefer, and one that they thought most women would prefer. They were also asked to rate each photograph they had chosen on five 7-point scales (beautiful–ugly, liked–disliked, controlled–uncontrolled, energetic–lazy, and successful–unsuccessful). The "ideal" photograph chosen was significantly thinner than the picture chosen as the "actual size." This discrepancy in size between "actual" and "ideal" bodies was mirrored in favorability ratings, which were higher for the ideal. It was interesting to note that the women perceived "most women's" ideal to be thinnest, followed by "most men's," followed by their "own ideal," followed by their "actual size." Huon suggests that this shows that women who wish to be thin are mostly influenced by what they think other women prefer, rather than by what they think that men prefer. However, the perceived men's preferred size was thinner than the "ideal" reported by these women, suggesting that pressures are perceived to come from men as well as from women.

British work has also found that women want to be thinner than they actually are. Jane Wardle and her colleagues (1993) investigated body satisfaction in 274 white and Asian women, using the Stunckard *et al.* drawings. Participants were asked to indicate the figure that looked most like themselves, the figure they thought men would find attractive, the figure they would most like to look like, and the figure that most women would find most attractive. There was a consistent tendency to choose a slimmer "ideal" than "current" shape, with "shape that men like" coming somewhere in between, and "shape that women like" being slimmest for both white and Asian groups. The investigation demonstrated that normal-weight, young British women tended to feel fat and wanted to lose weight.

Michelle Cororve-Fingeret and colleagues at Texas A&M University have taken a critical look at figural rating scales, and in particular at potential demand characteristics inherent in the design of studies in which women are asked to choose their ideal and current sizes and the size that they think that men prefer. Reasoning that making all three choices in the same test session might encourage women to give socially appropriate responses, they compared what happened when their 17–33-year-old participants made all the choices in the same test session with other conditions in which they picked only some of the target figures. They found that the ideal–current discrepancy was robust when measured in different formats, suggesting that this technique is a valid measure of ideal–current discrepancy and they concluded that "the findings do provide evidence of robust and large effects for the current–ideal discrepancy as measured by figural rating scales" (Cororve-Fingeret *et al.*, 2004: 207).

*Questionnaire studies*

Another way to assess body image is to ask women to complete self-report questionnaires. Body image questionnaires are designed to provide quantitative measures of aspects of body image, including body attitudes. The main focus here will be on measures designed to assess global body satisfaction For an excellent review of alternative questionnaire measures designed to investigate all aspects of body image, including the Appearance Schemas Inventory (Cash and Labarge, 1996) and the Body Image Ideals Questionnaire (Cash and Szymanski, 1995) see Kevin Thompson and Patricia Van den Berg's review (2002).

Most body satisfaction measures ask respondents to indicate degree of agreement or disagreement with statements relating to satisfaction with particular body parts or with the body as a whole. The Body Cathexis Scale was developed in the 1950s by Secord and Jourard (1953). It is one of the earliest measures for assessing the degree of satisfaction with the body and is still widely used. Participants indicate satisfaction with a wide variety of body parts, and the scale is scored so that each person ends up with a score indicating body satisfaction. Secord and Jourard argued that body satisfaction is highly associated with general self-esteem, so that a person who scores highly on the body satisfaction scale would also be likely to score highly on self-esteem scales. This link has been confirmed in many studies in women, men, and children (see Ben-Tovim and Walker, 1991, for a review). Researchers have tended to modify the scale, losing the items that relate to height, ankles, calves, and neck length, which tend to produce unreliable results, and adding other body areas. For instance, Adrian Furnham and Nicola Greaves (1994) added lips, ears, biceps, chin, buttocks, arms, eyes, cheeks, legs, stomach, body hair, and face. Fifty-five British women aged 18–35 were asked to rate, on a 10-point scale, how satisfied they felt with each body part (where 1 = complete dissatisfaction and 10 = complete satisfaction). Compared to a sample of 47 British men in the same age range, the women were significantly less satisfied with all body parts, and especially with thighs, buttocks, and hips. Dissatisfaction with the lower part of the body, where flesh tends to accumulate in women, is widely documented in studies using various methods, as will be seen below.

The Multidimensional Body-Self Relations Questionnnaire Appearance Scale (MBSRQ–AS) (Cash, 2000) measures appearance evaluation (seven items; e.g., "I like my looks just the way they are"), appearance orientation (12 items; e.g., "Before going out in public, I always notice how I look"), overweight preoccupation (four items; e.g., "I constantly worry about being or becoming fat"), and self-classified weight (two items; e.g., "I think I am very underweight–very overweight"), all scored on a five-point Likert scale. The Body Areas Satisfaction Scale asks about dissatisfaction with various parts of the body. This questionnaire is internally reliable (alphas for subscales range between .70 and .94), has been well validated on male and female samples in various Western populations, and has been used extensively in body image research (Cash, 2000). Women tend to score lower than men on appearance evaluation (satisfaction), and higher on overweight preoccupation and appearance orientation. According to Cash *et al.* (1986) and Garner (1997), the areas of the body that present most concern for women are mid-torso (stomach) and lower torso (hips and buttocks).

An awareness that women tend to be most unhappy about the lower parts of their bodies has led to the development of scales clearly derived from the Secord and Jourard scale, but with a narrower focus. David Garner and colleagues developed the Eating Disorders Inventory to assess eating and body image in people with problematic relations with food (Garner *et al.*, 1983b). One of its subscales is the Body Dissatisfaction Scale, which consists of items asking whether the lower parts of the body are just right or too big, and one question that asks about overall satisfaction with the whole body. At least 50 percent of women register a "dissatisfied" response on this scale (Garner *et al.*, 1983b).

The Body Shape Questionnaire (Cooper *et al.*, 1987) was designed specifically to study body image in women with "eating disorders." It includes 34 questions relating to antecedents and consequences of body shape concern, and asks the respondent how she has felt over the last four weeks, to look at long-term dissatisfaction. Items include "Have you felt ashamed of your body?" and "Have you pinched areas of your body to see how much fat there is?" Evans and Dolan (1992) have produced shortened versions of the scale with 16 and eight items that retain the reliability and validity of the original version but have the advantage of greater ease of completion for participants. In a population of normal-weight women with no history of "eating disorders," 17 percent scored high levels of body shape concern on the original Cooper *et al.* (1987) questionnaire, showing—as might be expected—that body shape concern is not restricted to women with "eating disorders" but affects a significant proportion of women with no history of such problems.

The Body Attitudes Questionnaire (Ben-Tovim and Walker, 1991) covers six distinct aspects of body experience: fatness, self-disparagement, strength, salience of weight, attractiveness, and consciousness of lower-body fat. The scale is specifically designed for women, produces separate scores on each of the subscales, and covers a wider range of body-related attitudes than alternatives such as the Cooper *et al.* (1987) scale. Sample questions include, "I worry that my thighs and bottom look dimply" and "I try to avoid clothes that make me especially aware of my shape." The authors found that concern about being fat was central to women's attitudes about their bodies, and that this was particularly marked in relation to concern with the lower half of the body. They also found that "body disparagement" (where the woman agrees to statements such as, "My life is being ruined because of the way I look" and "I prefer not to let other people see my body") was common in their sample of 504 Australian women respondents.

Questionnaire studies suggest that many women are dissatisfied with their bodies, particularly the lower half of the body (stomach, hips, and thighs). These data support the results of silhouette studies, and also add detail on the specific body areas that present cause for concern. One of the problems with figural rating scales work is that women are forced to choose a whole-body silhouette, which obscures perception of individual body parts. Questionnaires that ask specifically about different body parts allow a more detailed assessment of satisfaction with different parts of the body, and reveal that most women participants in the studies may be quite satisfied with the top half of the body while being dissatisfied with the lower torso and thighs.

*Interview studies*

Another way to find out how women feel about their body shape and size is to ask them how they feel in a semistructured or unstructured interview. Using these techniques, interviewers talk to women in an informal way about experiences of body (dis)satisfaction, usually guided by a list of topic areas that the interviewers want them to discuss. The advantage of doing this (rather than asking women to complete a questionnaire that asks specific questions) is that women are given the freedom to express how they feel, rather than just answering preplanned questions. This allows them to set their own agenda and address issues that are important to them, giving this technique more flexibility than questionnaire work.

In a classic study conducted in the 1980s, Nickie Charles and Marion Kerr (1986) carried out an interesting investigation using the semistructured interview technique. As part of a study on eating in the family, they interviewed 200 British women about their attitudes and experiences of dieting, and their satisfaction with their current weight. Their results showed that most women were dissatisfied with their body image. Of the 200 women they interviewed, only 23 had never dieted or worried about their weight. Of the 177 who had been concerned about their weight, 153 had been concerned enough to diet. When speaking about their ideal body, most were dissatisfied with the way that they looked at the time of the interview. Charles and Kerr concluded:

> What emerges from these comments is a strong dissatisfaction with their body image, a dissatisfaction which was not confined to women who were dieting or trying to diet but was shared by almost all the women we spoke to.
>
> (Charles and Kerr, 1986: 541)

The women who were interviewed by Charles and Kerr seemed to have a mental yardstick for how they would like to look. For some of them, this was how they had looked when they were younger. For many, losing a "magic half-stone" (7 lb) was the goal. Most had not managed to accept their bodies as they were. The areas of the body that caused most dissatisfaction were breasts (too small or too large), legs (too fat or too thin), abdomen (not flat enough), and buttocks (too flabby or too skinny). Not all women felt too fat, but the majority did. Although being slimmer was linked with good health, women cited looks rather than health as the main reason for dieting. One woman needed to diet for medical reasons, but said that the main reason for losing weight was to look better.

The interview data in Charles and Kerr's study suggested that adult women tend to be dissatisfied with the way their bodies look, and that they see the main way to change body shape to be dieting. Charles and Kerr linked body dissatisfaction to women's inferior position in society, seeing control of the body as a realizable goal for women who may find it impossible to exert power externally:

> Women are constantly trying to reduce, or increase, their body size so that it will conform to the ideal, abnormally slim conception of female beauty which dominates our culture. At the same time their social position is often one of powerlessness and the body, something which can be brought under control and which power can be exerted over, bears the brunt of women's rage and feelings of impotence.
>
> (Charles and Kerr, 1986: 570–1)

In a series of interviews with women carried out at Manchester Metropolitan University in the 1990s, it was found that women of various ages reported body dissatisfaction. Fifty women, aged 16–63, were interviewed by Penny Cortvriend, Lisa Bradley, Helen Richards, Debbie Mee-Perone, and me between 1994 and 1996. The women were encouraged to talk about their experiences of body shape and weight, diet, and exercise. They reliably reported dissatisfaction with stomach, buttocks, and thighs, irrespective of their ages. Pseudonyms and ages are noted here before the quotations:

*Jane (age 35):*    All my bottom part. From my knees upwards and from my chest downwards. My, um, my what's it called, trunk. The whole of my trunk I am dissatisfied with.

*Sheila (age 34):*    All the blub around my belly. I don't like that one bit.

*Dawn (age 17):*    I'd like my thighs to be smaller. And my bottom's too big.

These findings supported those from quantitative questionnaire work, suggesting that stomach, thighs, buttocks, and hips present most concern to women. Such comments were presented in almost all the interviews, irrespective of the objective size of the woman who was being interviewed. Both slim and heavier women of all ages reported concern that their hips, buttocks, and thighs were too big. In fact, there is some evidence from work on body size estimation that women also tend to overestimate the size of these body parts (see later this chapter). These are areas of the body where women store fat, and also areas which are often the focus of media attention in advertisements for slimming products (Bordo, 2003).

The discourses used by women when asked to talk about their bodies are interesting. Most women seem to objectify their bodies. Most are able to describe what is "wrong" with their body with no difficulty, but find it difficult to identify any part that is satisfactory. Most of the women interviewed, irrespective of their body size, reported that they would be delighted to lose half a stone (7 lb). For instance, one 26-year-old woman said, "I'd kiss you!"; another, aged 25, said, "I'd be so delighted." The women reported that they would be more confident if they lost weight. Many women reported that they would change the way that they dressed if they lost weight, and that they would become like a different (better) person. For instance:

| | |
|---|---|
| *Susie (age 26):* | Yes. I'd be confident as hell. Oh, I'd wear stuff that was shorter and tighter. |
| *Jodie (age 27):* | I'd completely change. My clothes, everything. I'd be a different person. |

Women who had experienced weight loss reliably reported increased confidence. For instance:

| | |
|---|---|
| *Frankie (age 43):* | I remember once I did a diet from a magazine going back, er, 14 years now when I was so slim. I felt so good, I felt like a different person. I felt so confident. |

Feeling slender and feeling confident were intrinsically linked for most of the women interviewed. This was the case for heavier and slimmer women. When asked to imagine putting on half a stone (7 lb) in weight, many women said that this would make them feel like hiding away and not going out.

| | |
|---|---|
| *Ruth (age 26):* | Oh God, no, I'd be gutted [really upset]. I wouldn't go out. |

These feelings were expressed by women across the age range, who said that they would "feel fat" and avoid social activities if they put on 7 lb. The significant social effect of this relatively small increase in weight shows the importance of not increasing weight to most of the women we interviewed. This is particularly interesting, since researchers have shown that judges do not rate women's attractiveness higher when they lose (compared to when they gain) between 0.5 and 18 lb (Alley and Scully, 1994).

Many women reported that they felt happiest about their body first thing in the morning (before they had eaten), when they felt lightest and slimmest. For instance:

*Caroline (age 32):* When I first get up, my tummy looks flatter but then as soon as I have had a drink or a slice of toast or something, there it goes, there it is [laughs].

Women referred to media models as influences on body satisfaction. Many women said that models (in general) were too thin. For instance:

*Jade (age 17):* I used to think, oh models, perfect figure. And now sometimes I look at them and I think no. Too skinny. Definitely too skinny.

However, other women tended to be ambivalent about skinny models, saying that they were too thin, but also that they would like to look like them. The discourse "they make me sick" was used repeatedly by respondents in these interviews. For instance:

*Beth (age 25):* They make me sick. They are too thin. But I would kill for one of their bodies.

*Joanne (age 35):* Some [models] I think, no, I wouldn't like to be like that. But I suppose the Naomis and the Claudia Schiffers, and things like that ... that seems reachable. You know, I mean, obviously, you couldn't get the youth and the flowing hair and that lot. But they make you sick, really, don't they [laughs]? Why her, not me?

The idea of "skinny but shapely" being the most attractive body shape was a recurring theme. For instance:

*Sally (age 17):*   I like a balance. A bit of curves but skinny curves.

*Nicki (age 43):*   I don't like thin thin at all. I mean I would hate to be like that. But the shapely slim models, I might look at them and think it would be nice to look like that.

Women of all ages cited models as influential in determining body satisfaction. The ideal body for women from 16 to 60 was the tall, slim, cultural ideal. For instance:

*Sandi (age 26):*   I'd like firm breasts, thin legs, little tiny hips.

Many women cited pressure from the fashion industry to be slim, saying that fashionable clothes only come in small sizes (British size 14 or below), so that to dress fashionably you have to be slim. For instance:

*Suzanne (age 26):*   Fashion dictates really what size you are, because none of them go over a size 14 anyway, so you couldn't be fat and fashionable.

Many women said that the fact that their clothes became uncomfortable if they put on weight acted as a motivator to lose weight again. This was seen by many women as more important than how much they actually weighed. For instance:

*Betty (age 63):*   The fact that clothes get uncomfortable really. That's basically what it is, 'cos I don't look in the mirror to see how fat I am. And when I put on clothes that are tight around the waist. And the clothes that I've got that are nice but that I can't get into. That's what motivates me to get my weight down. It's clothes.

*Sharron (age 46):*   I don't feel comfortable at the moment in my jeans. That three pounds [recent weight gain] has made a tremendous difference on a skirt or a pair of jeans. That's the only thing. If you've got a pair of jeans, three pounds makes a difference on the waist. That's the only thing that I would diet for if I went out of my clothes size. I would have to diet, because I could never afford to replace all my clothes. If I was growing out of my clothes I would definitely try and cut down.

*Toni (age 27):*    I don't long to be under nine stone [126 lb] again, because I think that is an unrealistic weight for me, but I think just so that my clothes fit me nicely. Do you know what I mean? And I think that the emphasis has changed now in that I don't really weigh myself that often because it is not actually the weight that matters to me. It is how I feel myself and what I feel I look like.

The physical changes associated with the aftereffects of pregnancy presented particular concerns. Although recent Australian data (Skouteris *et al.*, 2005) have suggested that women may feel less fat in late pregnancy than prior to, or in the earlier stages of, pregnancy (probably because this is a time when women are expected to put on weight to ensure the health of their baby), women felt that their bodies had become less aesthetically pleasing after pregnancy, and that they had been relatively attractive in the "golden days" before pregnancy and childbirth. For instance:

*Sarah (age 27):*    You don't realize at the time before you've had kids [how relatively attractive you are], but when you have had them [children], you think, oh, I was Page Three [referring to looking like images presented in *The Sun* newspaper, which traditionally features a young, slim, partly clothed woman on page 3].

Pregnancy did not result in any positive effects that these women could identify. The main negative effects were stretched skin around the stomach and drooping breasts. For instance:

*Jude (age 25):*    I've got more stretch marks than I don't know what. I've got millions of them.

*Helen (age 35):*    All this breast feeding has just ruined my boobs [breasts]. Yes, I'd change those if I could.

Interviews with women across a wide age range have shown that most women are dissatisfied with their body size, in particular the lower torso. Many report comparing themselves to models or actresses, and most have a body ideal that is skinny but shapely, epitomized by models such as Claudia Schiffer (who was the model most admired by our respondents across the age range). Very skinny models (such as Kate Moss) were not so admired, since they were seen as "too skinny" by some, and as an unrealistically slim target shape by others. Being slim was linked with self-confidence for most of the women we spoke to, and most believed that their life would change for the better if they lost weight (irrespective of current body size). One interesting aspect of the interviews was that none of the women we interviewed reported wanting to put on weight (even those who were objectively very thin). And all the women interviewed could identify one body site where they wanted to lose weight. It seemed that many women perceived their body to be heavier than it appeared to the outside observer. Some psychologists have suggested that women tend to overestimate the size of their body (particularly the lower torso). This phenomenon will be investigated next.

### Body size estimation techniques

Interest in body size estimation originated in the 1960s when Bruch (1962) suggested that anorexic women showed a marked distortion in their size perception, perceiving themselves as fat even when very thin. We might expect that these women are exceptional and that the majority of women have a pretty good idea of their body size and shape. After all, we are accustomed to looking at ourselves in mirrors, and buying clothes that fit. In fact, research on body size estimation suggests that most women are poor at estimating the size of their body as a whole and the size of individual body parts, tending to think that they are larger than they really are.

Body size estimation techniques allow women to estimate the size of their bodies, and give a quantitative measure of the degree of distortion. Estimation techniques generally fall into two categories: "part body" and "whole body." Part-body methods involve estimating the size of specific parts of the body, usually by adjusting the width of light beams projected onto a wall. Whole-body estimation techniques involve looking at an image (usually a photograph of the woman's own body) made either fatter or thinner than actual size, and adjusting the image to match perceived size.

**Part-body estimation techniques**

Part-body techniques, which allow the participant to estimate the size of specific body parts in turn, were popular in the 1970s and 1980s, but are less so now that more sophisticated measures have been developed. The movable caliper technique (Slade and Russell, 1973) involves asking the participant to adjust two horizontally mounted lights to match the width of a particular body part. This technique was modified in the 1980s by Thompson and Spana (1988) to include a simultaneous presentation of four light beams representing the cheeks, waist, hips, and thighs. They called this instrument the adjustable light beam apparatus. The participant is required to adjust the width of all four light beams to match her own estimate of the width of her cheeks, waist, hips, and thighs. An assessment of the participant's actual width (measured with body calipers) is compared with her estimate; and a ratio of over- or underestimation is calculated. Kevin Thompson has found that women tend to overestimate the size of all four body parts by about 25 percent, and that the waist is overestimated to the greatest degree (Thompson *et al.*, 1990). Dolan and colleagues (1987) also found that women showed a tendency to overestimate the size of the waist region.

**Whole-body estimation techniques**

These methods involve presenting the participant with real-life images that are objectively thinner or fatter than her actual size. She is asked to select the image that matches her perception of her current size. For example, David Garner has used the distorting photograph technique, in which participants are asked to indicate their size by adjusting a photograph that is distorted in a range from 20 percent under to 20 percent over actual size. Degree of distortion in body image (i.e., the extent to which the woman overestimates the size of her body) is measured by the discrepancy between actual size and perceived size. Women show a reliable tendency to overestimate the size of their body, slimmer women showing more of a distortion tendency than heavier women. Other researchers in Australia (Touyz *et al.*, 1984) and the USA (Gardner and Moncrieff, 1988) used the distorting video technique, in which participants indicate their perceived size by adjusting a video image that is distorted by from 50 percent under to 50 percent over their actual size. Women tend to overestimate their size in this procedure, perceiving themselves as heavier than they actually are. Whole-body techniques have been criticized. It has been argued (Thompson *et al.*, 1990) that confrontation with a real-life image that increases in size may be very upsetting to an individual sensitive to appearance. Moreover, the techniques do not allow the participant to manipulate individual body sites separately. This is important because size estimation may be site-specific and not constant to the whole body (Thompson and Spana, 1988), so that a woman may overestimate the size of hips, stomach, and thighs, but not the rest of the body, and this is not possible to demonstrate if images can only be altered to be generally thinner or fatter. An answer to this second problem may be found in computerized techniques that allow participants to alter specific areas of a visual image on the screen to match their body shape and size.

### Combined whole- and part-body estimation

Emery and his colleagues (1995) from Newcastle and Oxford universities produced a sophisticated, computerized measure in the 1990s that enabled them to "grab" a frame from a video of the participant in a leotard. The participant can observe the frame-grabbed image on the VDU screen, and use the cursor to modify the shape of different parts of the image to produce what she feels is an accurate representation of her own body shape. The program can then calculate for each body part the degree of under- or overestimation of size. A study of 20 women 19–32 years of age showed that the women tended to overestimate the size of legs, buttocks, and abdomen, and underestimate the size of other body parts. The advantages of this method are that it allows study of the particular areas of the body that are over- or underestimated and allows the participant to look at an image that realistically mimics weight loss or gain, rather than just widening or narrowing the image.

These techniques have become more and more sophisticated over the years. Recently, Marita McCabe and colleagues (2006) have used a digital body image computer program that enables participants to manipulate a full frontal image of their entire body at five specific sites (chest, waist, hips, thighs, and calves). The degree of over- and underestimation at each site is compared with the ability to manipulate the size of an on-screen, 10-cm image of a vase (to check the accuracy of perception when perceiving non-body-related images). They have found that their sample of 107 Australian women (mean age 25 years) overestimated the size of their body. Although they also tended to overestimate the size of the vase, overestimates of body regions were significantly greater for all body regions. Actual size (BMI) did not predict degree of overestimation for women, consistent with the view that women of all shapes and sizes may be likely to overestimate their size. McCabe *et al.* conclude that estimation inaccuracies are not confined to women with eating disorders, but are also found in the normal population of women. Studies using these techniques show that the majority of women tend to perceive their bodies as heavier than they actually are. There is some disagreement over whether women who differ in weight/BMI differ in degree of overestimation. In a review of relevant literature, Kevin Thompson *et al.* (1990) argue that thinner women overestimate more than heavier women. However, recent studies have failed to find a significant relationship between BMI and estimation accuracy (Bergstron *et al.*, 2000; McCabe *et al.*, 2006), although other factors may predict accuracy of estimation. The stage within the menstrual cycle may have an effect, and it has been suggested that the size of the waist may be overestimated in the days prior to menstruation (Thompson *et al.*, 1990). Depressed mood also predicts size overestimation (Taylor and Cooper, 1986; McCabe *et al.*, 2006).

So, to conclude, evidence suggests that most women overestimate the size of (at least) parts of the body. It is important to bear in mind this tendency to overestimate body size when assessing data from studies of body satisfaction, because they need to be understood in the context that many women have unrealistic images of their body, particularly their waist, hips, and thighs. These data also emphasize the importance of focusing on women's perceptions of body size, and discrepancy from the slim ideal, rather than on objective size. Perception of size is likely to be a much better predictor of body satisfaction than objectively measured body weight, a prediction borne out in studies that have found that perceived size is a better predictor of body satisfaction and self-esteem than the BMI (e.g., Furnham and Greaves, 1994; Tiggemann, 2005).

## Behavioral indicators of body dissatisfaction

One way to investigate body image is to monitor behaviors that would be expected to result from body dissatisfaction. Interview work has suggested that women engage in dieting and exercise as ways of trying to change body size and shape. This section will investigate body-relevant behaviors in women, including dieting, exercise, and cosmetic surgery.

### Dieting

One behavioral indicator of body dissatisfaction is inclination to try to change body shape through diet. Most women have attempted to change weight and shape at some time in their lives by reducing the amount of food that they eat, and women's magazines continue to promote dieting as an effective way to lose weight with front-page headlines such as "Lose 4 pounds in 24 hours: 4 new crash diets—nutritionist approved!" (*Eve* magazine, December 2006). Estimates of the frequency of dieting in American and British women show that about 95 percent of women have dieted at some stage in their lives (Ogden, 1992); and that about 40 percent of women are dieting at any one time (Horm and Anderson, 1993). Recent statistics from surveys carried out in Britain in 2001 showed that 86 percent of women have dieted (Wykes and Gunter, 2005). In a study of British women aged 18–35, Furnham and Greaves (1994) found that 48 out of 55 (87 percent) had dieted or were currently dieting. When asked their reasons for dieting, women were more likely than men to say "to be slim" and "to increase confidence and self-esteem."

Most researchers find that diets lead to long-term weight loss in only about 5 percent of nonobese dieters (see Chapter 2). The other 95 percent are likely to feel that they have failed. Nickie Charles and Marion Kerr (1986) found that most of the women they interviewed had dieted as a way to lose weight, and most felt that they had failed because they had been unable to keep to the diet. Most of the women interviewed at Manchester Metropolitan University used dieting as their primary way to try to lose weight. For instance:

*Judy (age 43):*      We know we've got to diet to keep slim.

*Sadie (age 34):*      The only way to get rid of it [weight], to feel more comfortable with yourself, is to diet.

Dieting was usually self-motivated, and women were keen not to be seen to have been duped into dieting by men:

*Betty (age 63):*      I don't diet for anyone else. Just me.

However, some women reported that their partners had encouraged them to lose weight and that they had been sufficiently upset, when their partners commented negatively on their weight or shape, to lead them to change their eating habits:

*Caroline (age 32):*      He said, "God, you aren't half getting fat." The cheeky pig. I cried and slept downstairs that night.

Continuous vigilance and awareness of body size were a common feature of women's discourse. Most reported dieting in cycles, losing weight by dieting for 2–6 weeks, and then putting on the weight again when they started eating normally. For instance:

*April (age 35):* Well, I can't cut down. I have to go to extremes. I have to once I manage it. I keep trying and trying, and once I start a diet, I can keep it going for six weeks as long as I don't cheat at all. If I have any cheats, that's it. I have to keep to a steady routine, so I'd have branflakes for breakfast, cottage cheese and soup for lunch, and a diet meal for tea [evening meal], and at weekends I'd probably allow myself to binge. But if I broke that pattern during the week, that's it. I'd start eating excessively then. From one extreme to another. When I do it, I go over the top really. So I can lose it quick, but that is probably why it goes on so quick.

*Jackie (age 43):* My whole life, I think, is going to be dieting and then nondieting, then dieting, and I know it's not good for your health.

Most of the women interviewed distinguished clearly between "normal" dieting (cutting down on fatty foods, generally eating less, and calorie counting) and what most of them referred to as "fad" (or "faddy") diets, which were usually liquid protein diets or all-fruit diets. As such, they presented themselves as experts on dieting who could distinguish between "real/normal" diets and "fad" diets. Liquid protein diets, which originated in the mid-1970s, involve replacing meals with low-calorie protein drinks (powder mixed with water), and are usually claimed to provide all the protein needed to be healthy while reducing calorie intake. There is some evidence that these diets, which were originally designed for obese people, may be dangerous for those who are within the normal range but "feel fat," although, as Jane Ogden (1992) says, these diets are so boring that most people give them up before they can do any real harm. A similar argument can be made for the all-fruit diets, whose authors recommend periods of starvation when only fruit is eaten. These could be dangerous for health. The authors often encourage dieters to engage in bulimic-type behavior, bingeing (on off-diet days), then purging (on diet days), and eating fruit, which acts as a diuretic, to encourage weight loss.

In interviews, most women said that they were against what they called "fad dieting," because such diets were seen to be ineffective in the long term (because they are boring and lead to cravings for other foods) and bad for health (because they do not contain necessary nutrients). For instance:

Paula (age 46):    I think that fad diets are absolutely stupid. The only way to lose weight is to cut down generally and to exercise.

Rosie (age 30):    When I go on one of those silly diets, I actually feel tired. I'm obviously not getting enough energy.

However, women commonly reported dieting to lose weight for special occasions, such as nights out with friends. For instance:

Heidi (age 27):    Say you've got something tight on and you don't want it to be so tight, you'd watch what you ate all week so that you could wear it for a night out. You tend to starve yourself till the night, then binge after 'cos it doesn't matter then until the next night out.

Wendy (age 25):    It's like when I go out on a Friday night I can't eat so I can look slimmer that night when I go out. My belly is flatter if I don't eat.

This short-term change in behavior was not usually seen as "dieting," which was characterized as a more long-term change in behavior. Restriction of food, even when hungry, to look slimmer was reported by most of the women we spoke to.

Dieting is common among women. Many women deny themselves food, especially before a special occasion, to look slimmer. Women diet to look thinner, in the belief that thinness is associated with confidence. The slimming industry promotes this association, with images of self-confident-looking, thin models, and the rhetoric of a "new you" after the commercially available diet has helped the dieter to lose weight.

*Exercise*

Another behavioral indicator of dissatisfaction is exercising as a means to change body shape and size. Fewer women than men exercise in the USA, Canada, and Britain, and the majority of women do not exercise sufficiently to achieve significant health benefits (Choi, 2000a). The British Heart Foundation (2003) suggests that, in order to protect heart function, we should all engage in moderate exercise at least three times a week, and ideally five times per week. Physical exercise has well-documented effects on the incidence of coronary heart disease, colon cancer, and diabetes in women (Choi and Mutrie, 1997) as well as the potential to improve body satisfaction.

Women's motivation for exercise differs from that of men. In a recent study of exercise motivations in 93 British bar staff, we found that weight loss is a more important motivator for women who exercise than for men, and that women and gay men are more likely than hetero-sexual men to exercise to improve their appearance in general (Grogan *et al.*, 2006b). This supports work by Adrian Furnham and Nicola Greaves in the 1990s showing that women are more likely than men to cite exercising for weight control, altering body shape, attractiveness, and health (Furnham and Greaves, 1994). In interviews conducted at Manchester Metropolitan University in the late 1990s, all women who were interviewed either intended to use, or actually used, some form of exercise (usually walking, going to the gym, or aerobics) as a way to lose weight and "tone" their bodies. The primary motivator to exercise for all the women interviewed was to improve muscle tone and lose weight, rather than for health (e.g., to improve cardiovascular fitness) or other (e.g., enjoyment) reasons. For instance:

*Caroline (age 32):*  [I exercise] entirely for weight. To try to firm up and try to use some calories, and I'm always thinking I'm not doing enough. Afterwards, like after I've been swimming, I feel great. I actually feel slimmer.

*Jade (age 17):*  I want to make my legs smaller. I do exercises for that.

The positive effects of exercise are not limited to changes in muscle tone and "feeling slimmer" (although this might be what motivates exercisers in the first place). Researchers have argued that women who exercise also experience positive changes in body image and self-concept due to an increase in physical mastery of the body through exercise. Precilla Choi (2000a, 2000b) argues that exercise has the potential to develop physical mastery in women, leading to more positive body image and self-esteem, but that the construction of exercise as a beauty product may lead to unrealistic expectations (which may lead to women quitting exercise when these are not realized) and that the competitive nature of sports environments may alienate women who do not conform to the slender, sporty ideal. She argues:

> The potential for true physical and psychological health, as opposed to beauty, must be emphasised and the exercise culture must facilitate empowerment by emphasising mastery over outcomes, by celebrating the physical achievements of all participants, and by including all participants whatever their shape and size.
>
> (Choi, 2000a: 377)

Adrian Furnham and colleagues (1994) selected 60 white British women to take part in the study, split into four groups of 15. The first group (nonexercisers) were women who did not take part in any regular exercise (most exercised less than once a week). The three groups of exercisers all exercised at least three times per week. The first of these were netball players, the second were rowers, and the third were bodybuilders. Participants were asked to rate nine sketches of naked female shapes (Figure 3.2), ranging from extremely thin to hypertrophic (extremely muscular) on 10 attributes (confident, feminine, healthy, masculine, popular, sexy, unattractive, unfriendly, unhappy, and unnatural). They were also asked to rate their own body on similar measures, and to identify the sketch closest to the way they would like their body to look.

The researchers found that women who exercised tended to perceive thin shapes more negatively, and more muscular shapes more positively, than did nonexercising women. Moreover, women who exercised had a more positive perception of their own bodies than those who did not exercise, even though they were heavier on average than nonexercisers. This may be because exercise contributes to a more toned body. It is also likely that physical mastery increases self-esteem. Bodybuilders and rowers viewed the muscular body shapes more positively than the other two groups, suggesting that they set less rigid definitions of desirable body shape in women. As might be expected, the bodybuilders rated the highly muscular figures most positively, rating them as more feminine, sexy, and attractive, and less unnatural and masculine, than did the other groups. This will be considered again in Chapter 7 in relation to improving body image.

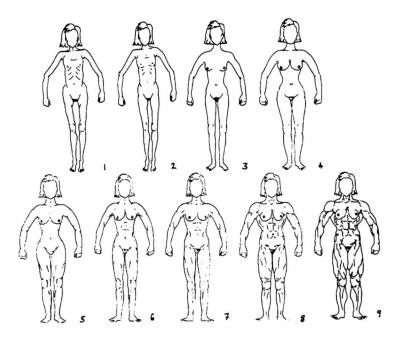

*Figure 3.2* Female body shapes.

*Source*: Adapted from Furnham *et al.*, 1994 with permission.

## Bodybuilding

The bodybuilders in the Furnham *et al.* (1994) study challenged traditional stereotypes of femininity as represented by the slim, shapely ideal
currently in vogue. Bodybuilding is not generally seen as appropriate for
women, and women who engage in this sport may face discrimination
(Mansfield and McGinn, 1993). Various authors have documented the
struggle faced by pioneering women bodybuilders as they entered the
competitive bodybuilding world in the 1970s (St Martin and Gavey,
1996). The first widely publicized women's bodybuilding event was held
in 1979 in Los Angeles (previously the only choice for women bodybuilders was the "beauty pageant" added to the men's competitions).
In the 1980s, the Ms Olympia competition started in the USA, and
in Britain, NABBA (National Amateur Body Building Association)
renamed its "Miss Bikini International" competition "Ms Universe." In
1986, the Ms Universe competition was divided into "physique" and
"figure" classes. The "physique" class caters for those aiming for a more

muscular physique and less traditionally feminine presentation (minimal makeup and bare feet), and "figure" for those who want traditionally feminine presentation (moderate degrees of muscularity, makeup, and shoes with high heels). In the 1990s, fitness competitions were set up for women who engage in weight training as part of a general fitness regime. Fitness competitors engage in an aerobic performance as well as posing to reveal body shape and tone.

Women's bodybuilding has been conceptualized in many different ways by feminist writers. Sandra Lee Bartky (1990) sees it as a direct challenge to the cultural restrictions placed on women in terms of how their bodies should look, and argues that women bodybuilders represent a radical cutting edge of feminist resistance to cultural ideals. She represents an optimistic view of bodybuilding as a way to challenge dominant ideologies that represent women as physically weak, showing that muscularity (and, by inference, strength) is mostly a product of cultural practices. By showing that women's physical weakness is (mostly) culturally produced, she opens up the possibility that it is surpassable. This view sees bodybuilding as an empowering practice that challenges the cultural association of muscularity (and strength) with masculinity. An alternative view is presented by Susan Bordo (2003), who sees bodybuilding as women's response to cultural pressures to control their bodies into a culturally acceptable, firm, toned, solid form. She links bodybuilding with anorexia, seeing both as attempts to avoid "the soft, the loose, unsolid, excess flesh" (191). She sees women bodybuilders as responding to cultural pressures to have a slim, firm body, but doing so in a different way from women who choose to try to attain the ideal through the usual means of restriction of food intake. For Bordo, these women are not challenging cultural ideals, but merely responding to them in a different way.

Leena St Martin and Nicola Gavey (1996) argue that, in competition, bodybuilding women are required to be "feminine," producing pressures for "almost hyper-feminine ornamentation, posture and demeanour" (54). They show how women bodybuilders undergo cosmetic surgery (such as breast augmentation) to emphasize their femininity, and are expected to ornament themselves as "feminine" in their posing suits, makeup, and hairstyles. Still, they argue that:

> While the femininity control institutionalized in competitive bodybuilding cannot be denied, this feminine overlay on a highly muscularized body doesn't automatically prevent it from disrupting the sex/gender system. If we read body-building and bodybuilders' bodies as cultural texts, then it is possible to interpret

women's body-building as a challenging and destabilizing cultural practice.

(St Martin and Gavey, 1996: 54)

St Martin and Gavey argue that women's bodybuilding requires bodies that transgress the feminine, and that the requirement for hyperfemininity in competition could be seen as the result of the attempt to bring these women back into the feminine fold, to make them acceptable to the dominant culture. However, ironically, this has the effect of posing more of a challenge to traditional ways of understanding gender than is presented by women engaged in other sports where they are not emphasizing their femininity, because the conflict between their bodies and cultural expectations of what their bodies should look like cannot just be explained by denoting them as "not really women."

We have recently interviewed an opportunity sample of women bodybuilders who all compete (or have competed in the past) in the physique class (Grogan *et al.*, 2004), to investigate their motivation for bodybuilding. These women were engaging in behaviors that place them outside the mainstream norms of how it is appropriate for women to look, and were resisting the social pressures to be more slender that other women report. We were interested in what motivated them to start bodybuilding and what maintained their bodybuilding. Given that mainstream Western culture expects women's bodies not to take up space (Orbach, 1993), we were also interested in these women's experience of other people's reactions to their increased size. We wondered how they experienced the reactions of those outside, and also inside the bodybuilding world, and what sources of social support these women used.

The women who took part in our interviews presented accounts in which they represented themselves as feeling better about their bodies, and about themselves generally, than in their pre-bodybuilding days, stressing control of the body. This is a traditional feminine discourse, drawing on notions of bodily restraint (Bordo, 2003), although in this case the women were talking about increasing rather than reducing the size of their bodies. These women had shifted their body ideal (with support from within the bodybuilding community) to a more muscular figure, and the only people whose reactions concerned them were other bodybuilders and competition judges. This effectively negated the importance of reactions from those who may not find a hard and muscular body appealing, enabling these women to feel physically and mentally strong, and raising their self-esteem and self-confidence. However, they also reported that they were under constraint from the bodybuilding community in terms of what size was acceptable, and this restricted how muscular they could get and still be able to succeed in competition. This raises the crucial question of whether these women should be seen as complying with mainstream social pressures to be "feminine," as Jane Ussher (1997) puts it, to "do girl"; or whether, as Sandra Bartky (1990) and Leena St Martin and Nicola Gavey (1996) argue, they are resisting these pressures. We suggest that they are doing both. In actively changing their bodies to be "unacceptably" muscular, and by explicitly rejecting the judgments of mainstream views of their bodies, these women are resisting mainstream cultural norms. They are also complying with a narrow set of ideals, determined by the largely male bodybuilding community. If we had interviewed women who had not competed, we may have identified more evidence of resistance and individuality, since they would be likely to be under less pressure from the bodybuilding community.

These women bodybuilders were engaged in a complex balancing act in which they want to be muscular, toned, and athletic looking, but not to get unacceptably muscular. Their experiences provide a model of how women can resist mainstream cultural pressures to be slender, providing they have support from a salient subcultural group. They show that contesting the dominant slender ideal can lead to feelings of empowerment and the forging of alternative body ideals. The fact that these women are subject to alternative pressures from within the bodybuilding community to present as "feminine" should not detract from the fact that they have found a way to resist mainstream pressure to be slim, and to feel good about the look and feel of their bodies.

### Anabolic steroid use

The use of anabolic steroids as an aid to bodybuilding is becoming more and more prevalent in Britain (Lennehan, 2003) and the USA (Pope *et al.*, 2000). Steroids help to maximize the effects of weight training in increasing muscle mass, but carry with them risks of serious side effects, such as kidney and liver damage and hypertension, as well as risks of HIV infection and hepatitis for those who use injectable steroids (Institute for the Study of Drug Dependence, 1993). Many competitors in mainstream bodybuilding competitions take steroid drugs in the lead up to competition (Korkia, 1994). Indeed, anabolic steroids are so much a part of bodybuilding culture that "natural bodybuilding" competitions have been set up specifically for bodybuilders who choose not to take steroid drugs, and so could not realistically compete in mainstream competitions because they could not attain the kinds of muscle bulk attained by steroid users (St Martin and Gavey, 1996).

Most work on anabolic steroid use has focused on men, as most body-builders are men, and most steroid users are male (Lennehan, 2003). However, women's use of anabolic steroid drugs for bodybuilding has increased recently, in tandem with the increase in women's bodybuilding competitions. Pirkko Korkia (1994) looked specifically at the degree of anabolic steroid use in British women using bodybuilding gyms. Twenty-one weight-training gyms, in London, Merseyside, Swansea, and Glasgow, were surveyed. All women using the gyms over a two-day period, on days when the maximum number of clients could be expected, were asked to complete a questionnaire, and 349 women were surveyed. Of these, eight women (2.3 percent) had used anabolic steroids at some time, and five (1.4 percent) were currently using them. In interviews, most women reported that they used oxandrolone, methandrostenolone, and stanozolol. In the second part of this study, Korkia interviewed 13 women currently using anabolic steroids. One woman suffered menstrual irregularities through steroid use, and two reported that they had suffered permanent side effects from steroid use. This study suggests that a significant minority of women are using steroids to help to build muscle mass. US studies have tended to find slightly higher incidences of steroid use among women. Charles Yesalis and Michael Bahrke (1995) place the incidence of use in women at 1–6 percent, with highest use among athletes and bodybuilders. The main side effects in their study included menstrual abnormalities, deepening of the voice, shrinkage of breasts, baldness, acne, and increased body hair. These side effects run directly counter to current cultural ideals for women's body image, so could be expected to lead to negative responses from others.

In order to try to understand why women engage in anabolic steroid use, risking their health to become highly muscled, we have investigated experiences of steroid use in interviews with women who use anabolic steroids as part of their bodybuilding regime (Grogan *et al.*, 2006a). Social support, especially from within the bodybuilding community, was an important motivator for use, and these women believed that it would be impossible to compete in bodybuilding without steroids. The masculinizing effects of steroids (male pattern baldness and deepening of the voice) and the threat to reproductive health were cited as the biggest disincentives for women, and more of a disincentive than more serious long-term risks such as kidney and liver damage, or risk of blood-borne diseases caused by sharing needles. For instance, one respondent was concerned about her fertility:

> [reproductive health] is a bit of a worry but I've had kids before and to be quite honest I haven't been on the pill [oral contraceptive] for

three years. But when you've been dieting and taking gear [steroids], it's not a good time. So we need to have a full term to be clean, and you know what I mean. You know we'll go to the doctors and get everything checked out anyway.

The main problems voiced by women in relation to steroid use were the masculinizing effects of some steroids, such as lowering of the voice, male pattern baldness, and increased hair growth on the body and face. For instance, one of the women reported:

I could sing before and I can't now. Umm, I find if I try and sing, it breaks, which is not particularly great. Also I've found I have been quite lucky on the hair side, as on my body my hair hasn't grown, but I have found on my face, umm, I had what you would call downy hair, which was like fair downy hair. When I competed, it was noticeable and it was the steroid use and it was my own fault for shaving it off a couple of years back, which caused my hair to grow back even worse. You could argue whether it was or it wasn't steroid use, that. But I do have hair problems now so I do have to shave in certain areas, which is a disadvantage, I feel. Skin—my skin has never been particularly good either on steroid use.

No women reported concerns about liver or kidney damage. Nor did they express concerns about contracting HIV/AIDS through infected needles. The only side effects that were experienced as significant deterrents were those that had a direct effect on body image and fertility. However, these (and fertility problems) were outweighed by the importance of wanting to gain muscle for competition. An unexpected finding in this study was that the women's primary concern about maintaining a "feminine" look was to increase their chances of winning in competition through being able to present on stage as looking "feminine" (defined as having a hair-free body and clear skin). Interventions designed to reduce or prevent steroid use in women need to take into account the fact that the desire to maintain a traditionally feminine look and reproductive health may act as a disincentive for their use.

### Cosmetic surgery

The 1990s and 2000s have seen a significant increase in the numbers of women having cosmetic surgery in Britain, Australia, Canada, and the USA (Gillespie, 1996; Haiken, 1997; Viner, 1997; Cepanec and Payne,

2000; Villeneuve *et al.*, 2006). More and more women are turning to cosmetic surgery as a way to change the shape of their bodies. Susan Bordo (2003) notes that the increased availability of cosmetic surgery has changed expectations about how women's bodies should look as they age, and has reduced the range of body and facial types considered acceptable. Cosmetic procedures are now "normal" and accessible, with the most frequently requested operations worldwide being liposuction and breast augmentation procedures on women:

> These homogenised images normalise—that is they function as models against which the self continually measures, judges, "disciplines" and "corrects" itself. Cosmetic surgery is now a $1.75-billion-a-year industry in the United States, with almost 1.5 million people a year undergoing surgery of some kind from face lifts to calf implants.
>
> (Bordo, 2003: 25)

Cosmetic surgery is not a recent phenomenon. It is possible to trace its history from 1000 BC; the first plastic surgery was reported in India, when rhinoplasty (nose reconstruction) was carried out on individuals whose noses had been cut off as a form of punishment (Haiken, 1997). However, it was not until the mid-twentieth century that cosmetic surgery (surgery performed for the aesthetic improvement of healthy bodies) emerged. Naomi Wolf (1991) traces the beginnings of what she calls the "Surgical Age," in which cosmetic surgery became a mass phenomenon, showing how it became more and more accessible to women who were dissatisfied with the way that they looked, partly fed by the promotion of cosmetic surgery techniques aimed at women. Fabienne Darling-Wolf (2000) notes that cosmetic surgeons and popular media promote the idea of the female body as inherently flawed and in need of technological reconstruction in order to create a demand for their services, and that there has been a disturbing shift in the 1990s from an emphasis on ornamentation of the body to actual reshaping of the "flawed" female body:

> Such a construction contributes to an ideology—clearly present in the language used by plastic surgeons—of the female body as inherently flawed and pathological. In the United States the American Society of Plastic Surgeons managed to convince the Federal Food and Drink Administration to let silicone breast implants stay on the market by arguing that the condition of having small breasts was actually a disfiguring disease called "micromastia."

Cosmetic surgery journals similarly abound with references to "abnormalities" and deformities' needing to be corrected.

(Darling-Wolf, 2000: 285–6)

This trend has progressed in the 2000s with the genesis of reality television shows in which women receive "extreme makeovers" including cosmetic surgery to correct perceived flaws. *Ten Years Younger* in Britain and *The Swan* in the USA give viewers access to before, during, and after footage of cosmetic procedures. These have the effect of normalizing these procedures and also raise women's awareness of cosmetic procedures that would be available to them if they could afford them. The fact that these are televised with a focus on positive outcomes makes these a worrying new trend.

The question of why women are willing to undergo unnecessary surgery to make their bodies conform more closely to accepted norms may help us to understand the nature of body dissatisfaction in women. Kathy Davis (1995) in *Reshaping the Female Body: The Dilemma of Cosmetic Surgery* looks at cosmetic surgery from a broadly feminist viewpoint. She argues that understanding why women engage in a practice which is painful and dangerous must take women's explanations as a starting point. She attempts to explore cosmetic surgery as one of the most negative aspects of Western beauty culture without seeing the women who opt for the "surgical fix" as what she calls "cultural dopes" (i.e., by taking seriously their reasons for having cosmetic surgery). She carried out her work in The Netherlands, where there had been a general increase in cosmetic surgery in the preceding years (to more than 20,000 cosmetic operations in 1994—more per capita than in the USA). Since cosmetic surgery is freely available to all women in The Netherlands, provided their appearance is classified as falling "outside the realm of the normal," it was possible to investigate women's decisions without financial considerations being an issue.

She spoke with women who had had a variety of different kinds of cosmetic surgery. She found that women gave accounts that dispelled the notion that they were simply the duped victims of the beauty system. They had long histories of suffering with bodies that they experienced as unacceptable, different, or abnormal. She argues that cosmetic surgery is about wanting to be normal rather than wanting to be beautiful. Women she interviewed reported that they experienced the decision to have cosmetic surgery as a way of taking control of their lives, and that cosmetic surgery was something that they had decided upon for themselves, rather than under pressure from partners or knife-happy surgeons. They were clear that they had made informed choices, based on weighing up the risks and possible benefits of surgery. Davis takes the position that cosmetic surgery may be an informed choice, but it is always made in the context of culturally limited options. She argues fiercely against the idea expressed by many authors, including Kathryn Morgan (1991), that women who opt for cosmetic surgery are victims of male lovers, husbands, or surgeons. She also disagrees that women who opt for cosmetic surgery are the dupes of ideologies that confuse and mystify with the rhetoric of individual choice.

Davis (1995) sees women as active and knowledgeable agents who make decisions based on a limited range of available options. She argues that women see through the conditions of oppression even as they comply with them. The women she interviewed reported that they had made free choices, although these "choices" were limited by cultural definitions of beauty and by the availability of particular surgical techniques. The "choices" need to be placed within a framework that sees women's bodies as commodities. Davis's arguments echo arguments about surgery in transsexuals when she talks about being "trapped in a body that does not fit her sense of who she is" (1995: 163), and about "a way to reinstate a damaged sense of self and become who they really are or should have been" (1995: 169), seeing surgery as a way to renegotiate identity through changing the appearance of the body. This raises interesting problems for those who object to cosmetic surgery on grounds of political correctness, since there are parallels between the (probably politically correct) right of individuals to have gender reassignment operations because of identity conflict, and the accounts of women who have (probably politically incorrect) plastic surgery for the same reason. She argues against opting for the comfortingly clear, politically correct feminist line that cosmetic surgery is self-inflicted subordination to the beauty system, and suggests that we should try to understand cosmetic surgery as a dilemma for women, desirable and problematic for those who choose the surgical route. She cautions against closing the debate by accepting the politically correct line, and suggests that:

> As concerned critics of the explosion in surgical technologies for reshaping the female body and of women's continued willingness to partake in them, we simply cannot afford the comfort of the correct line.
>
> (Davis, 1995: 185)

In 2006, Jo Ann Campbell at Staffordshire University recruited 59 women who were due to undergo cosmetic surgery through Internet websites (Campbell, 2006). The women answered a series of open-ended questions about expectations and experiences of cosmetic surgery before and one month after having cosmetic surgery. She found that most of these women argued that they had been motivated to undertake cosmetic surgery by the feeling that the targeted body part was socially unacceptable and abnormal. For instance:

> I want to feel normal. All my life (since childhood), I was called names and pointed out for being ugly and flat chested. I know I can never be pretty. But normal would be heaven for me.

These accounts supported suggestions from other authors that women referred for cosmetic surgery are not necessarily dissatisfied with the whole of their bodies but tend to focus on one rogue body part as in some way out of line with the rest of their body (e.g., Cepanec and Payne, 2000). Although women referred for breast reduction surgery tended to cite health problems as the primary motivator for surgery (pain, rashes), aesthetic reasons were the main motivator for all other kinds of cosmetic surgery. Most women reported a significant improvement in quality of life and self-esteem postoperatively. Many women had spent considerable time researching the surgeon and surgery involved. Consistent with suggestions by Kathy Davis (1995, 2002), women argued that cosmetic surgery was a personal choice and a way to become "normal" and to take control over their bodies. For instance:

> Cosmetic surgery has given me a sense of power and control over my life for the first time. It gives me hope that I can be the real me.

It may be difficult for women to express wanting to be attractive and not open themselves to socially unacceptable charges of vanity. It may also be challenging to report anything other than agency over the decision to have surgery and still ensure that one is not seen as a "cultural dope." Diane Cepanec and Barbara Payne (2000) argue that the claim that women are taking their lives into their own hands deflects attention from the sociocultural contact in which women's agency operates. They are also critical of Davis's position that cosmetic surgery can be both disempowering and a road to empowerment, as this position can be used to endorse cosmetic surgery. Kathryn Morgan (1991) also argues that, although women may feel that they are making a free and informed choice, they are not really free to make a genuine choice because of patriarchal cultural pressures on them; that, although women may say that they are creating a new identity for themselves, they are really conforming to traditional (male-dominated) ideologies of how women's bodies should look. She suggests that women who believe they are somehow taking control over their bodies (and their lives) by opting for cosmetic surgery have really been coerced by family, friends, partners, and, indirectly, the medical profession, and she believes that the rhetoric of choice that is found in advertising materials for private plastic surgery is "ideological camouflage" which hides the real absence of choice. She believes that cosmetic surgery can never be an acceptable course of action for an individual woman, since to have plastic surgery is to support a system that is oppressive to women. This argument is supported by Susan Bordo (2003):

> Unlike Davis I do not view cosmetic surgery as being first and foremost "about" self-determination or self-deception. Rather my focus is on the complexly and densely institutionalised system of values and practices within which girls and women—and increasingly boys and men as well—come to believe that they are nothing (and are frequently treated as nothing) unless they are trim, tight, lineless, bulgeless, and sagless.
>
> (Bordo, 2003: 32)

Morgan's (1991) examples come from women's magazine and newspaper articles, including personal accounts of experiences of plastic surgery. It is not difficult to find similar examples of media promoting women's "choice" to "resculpt" their bodies in the 2000s. A random selection of advertisements in women's magazines in Britain shows how the advertisers stress improvements in confidence (BUPA: "The real secret to looking good is feeling good"; Transform: "Years of development in plastic surgery enables women to have beautiful breasts and the confidence to enjoy life to the full") and in rationality (the Hospital Group: "If you're not happy with the way you look . . . change it!"; the Pountney Clinic: "[Liposuction] is the logical way to complete a 'trim' figure"), and avoid any mention of pain, stressing instead the virtues of care and reassurance (Transform: "With 30 years' experience and highly qualified and experienced surgeons, we've transformed the lives of over 150,000 patients so you can be confident you're in safe hands"). Pictures of conventionally attractive models appear in the advertisements, along with statements such as "For making me comfortable in sleeveless tops, for letting me relax in photographs, for showing me my best asset is me. Thank you" (BUPA); and "Cosmetic surgery changed my life" (Belvedere Private Clinic). It is also easy to find examples of articles encouraging cosmetic surgery. For instance, one article headed, "Bigger breasts, cheek implants, nose jobs, tummy tucks . . . You'll be surprised at what's available on the NHS [UK National Health Service] —and how easy it is to get it" (*Company*, February 1995) gives readers "nine steps to getting plastic surgery on the NHS." Although the article warns about having unrealistic expectations ("If you're expecting bigger breasts to bring back a straying man, or suddenly give you more confidence in life, you're in for a real disappointment"), telling women how much each operation costs and how to go about getting operations done on the National Health Service suggests general approval of the principle of cosmetic surgery. In conjunction with carrying advertisements for plastic surgery (I have been unable to find any British magazine aimed at young women that does not do so), women's magazines promote the practice.

## Social construction of femininity

Susie Orbach (1993) argued that women are taught from an early age to view their bodies as commodities. She showed how women's bodies are used to humanize and sell products in Western consumer culture, and how the fact that women's bodies themselves are objectified creates body image problems for women:

> The receptivity that women show (across class, ethnicity, and through the generations) to the idea that their bodies are like gardens—arenas for constant improvement and resculpting—is rooted in the recognition of their bodies as commodities. A consumer society in which women's bodies perform the crucial function of humanising other products while being presented as the ultimate commodity creates all sorts of body image problems for women, both at the level of distortion about their own and others' bodies, and in creating a disjuncture from their bodies.
>
> (Orbach, 1993: 17)

Orbach linked the objectification and distancing of the body to the rise of anorexia nervosa, which she characterizes as "a metaphor for our age," in which women use their bodies as statements about their discomfort with their position in the world. This position has been supported through proponents of objectification theory (Frederickson and Roberts, 1997). According to this theory, women's bodies are socially constructed as objects to be watched and evaluated. In order to gain social approval, girls learn to practice self-surveillance, watching themselves and judging themselves against prevailing societal standards as though they were an outside observer. This habitual self-monitoring leads to body shame and dissatisfaction. In one study, Frederickson *et al.* (1998) randomly assigned US student women to conditions in which they were asked to try on either a swimsuit or a sweater (the swimsuit condition was intended to increase self-objectification). When the groups were compared, the swimsuit group had higher levels of body shame on average, ate less when food was available, and performed more poorly on a mathematics test. These data suggest that body surveillance can cause body shame and reduced performance in cognitive spheres, probably due to distraction and deflection of cognitive resources.

Many feminist researchers see women as victims of a society that controls them through their bodies. In the 1980s, several feminist authors suggested that a system of beauty norms set up impossible ideals for women, who were expected to be slender but large breasted. These unrealistic ideals were seen as an ideal way to keep women in a subordinate position, by ensuring that they put their energies into vigilance over their bodies. Women's energies are channeled into the "fight" for a perfect body. Susan Brownmiller (1984), in *Femininity*, presented a seemingly light-hearted but intelligent and hard-hitting analysis of women's relationships with their bodies. She traced the development of women's concern with the body from childhood into adulthood. Drawing on her personal experiences as a woman developing in the USA, she noted how changes in fashions meant that parts of her anatomy that did not change in themselves became more or less problematic depending on current trends. Taking a critical look at the importance of body size in relation to cultural expectations for women, she noted that masculinity is tied to concepts of "powerful" and "large," whereas femininity is linked to "small" and "weak." She argued that pressure on women to be slight and small is driven by men's desire to dominate:

> When a woman stands taller than a man she has broken a cardinal feminine rule, for her physical stature reminds him that he may be too short—inadequate, insufficient—for the competitive world of men. She has dealt a blow to his masculine image, undermined his footing as aggressor-protector.
>
> (Brownmiller, 1984: 13–14)

Brownmiller noted that, in the majority of species, females are in fact the larger sex, despite the anthropomorphic assumptions made by illustrators of children's books. Nevertheless, the associations of maleness with largeness and femaleness with smallness are firmly embedded in our consciousness, leading to discomfort when these expectations are challenged. She argued that this discomfort extends to fleshiness in women, since fat means additional bulk, a property associated with solidity and power, which are not culturally acceptable feminine characteristics. This is despite the fact that women's bodies typically carry 10 percent more fatty tissue than men's. She shows how women's bodies have been controlled and restricted across civilizations to conform to prevailing aesthetics, and how these practices served to weaken women physically, making them more dependent on men.

Brownmiller traced the history of the prevailing current vogue for extreme slimness, showing how ideals of feminine perfection have changed over the years and pointing to the voluptuous nudes portrayed by Ingres in *The Turkish Bath* (Plate 11), and the women of the Ziegfeld Follies with their 36–26–38 figures and the accent on their hips.

She also noted the importance of the bikini (which looks most

*Plate 11* Jean-Auguste-Dominique Ingres, *The Turkish Bath* (1863).

*Source*: Musée du Louvre © Photo RMN, Gérard Blot.

pleasing on a skinny body), and of both Jacqueline Kennedy (a determined dieter) and Twiggy (Plate 5), in determining the fashion for slimness in the USA in the 1960s. Slenderness became identified with refinement, willpower, and chic, and success at dieting became an important form of competition among women within a context where women were encouraged to compete in physical appearance. She argued forcibly that striving for physical perfection (a physical vulnerability that is reassuring to men) was a constant distraction for women, causing us to be self-conscious, and constantly self-monitor:

> [We are] never quite satisfied, and never secure, for desperate unending absorption in the drive for a perfect appearance—call it feminine vanity—is the ultimate restriction on freedom of mind.
>
> (Brownmiller, 1984: 33)

Wendy Chapkis (1986) argued that women are oppressed by a "global culture machine" (made up of the advertising industry, communications media, and the cosmetic industry) that promotes a narrow, Westernized ideal of beauty to women all over the world. Chapkis looked at the rituals that women go through to try to attain the ideal, and used these to demonstrate how oppressive these beauty regimes are of women. She argued that women are entrapped in the beauty system, but that there are opportunities for change if women are willing to accept themselves and their bodies as they really are. This would involve close examination of "beauty secrets" (the rituals that most women undertake to try to conform to the cultural ideal) and rejection of these in favor of a celebration of the "natural" body.

Susan Bordo (2003) argued that preoccupation with fat, diet, and slenderness in women is normative. She suggested that Western culture surrounds women with clear messages that overweight (described as "bulges" and "bumps") must be "destroyed," "eliminated," or "burned." The ideal is a body completely under control, toned, and contained, an ideal that can be achieved through dieting or extreme exercise and bodybuilding. She argued that the seemingly disparate areas of bodybuilding and compulsive dieting are linked in their rejection of loose, soft flesh:

> The two ideals, though superficially very different, are united in a battle against a common enemy: the soft, the loose, unsolid, excess flesh. It is perfectly permissible in our culture (even for women) to have substantial weight and bulk—so long as it is tightly managed.
>
> (Bordo, 2003: 191)

Bordo's analysis places women's preoccupation with slimness into a cultural context in order to explain why women are especially susceptible to pressures from the beauty system. She is pessimistic about women's ability really to resist these pressures. She argues that women cannot help but collude in the system because they are submerged in the culture in which slimness in women is associated with a specific (positive) set of cultural meanings. She says that feminists should be skeptical about the possibility of developing free, feminine identities that are independent of the mainstream beauty culture, and she shows how women's attempts to escape the system may be reabsorbed into negative discourses of femininity. Citing the Foucauldian position that individual self-surveillance and self-correction to prevailing social norms may be just as effective at controlling behavior as physical violence and material constraints, she relates this to appearance-related behaviors:

> When it comes to the politics of appearance such ideas are apt and illuminating. In my work they have been extremely helpful both to my analysis of the contemporary disciplines of diet and exercise and to my understanding of eating disorders as arising out of and reproducing normative feminine practices in our culture, practices which train the female body in docility and obedience to cultural demands while at the same time being experienced in terms of power and control.
>
> (Bordo, 2003: 27)

In contrast, Dorothy Smith (1990) saw women in an active role in interpreting cultural messages. She argued that women "do femininity" in an active way. She represented "femininity" as a skilled activity. One of the sources of learning the skill of "being feminine" is to read appropriate materials (especially women's magazines) in which information is actively presented on how to be more attractive. The material itself requires prior knowledge in the area to place it into context. Smith showed how women's magazine articles assume agency in the reader, and how they work by presenting the woman with a specific ideal (in the representation of a "perfect" model body), and telling her what she needs to do to attain the ideal (diet, exercise, and use cellulite creams and makeup). She argued that the creation of dissatisfaction in women leads to active attempts to rectify the perceived deficiency. Women objectify their bodies and are constantly planning and enacting measures to bring them closer to the ideal.

Sandra Bartky (1990) also saw women as engaging actively with the representation of the female body. She argued that what she called the "fashion–beauty complex" seeks (on the surface) to provide opportunities for women to indulge themselves, but covertly depreciates women's bodies by constantly presenting messages that women fail to measure up to the current ideals:

> We are presented everywhere with images of perfect female beauty— at the drugstore cosmetics display, the supermarket magazine counter, on television. These images remind us constantly that we fail to measure up. Whose nose is the right shape, after all, whose hips are not too wide—or too narrow? The female body is revealed as a task, an object in need of transformation. . . . The fashion–beauty complex produces in women an estrangement from her bodily being: on the one hand, she is it and is scarcely allowed to be anything else; on the other hand, she must exist perpetually at a distance from her physical self, fixed at this distance in a permanent posture of disapproval.
>
> (Bartky, 1990: 40)

Bartky noted that every aspect of women's bodies is objectified, so that women feel estranged from their bodies. She suggested that the pleasures that women report in body-maintenance procedures result from the creation of "false needs" by the fashion–beauty complex, which produces the needs themselves (through indoctrination, psychological manipulation, and the denial of autonomy), and also controls the conditions through which these needs can be satisfied. She argued that the repressive narcissistic satisfactions promoted by the fashion–beauty complex stand in the way of authentic delight in the body. She suggested a revolutionary aesthetic of the body, which allows an expansion of ideas of beauty and allows body display and play in self-ornamentation. She promoted the release of our capacity to apprehend the beautiful from the narrow limits within which it is currently confined, to produce an aesthetic for the female body controlled by women. She proposed that women should produce a model of feminine beauty that celebrates diversity. This could be an ideal that actually makes women feel better about themselves, rather than one that breeds body insecurity among those who do not conform to the slender, well-toned, mainstream cultural ideal.

Feminist accounts of women's experience of the body are important in helping to make sense of why women in particular show normative body concern. There can be no doubt that Western culture in the 2000s promotes unrealistic body ideals to women, and that nonconformity to these ideals leads to social disapproval. The question of women's active involvement in restrictive beauty practices (such as dieting and cosmetic surgery) is more complex, and writers such as Sandra Bartky have provided useful critiques of women's active involvement in the process of "doing femininity," seeing women as active agents who make knowledgeable choices about body practices within a restricted range of cultural options. Women's bodies are subject to critical evaluation to the extent that they differ from an established norm based on a youthful, slender ideal. Women who have social support for an alternative body type (such as the physique bodybuilders whose interviews are described above) report relative satisfaction with their bodies, but only to the extent that their bodies comply with an alternative norm (too muscled or too much body hair and they will no longer be satisfactory). Chapter 6 investigates factors that may predict higher satisfaction in some groups of women. Chapter 7 investigates ways of using what we know about body dissatisfaction to promote a more positive body image in women.

## Summary

- Many women in Western societies are dissatisfied with their bodies, particularly their stomach, hips, and thighs.
- Most women would choose to be thinner than they currently are and tend to overestimate the size of key body sites, irrespective of current size.
- Questionnaires and interviews have found a similar pattern of dissatisfaction in British, Canadian, US, and Australian women.
- Feminist approaches to understanding women's dissatisfaction suggest that social pressure on women to strive for the slender, toned body shape that is associated with youth, control, and success encourages the objectification of the body and the disproportionate allocation of energies to body maintenance.
- A positive way forward is indicated by feminist scholars such as Susan Bordo, Naomi Wolf, and Sandra Bartky, who promote the development of a new aesthetic of the female body that would push back the limits of acceptable body shape and size in Western societies.

# 4    Men and body image

The study of the psychology and sociology of the male body is a relatively recent phenomenon. Until the 1980s, the study of body image was largely restricted to women. Women's bodies have historically been represented more frequently in the media than men's, and descriptions of women tend to be more embodied than those of men (Bordo, 2003). Over the last two decades, psychologists (see reviews by Pope *et al.*, 2000; McCabe and Ricciardelli, 2004; Cafri *et al.*, 2005; Thompson and Cafri, 2007) and sociologists (see Monaghan, 1999, 2005a, 2005b) have become increasingly interested in men's body image and male embodiment. This is largely due to the fact that the male body has become more visible in popular culture, producing interest in the effects of this increased visibility on men's image of their bodies. This chapter summarizes current research and assesses what we know about men's body image in the mid-2000s.

There is a general consensus that most men aspire to a muscular mesomorphic shape characterized by average build with well-developed muscles on chest, arms, and shoulders, and slim waist and hips, rather than an ectomorphic (thin) or endomorphic (fat) build. Harrison Pope and colleagues in *The Adonis Complex* (2000) have argued that men idealize the slender, muscled physique presented in popular Western media. Low body fat levels are a crucial part of this ideal physique, as they allow muscles to be more visible (Cafri and Thompson, 2004). Having a flat and toned stomach is seen by some as a status symbol in its own right. For instance, in an interview with *The Observer Magazine* in Britain, David Zinczenko (author of *The Abs Diet*) says:

> In some ways being thin is more of a status symbol than it's ever been because of how overweight some people are. If you have a flat stomach, you're probably in control under very trying circumstances. These days, everybody has an iPod. Everyone can afford a

plasma TV. A flat stomach is a much more difficult thing to come by. It's a way to stand out.

(Leith, 2006: 33).

The slender, muscular shape is the masculine ideal because it is intimately tied to Western cultural notions of maleness as representing power and strength. Mansfield and McGinn (1993: 49) argue that "muscularity and masculinity can be, and often are, conflated." However, although moderate muscularity is rated highly, extreme muscularity (such as seen in male bodybuilders) is not universally acceptable, being perceived as unnatural and as reflecting narcissism by many men (Aoki, 1996; St Martin and Gavey, 1996). The Western cultural ideal is generally slender and moderately muscular, without being overmuscled (Mansfield and McGinn, 1993; Monaghan, 2005a).

## Assessment of body image

A similar array of techniques has been used to assess body image in men to that used for women; indeed, most measures were developed for use with women and have been adapted for use with men. The exceptions are measures of drive for muscularity that have been designed in the 2000s for use with men (McCreary and Sasse, 2000), and some other measures that have been developed so as to be gender-free (Cash, 2000). Results from studies using a range of available measures will be considered in turn here to evaluate the degree and direction of body dissatisfaction in men.

### *Figural rating scales*

Studies using male silhouette figures, in which men have been asked to identify the figure most similar to their current body shape and their body shape ideals, have produced interesting findings. In a classic study conducted in the 1980s, April Fallon and Paul Rozin (1985) showed nine male silhouettes (Figure 4.1) to 248 US undergraduate students and asked them to indicate the figures that approximated their current figure, what they would like to look like, and what women would prefer. There was no significant discrepancy between these men's ideal, the figure they would expect women to prefer, and their perceived current shape. Fallon and Rozin conclude that men's perceptions serve to keep them satisfied with their figures, and relate the findings to the lower incidences of dieting, anorexia, and bulimia in US men than in US women. In line with most other researchers working with figural rating

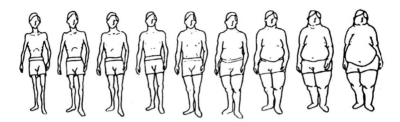

*Figure 4.1* Figural rating scale for men.

*Source*: Adapted from Stunckard *et al.*, 1983 with permission.

scales at this time, Fallon and Rozin based their conclusions on scores averaged across their samples. However, although body dissatisfaction in women usually relates to feeling overweight, body dissatisfaction in men may relate to feeling either overweight or underweight. Averaging has the effect of combining together men who believe they are either overweight or underweight compared to their ideal, so that on average they may appear to have no discrepancy between their ideal and current body (Drewnowski and Yee, 1987). Data need to be considered in terms of discrepancies between current and ideal shape whatever the direction of those differences, to take account of those who are dissatisfied because they feel too thin as well as those who are dissatisfied because they feel too fat.

Marc Mishkind and colleagues (1986) took this methodological problem into account when designing their study. They found that, when shown a similar set of silhouette drawings of male body types ranging from very thin to very fat, 75 percent of men reported that their ideal was discrepant from their current body size. Roughly half wanted to be bigger, and half wanted to be thinner than they were. In this respect, there is an important difference between men and women on these silhouette tasks. Women reliably pick a slimmer ideal than their current shape. Men are equally likely to pick a thinner or a larger ideal. Wanting to be larger and wanting to be thinner both represent body dissatisfaction. These differences between men are lost when researchers average across groups. Mishkind *et al.*'s data suggest that a significant proportion of men are dissatisfied with their body shape.

Another problem with the figural rating scale methodology when applied to men is that men may be primarily concerned with the degree of muscularity of the target figures rather than size per se. Shawn Lynch and Debra Zellner (1999) investigated the effects of increased levels of muscularity by producing a set of male figures with the same body fat levels but increased muscularity, and they found that their sample of US male college students chose ideals that were significantly more muscular than their current shape, and that these men assumed that women preferred a significantly more muscular body than the men's current size.

Lynch and Zellner's (1999) finding is interesting in showing that young men, on average, desire to be more muscular, but their methodology did not enable men to indicate any interaction in preference between fat levels and desired muscularity. In 1999, Amanda Gruber, in collaboration with Harrison Pope and colleagues, developed the Somatomorphic Matrix (Pope *et al.*, 2000). This is a computerized body image test that enables men to choose between male figures that vary along the two crucial dimensions of muscularity and fatness (Figure 4.2). Images are displayed on a computer screen, and men can adjust the image by clicking on "buttons" on the screen to make the image more or less muscular and more or less fat. This method has enabled Harrison Pope and colleagues to produce data on preferred degree of muscularity and body fat in samples of US, Austrian, and French men, finding that college-aged men in all three countries showed a preference for an ideal that was significantly more muscular than the men's current body shape, and believed that women preferred a significantly more muscular body for men than these men's current body. This result has been replicated in several other recent studies (Frederick *et al.*, 2005).

Most studies of men's figure preferences have been conducted with men in their twenties. The picture becomes more complex with older men, who may be less satisfied with their body fat but more satisfied with their degree of muscularity than younger men. Shawn Lynch and Debra Zellner found that their group of older men (averaging about 45 years old) did not show the same discrepancies between their current and ideal degrees of muscularity, suggesting that older men may be more satisfied with their bodies (Lynch and Zellner, 1999). However, Sue Lamb and colleagues (1993) administered silhouette scales to older and younger US men and found that older men (aged about 50) presented body ideals that were much thinner than their perceived size, suggesting that some middle-aged men may be dissatisfied with their fat levels. Possible reasons for these differences will be discussed in Chapter 6 in relation to changes in body satisfaction across the life span.

### Questionnaire studies

Most of the early body satisfaction questionnaires have been designed to look at body dissatisfaction in women, and contain items that are not

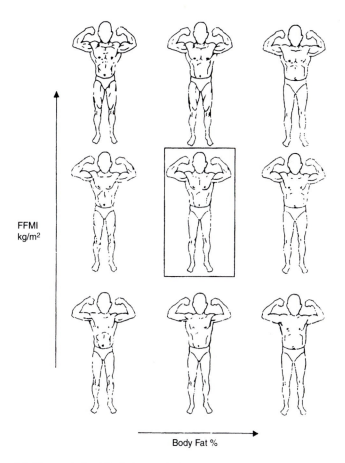

*Figure 4.2* Computerized body image test.

*Source*: Adapted from Pope *et al.*, 2000 with permission.

*NB*: FFMI = Fat Free Mass Index (see Pope *et al.*, 2000: 245)

relevant to men. Questionnaires aimed at women tend to be designed to assess desire to be thinner, and concern about lower-body fatness, whereas male body concerns tend to center on wanting to gain muscle from the waist upward (Cafri and Thompson, 2004). However, some of the early measures are equally appropriate for use with both men and women, and others have been developed recently specifically for use with men.

One of the earliest scales that could be used with male samples was the Body Esteem Scale (Franzoi and Shields, 1984), which assesses satisfaction with a number of body parts and can be applied to men as well as to women. According to Franzoi and Shields, the crucial determinants of men's body satisfaction are physical attractiveness (face and facial features), upper body strength (biceps, shoulder width, arms, and chest), and physical conditioning (stamina, weight, and energy level), and when the scale is used with a male sample, a 13-item physical condition and a nine-item upper body strength subscale score can be calculated in addition to the 13-item physical attractiveness subscale. These subscales have good internal reliability and validity (Franzoi and Shields, 1984), and the questionnaire has been used effectively in a number of studies with US and British male samples. For instance, in 1994, Adrian Furnham and Nicola Greaves administered the measure to 47 British men aged 18–35 (mostly university undergraduates). Participants were asked to rate (on a 10-point scale, from 1 = complete dissatisfaction to 10 = complete satisfaction) how satisfied they were with their nose, lips, waist, thighs, ears, biceps, chin, buttocks, width of shoulders, arms, chest, eyes, cheeks, hips, legs, feet, stomach, body hair, face, and weight. They were also asked to rate "attempt to change" each body part on a similar 10-point scale. Men were least satisfied with biceps, width of shoulders, and chest measurement, and were most likely to try to change these aspects of the body. This finding coincides with current ideals of male body shape, where the emphasis is on broad shoulders and well-muscled chest and arms.

Don McCreary and colleagues in Canada have developed a questionnaire that is specifically designed to assess attitudes and behaviors relating to drive for muscularity, so it is particularly appropriate for use with men (McCreary and Sasse, 2002; McCreary et al., 2004). The Drive for Muscularity Scale is a 15-item questionnaire that measures the extent to which people desire to have a more muscular body. The items are a mix of questions relating to attitudes and behaviors scored on a six-point Likert scale from "always" to "never." Sample questions include "I wish I were more muscular" and "I feel guilty if I miss a weight-training session." The questionnaire gives three scores: a total drive for muscularity score, and subscale scores for muscularity-related attitudes and behaviors. McCreary and colleagues report good levels of internal reliability (alphas between .87 and .92) and validity (McCreary et al., 2006). Scores on this questionnaire have indicated that drive for muscularity in men is unrelated to actual muscularity (McCreary et al., 2006), although it is related to psychological variables such as self-esteem and depression (McCreary and Sasse, 2002).

Tracy Tykla and colleagues (2005) have recently developed a body attitudes scale specifically designed for use with men. The Male Body

Attitudes Scale assesses three dimensions of body attitudes (muscularity, low body fat, and height), and has good internal reliability, test–retest reliability, and validity. Items include "I think I have too little muscle on my body" (muscularity subscale), "I think my body should be leaner" (low body fat subscale), and "I wish I were taller" (height subscale). Scores on all subscales and total score were correlated significantly with men's self-esteem, suggesting that low self-esteem is linked to body dissatisfaction in men as well as in women, supporting suggestions by other authors (McCabe and Ricciardelli, 2003) and contrary to suggestions that men's self-esteem is independent of their body image (Ogden, 1992). This scale is useful for assessing male body image, since it covers height, which has been largely ignored in body image research, but which has emerged in interviews as a determinant of men's satisfaction (Grogan and Richards, 2002).

Thomas Cash's Multidimensional Body–Self Relations Questionnaire (MBSRQ) (Cash, 2000), has a series of body area satisfaction subscales that enable the researcher to identify areas of the body that cause dissatisfaction in men and women. In their 1986 study, Tom Cash and colleagues found that 34 percent of men were generally dissatisfied with their looks, 41 percent with their weight, 32 percent with muscle tone, 28 percent with upper torso, 50 percent with midtorso, and 21 percent with lower torso. These percentages were higher than in a similar study in the 1970s (Berscheid *et al.*, 1973), which had found that only 15 percent of men reported general dissatisfaction with their looks, 35 percent with their weight, 25 percent with muscle tone, 18 percent with upper torso, 36 percent with midtorso, and 12 percent with lower torso. The difference between these two studies suggests that men in the 1980s were less satisfied than men in the 1970s. In 1997, David Garner replicated the study and found even higher percentages of dissatisfied men. In this study, 43 percent of men were generally dissatisfied with their looks, 52 percent with their weight, 45 percent with muscle tone, 38 percent with upper torso, 63 percent with midtorso, and 29 percent with lower torso (Garner, 1997). These data suggest a notable increase in dissatisfaction in US men completing these questionnaires in the journal *Psychology Today* over the 30-year period.

Clare Donaldson (1996) administered the MBSRQ body area satisfaction subscales and some additional body image items to 100 male students in Manchester, UK. They ranged from 18 to 43 years of age, with an average age of 28. The majority (85) were white. They ranged in height from 5 feet 4 inches to 6 feet 6 inches, and in weight from 7 stone 11 lb (109 lb) to 17 stone 12 lb (250 lb). She found that 27 percent of men in the sample were dissatisfied with their weight, showing that men in this sample were, on average, more satisfied than Cash *et al.*'s (1986) US men. However, 38 percent were dissatisfied with their muscle tone, 25 percent with lower torso, 28 percent with midtorso, and 37 percent with upper torso. When asked about general body satisfaction, only 10 percent of the men reported that they were generally dissatisfied with their body, and 65 percent said that they often liked themselves the way they were. However, when asked how often they felt depressed about their body image, only 47 percent said that they "never" felt depressed about their looks, 4 percent saying they "often" did, and 1 percent "very often." These data show these men to be clearly more satisfied with their bodies than equivalent groups of women, but nevertheless to have some dissatisfaction with body shape and size.

Helen Fawkner (2004) administered the MBSRQ (and other measures) to a sample of 369 Australian men aged 17–89 years, with an average age of 35 years. Average weight was 170 lb (standard deviation 27 lb). She found that 29 percent were dissatisfied with their weight; lower than Cash's 1980s American sample, and similar to Donaldson's British men. Twenty-four percent were dissatisfied with their muscle tone, 21 percent with upper torso, 41 percent with midtorso, and 18 percent with lower torso. Only 10 percent were dissatisfied with their overall appearance.

Some studies report much higher estimates of dissatisfaction in British men. For instance, a survey commissioned by *Men's Health* magazine was completed by 1,000 of the magazine's readers. A total of 75 percent were not happy with their body shape. Most wished their bodies were more muscular. About half were worried about their weight, aging, and going bald (Chaudhary, 1996). Such findings need to be interpreted with caution, since the readers of *Men's Health* may be a group of men particularly sensitive to body image issues whose views are not representative of the general population of British men. However, the findings do demonstrate significant body image concern in men who read magazines that promote a healthy lifestyle and present the slender, muscular male body as the ideal body shape.

In another study, body image questionnaires, including open-ended items asking about body satisfaction and some closed-ended items asking about thoughts, feelings, and behaviors relevant to body image, were administered to 100 men in Gainesville, Florida (Grogan, 1999). Respondents ranged in age from 16 to 48 (average age 23), in height from 5 feet to 6 feet 5 inches (average 5 feet 11 inches), and in weight from 8 stone 6 lb (118 lb) to 19 stone 9 lb (275 lb) (average weight 12 stone 5 lb (173 lb)). Only 6.3 percent reported that they were not generally happy with their body (slightly lower than the 10 percent estimate from Donaldson's British men). However, 72 percent would feel better if they became more muscular, and 80 percent would feel better if they became more toned. Only 22 percent would feel better if they were thinner. Muscularity and body tone were clearly important to these men, replicating Donaldson's British results and supporting Fawkner's Australian data. When asked about drugs they had taken to change body shape and size, 3 percent reported that they had taken anabolic steroids, suggesting significant use of steroids among this group of men. Ninety percent exercised regularly, 55 percent played team/ball games (mostly basketball and American football), 18 percent did aerobics, 68 percent did weight training, and 36 percent walked, cycled, or roller-bladed. When asked why they exercised, 23 percent said they did so for health and fitness, 41 percent for weight/shape/appearance, 21 percent for stress relief, and 30 percent for social reasons. These results replicated Donaldson's British findings in showing that a similar group of US men were also primarily concerned with muscularity and body tone, and that they were actively involved in trying to change their body shape and size through exercise (which more men did for cosmetic reasons than for any other reasons); dieting (which usually entailed either more "healthy" eating, i.e., more fruit and vegetables or restriction of food intake); and, in a small number of cases, taking diet pills, stimulants, or anabolic steroids to change body size.

Questionnaire findings have helped to build up a picture of body satisfaction in men. Most data come from samples of men in the 18–35-years-old range, who have been found to have significant areas of dissatisfaction related to muscularity and body tone, particularly relating to upper body size and muscularity. Dissatisfaction seems to have increased significantly since the 1970s, a relatively large number of men in Western cultures experiencing some dissatisfaction with the way that they look, and some men changing their behavior specifically to modify their appearance.

*Interview studies*

One of the limitations of the questionnaires measuring aspects of body evaluation is that they do not tell us why men are dissatisfied, and how this dissatisfaction affects the rest of their lives. Interviews enable men to explain more about their experiences of embodiment, and help to develop further our understanding of men's experiences of body dissatisfaction.

Jane Ogden (1992) reports interviews in which she asked men to talk about their bodies. The results were interesting. She found that the men she interviewed were clear on how the ideal man should look. He should be tall and well-built, with wide shoulders, V-shaped back, firm buttocks, and flat stomach. Men emphasized fitness and health as being important, and linked the slim, muscular ideal with being confident and in control. There are obvious parallels here with our interviews with women, where being slim was equated with being confident and in control.

In a recent British focus group study, men aged 16–25 years talked about body image and body dissatisfaction (Grogan and Richards, 2002). Older men in the sample (age 18–25 years) were in agreement that the ideal male body is toned and muscular. Being muscular was linked with being healthy and fit. These ideals correspond exactly to the cultural ideal of the well-toned mesomorph. These men believed that the ideal body was within their reach (through exercise), but were not motivated to exercise to change their body shape, since it was not sufficiently important to them. They believed that women were more likely to be motivated to exercise to change body image, but that body shape mattered less to men. They agreed that feeling that they were looking good affected their self-esteem, linking looking good (having a well-toned, muscular body) with feelings of confidence and power in social situations.

Similar findings emerged from focus groups with younger men aged 16–17 years (Grogan and Richards, 2002). These younger men's ideal build was muscular and relatively slender. Several of them said that they wished that they were bigger and had more muscle. The desire to be big and muscular was clearly distinguished from a fear of being big and fat. Being fat rather than muscular was related to weakness of will and lack of control. Two of the young men felt fat (although they were within the normal weight range), and explained how they laughed about excess weight as a way of covering up their embarrassment about feeling fat. All these young men were concerned with the way that they looked, believing either that they were too thin and needed to put on muscle, or that they were too fat and needed to lose weight. When asked whether they felt external pressure to look a certain way, all felt pressure from others. Pressure came mainly from male peers. Competing with peers and fitting in with the group in terms of size were given as an explicit reason by some of the interviewees, who wanted to be as big as their friends. We have rarely encountered such explicit competition with peers when talking to women. For instance:

> I need to be a bit bigger because my brothers are like six foot, and I'm a couple of inches shorter than all my friends as well, and I feel pressure.

If you've got friends who are, like, quite big in build, you want to be the same as them. Although you might not be able to do anything about it, it's on your conscience all the time. You want to be that sort of size.

However, these men were clear that they were only willing to put limited resources into trying to attain their ideal body shape. For instance:

It would be nice to look rather large, but I'm not really bothered if I don't look that big, and I wouldn't mind looking like that [the Chippendales dance troupe]. But I wouldn't put myself out to look like it, you know.

Reporting that they were not sufficiently concerned about the look of their bodies to exercise or diet reflects traditional male discourses on self-reliance and detachment, and may underestimate these men's investment in their bodies. Dieting in particular has been seen as a feminine activity and inappropriate for men, who are expected to eat heartily and not be concerned either with dieting or with healthy eating (Gough, 2007). Muscle tone and muscle mass were important to these young men, supporting suggestions that muscle tone is central to male physical attractiveness. Men compared themselves with their male friends, and wanted to "fit in" with them in terms of body size. To be smaller or fatter than the ideal was seen to be problematic, suggesting that men want to be "average," to have bodies that are not noticeable, supporting Ogden (1992).

Self-confidence and self-esteem were related to how good they felt about their bodies, supporting questionnaire work cited earlier and conflicting with Ogden's (1992) suggestion that men's body image is independent of their self-esteem. It is possible that the cultural shift in the importance attached to the appearance of the body for men in the 1990s and 2000s (Pope *et al.*, 2000; Thompson and Cafri, 2007) has led to an increased association between self-esteem and body satisfaction in men. This would explain the difference between Ogden's results from the early 1990s and other, more recent work that has found an association between self-esteem and body satisfaction in men (Grogan and Richards, 2002; McCabe and Ricciardelli, 2003; Tykla *et al.*, 2005).

Helen Fawkner (2004) ran focus groups with 34 Australian men in which they discussed body image and media imagery of the body. The results showed that many men reported that appearance was important to them and had considerable influence on their day-to-day interactions. The men reported that comments from partners or potential partners were influential in evaluating their own attractiveness and influencing their body image. Their ideal images were tall, slim, and V-shaped. All men reported some degree of comparison with media imagery. However, few men reported negative impacts of these comparisons, and few would modify their behavior to try to emulate these ideals. Exercisers and gay men were most likely to report negative affect as a result of comparisons with idealized media imagery, and were most likely to engage in unhealthy behaviors to try to change their body shapes. Fawkner (2004) suggests that exercise may increase narcissistic investment in one's body in vulnerable men, particularly in gay men. This will be investigated further in Chapter 6.

In another recent British interview study conducted by Gillian Adams and colleagues, men aged 18–32 took part in semistructured interviews in which they discussed experiences of body dissatisfaction (Adams *et al.*, 2005). The men interviewed described body dissatisfaction in cognitive, behavioral, and affective terms, and dissatisfaction was reflected in perceived discrepancy between their current and ideal bodies. Triggers for feeling dissatisfied were usually interpersonal. Negative feedback from others, especially sexual partners, was particularly salient, and comparison with other men's bodies also caused distress. In the absence of social contact, body dissatisfaction was not sufficient to promote behavior change, and most men did not engage in appearance-fixing behaviors, such as exercise and diet, simply because they were aware of a discrepancy between ideal and current body, supporting the findings of the Grogan and Richards (2002) and Fawkner (2004) studies described above.

### Body size estimation techniques

There have been fewer studies of size estimation with men than with women, probably because early work focused on size overestimation in young women with eating problems. However, recent work has suggested that men tend to overestimate their body size to a similar extent to women. There is some argument as to whether BMI affects the degree of overestimation, and although some authors have found that BMI is unrelated to overestimation (Monteath and McCabe, 1997), others have argued that heavier men tend to underestimate their body size more than thinner men, suggesting that individuals try to bring their body size estimate closer to a perceived average male figure (Smeets *et al.*, 1998).

In a highly sophisticated study on body size estimation, Marita McCabe and colleagues (2006) used their digital body image computer program to enable men to manipulate on-screen a full frontal image of their body at five points: chest, waist, hips, thighs, and calves. Their 82 male participants were aged 18–36 years, with BMI range of 18–36. Relative to a control condition in which the men estimated the size of a vase, they overestimated the size of all five body regions on average. The degree of overestimation was comparable to a female sample tested by the same procedure. The authors concluded that size overestimation may bring men's bodies more in line with the muscular male ideal, and so may have quite a different effect from size overestimation in women. Men with higher BMI were more likely to overestimate the size of their bodies, contrary to suggestions that heavier men underestimate the size of their bodies (e.g., Smeets *et al.*, 1998). Clearly, future work needs to go further in terms of differentiating between perceptions of own size and degree of muscularity, which may be particularly relevant to a male sample (McCreary and Sasse, 2000; Pope *et al.*, 2000). This work is informative in relation to gender and size estimation in showing that both men and women tend to overestimate the size of key body areas.

## Behavioral indicators of body dissatisfaction

There are a number of appearance-fixing (Cash, 2002) behaviors in which men might engage to try to change the look of their bodies and to reduce body dissatisfaction. The focus here will be on four kinds of body-relevant behaviors: dieting, exercise and bodybuilding, steroid use, and cosmetic surgery.

### Dieting

Dieting is significantly less frequent among men than among women, and is generally seen as not gender appropriate for men (Gough, 2007). A recent MINTEL survey in Britain found that 25 percent of men are dieting at any one time compared to 42 percent of women (Leith, 2006), although significantly more men in Britain are overweight than women (44 percent of men versus 34 percent of women) (Office of National Statistics, 2005). Dieting is generally perceived as a feminine-appropriate behavior, and men tend to exercise rather than diet if they want to lose weight (Grogan and Richards, 2002; Grogan *et al.*, 2006). However, a relatively small proportion of men within the normal weight range do diet to try to lose weight, and the number of men who refer for eating disorders is on the increase, particularly among gay men (Strong *et al.*, 2000). Dieting may be more frequent in men who are sensitive to health issues than in the more general male population. For instance, in a survey commissioned by *Men's Health* magazine in the 1990s, six out of 10 men who responded had dieted to lose weight, and all reported that they were successful in losing weight in the long term (Chaudhary, 1996). However, men who choose to respond to questionnaires in magazines may not be representative of the male population, and most estimates are much lower than this.

Clare Donaldson (1996) found that 20 percent of her sample of British male undergraduates had dieted. Eleven percent of the sample indicated that they "rarely" dieted, 4 percent "sometimes" did, 4 percent "often" did, and 1 percent "very often" dieted. Proportions of male students who diet in the USA may be higher than among British students. When the male Florida respondents to the survey mentioned earlier in this chapter were asked whether they had ever dieted, 40 percent replied in the affirmative. However, when asked specifically what they ate when they dieted, only 14 percent reported reducing food intake generally. The rest reported eating more fruit and vegetables and reducing fat intake, which sounds more like "healthy eating" than "dieting." Certainly, men's style magazines such as *Men's Health* and *Men's Fitness* tend to promote low-fat diets rather than calorie counting, and emphasize looking and feeling good rather than slimness. In a recent interview with *The Observer Magazine* in Britain, Morgan Rees, editor of *Men's Health*, is clear that the aim of the magazine is to encourage men to adopt more healthy eating patterns, rather than to diet:

> Pictures of six-packs, far from making you feel bad about how you are, exist to make you feel good about how you might become. Morgan Rees says, "We want the image to look achievable." And *Men's Health*, he adds, does not encourage men to diet. "We don't really favour diets," he says, "we favour healthy eating."
>
> (Leith, 2006: 32)

The Atkins diet, which focuses on high-protein, low-carbohydrate food, has had a relatively high uptake by men, and it has been suggested that this is because Robert Atkins focuses on health as well as weight loss, and because his diet is male-appropriate in that men can continue to eat meat:

> It was a lean, mean, hunter's diet. In a way it was like eating muscles.
>
> (Leith, 2006: 32)

Eating less to lose weight has generally been seen as a feminine activity (Bordo, 2003), and would not be expected to lead directly to the muscular physique that is the cultural ideal for men, so it is perhaps not surprising that men are less likely to diet than women. Men are more likely to try to bulk up by eating a high-protein diet, such as the Atkins diet, or to reduce the fat in their diets, than to reduce calorie intake in order to try to attain a slender physique (McCreary and Sasse, 2002; Leith, 2006). This may differ for heterosexual and gay men (Conner *et al.*, 2004), as will be addressed in Chapter 6.

*Exercise and bodybuilding*

Although men are significantly less likely than women to be motivated to exercise for appearance reasons (Grogan *et al.*, 2006a), a significant proportion of men use exercise to try to change the way that they look. This is particularly the case for older men. Caroline Davis and colleagues (1995) found that although younger women reported more weight-control motivation for exercise, older men were more likely than older women to use exercise to control their weight. These age differences will be explored further in Chapter 6.

In Clare Donaldson's (1996) study, 65 percent of her respondents reported engaging in sport specifically to improve their body image. The activities most obviously linked to improvement in body image for men are weight training and bodybuilding, activities that would be expected to lead to development of muscle mass, to bring the male body more into line with the slender and muscular ideal. Peter Baker (1994) reported that 500,000 British men regularly used weights to get into shape, and an increasing number use steroids to accelerate the effects of exercise. Harrison Pope *et al.* (2000) have also noted a significant increase in weight training in US men, linked with concerns about being insufficiently muscular (see also Thompson and Cafri, 2007).

Bodybuilding is becoming more and more popular worldwide as a way for men to attain the culturally valued slender, muscular body (Pope *et al.*, 2000; Thompson and Cafri, 2007). In 1996, Paul Husband and I carried out a study of body image in bodybuilders specifically for the previous edition of this book. We administered in-depth questionnaires and interviews to 10 male bodybuilders in their twenties and thirties in Manchester gyms. The men were between 5 feet 7 inches and 6 feet 3 inches tall (mean height 5 feet 10 inches), and ranged in weight from 9 stone (126 lb) to 17 stone (238 lb), with a mean of 12.7 stone (178 lb). They all trained with weights regularly (most days), although one had only recently joined the gym. When asked about activities engaged in specifically to improve body image, four out of 10 had dieted, one had cut out meals, five had cut out alcohol, three had played more sport, three had stopped eating carryout food, three had been running, four had used sunbeds, and one had used fake tan. The percentage of men in this small group who had dieted (40 percent) is significantly higher than most estimates of dieting in men: Clare Donaldson (1996) found that 20 percent of her sample of undergraduate students (in the same age range as these bodybuilders) had dieted, and Fallon and Rozin (1988) set their estimate at 25 percent. This is not surprising, since diet (and nutrition in general) is as important as weight training in the manipulation of fat-to-muscle ratios. Prior to competition (for instance), professional bodybuilders reduce body fat to an absolute minimum to reveal muscle definition and detail (Francis, 1989). These men were significantly more satisfied with their lower torso than with any other part of their bodies, in line with other work on men's body satisfaction (Donaldson, 1996; Garner, 1997; Fawkner, 2004). On average, they were "somewhat satisfied" with their weight; height; upper, mid- and lower torso; and overall appearance.

When asked whether they would like to look more like magazine models, these men, on average, said that they sometimes wished they could look more like the models (with a range from never to always); but when asked how satisfaction with their own appearance was affected by such images, these men, on average, said they were unaffected, and that such images did not make them feel like improving their physical appearance. It may be important here that we asked about images of male models in general (to which these bodybuilders may not aspire, since such models may be perceived to be insufficiently muscular). Interview work with these young adult male bodybuilders has suggested that they may compare themselves unfavorably to other highly muscled men, and this may motivate them to train harder. For instance:

> Before I started being interested in lifting weights, when I saw a competitive bodybuilder, when I saw the *Gladiators* on television, you know, it made you think, you know, it made you want to be like them.

These results suggest that other highly muscled men become a standard for comparison, against which these men compared themselves unfavorably, prompting the decision to weight train. All our interviewees described how they made unfavorable comparisons with other bodybuilders seen at the gym, and how these motivated them to try to gain more muscle. For instance:

> I remember one time when I was about 17 stone [238 1b], I thought I was getting really good. And a really, really big bodybuilder came

to work out at the gym, and he was absolutely enormous, and he had a big effect on me, you know, and I really kind of felt rubbish after that. I looked rubbish, felt crap. That kind of spurred me on to get bigger and bigger. In fact, it had that much influence on me, when I actually left the gym kind of looking at him, it was on my mind, and I got knocked off my bike on the way home. I was actually on the wrong side of the road. But, you know, I saw, not him, but, you know, the muscles, and that's how I wanted to be. It just completely dominated my thoughts.

Reports of other people's reactions when these men started to put on large amounts of muscle were interesting. Other bodybuilders were generally positive. For instance:

Other bodybuilders and bouncers and people like that, they kind of painted a picture of me and, you know, put me on a pedestal, and there was this big guy and he was strong, nothing could bother you, and I started to believe I had nine lives.

My friends and family . . . my friends in bodybuilding, you know, in that you meet a lot of, that's the good thing about going to a gym, you meet a lot of friends, so a lot of my friends do also train, you know, and some of the friends who don't train have respect in, you know, the way that I've done what I've done, you know, in the short period of time I've achieved it. The family are 100 percent behind me.

Some bodybuilders reported generally favorable comments from strangers:

I have noticed it on holiday in that people kind of look and nudge each other. I've not really had nasty comments. I've just had good comments. . . . You get the odd comment like "Do you weight train?" or "Do you do weights?"

However, men and women outside the bodybuilding culture tended to react negatively. For instance:

When I was about 18½, around Christmas time or whatever, people were quite different with me then. I was in a pub and one person pushed me, one person tripped me up as, you know, I was going past.

I found men found me threatening on the whole, even though I wasn't. I didn't get eye contact. I didn't talk to them. But if I was out socializing, I got quite a lot of ignorant remarks. I got people saying, "What are you taking?," you know, um. I got people who actually spat at me. I was pushed downstairs in a club. I felt that men were really offended and threatened by how I looked. Women reacted the same really. They felt threatened. They avoided me and just generally assumed that because I was big, I was nasty. I was using steroids, so therefore I was nasty and aggressive.

These reported negative reactions relate to a general social prejudice against bodybuilding men. Doug Aoki (1996) notes how even academics tend to present negative views of bodybuilders and bodybuilding in general:

> Usually circumspect about not denigrating minorities of any type, they nonetheless too often sneer at body-builders for the appearance of their bodies and for their presumed narcissism.
>
> (Aoki, 1996: 59)

It is interesting that bodybuilders attract negative reactions from others. It might be expected that an extreme form of the V-shaped body would be culturally favored. Alan Mansfield and Barbara McGinn (1993) note the strong cultural association between muscularity and masculinity. Perhaps there is a ceiling on acceptable levels of muscularity, or perhaps it is the narcissism—closely linked with the bulging muscles of the professional bodybuilder—that negates the effects of the hypermasculinity implied by the muscles. Bodybuilders are defying social expectations on a number of counts. Their behavior is assumed to be narcissistic, and therefore inappropriate for men (Aoki, 1996), for they spend time building up their bodies so that they look a certain way. Their bodies are at the same time hypermasculine (i.e., highly muscled) and feminine (with curves and the development of cleavage). Bodybuilding involves objectifying the body. This is a common phenomenon among women, who are taught to partition and objectify the body (Orbach, 1993), so it is seen as essentially feminine behavior (Aoki, 1996). The bodies of bodybuilders are seen as unnatural, especially when they are known to use anabolic steroids.

*Anabolic steroid use*

The use of anabolic steroids to improve athletic performance is well documented (see Lennehan, 2003). Anabolic steroids have long been used by professional bodybuilders to increase muscle bulk. The earliest documented use was by members of a Soviet weight-lifting team in the 1950s (Strauss and Yesalis, 1991). Recent data suggest that they are now being used by a number of young men who want to build up their bodies to a more pleasing muscular shape (Pope *et al.*, 2000; Wright *et al.*, 2001). Steroids enable the user to build muscle bulk much more quickly than is possible through weight training alone, so they are an attractive option to some young men who wish to become more muscular for cosmetic reasons.

It is not possible to know the extent of nonmedical steroid use. However, it is well known that steroids are widely available in public gyms and health clubs used by bodybuilders in Britain (Institute for the Study of Drug Dependence, 1993; Lennehan, 2003), the USA (Pope *et al.*, 2000), and Australia (Fawkner, 2004). Data from needle exchanges in Britain show that steroid users constitute a significant proportion of the group which makes use of the service, and these statistics probably underestimate use, since users often share needles in the gyms to avoid having to access appropriate needles themselves (Lennehan, 2003). US figures suggest that usage there may be more widespread, recent studies suggesting that most professional bodybuilders, weight lifters, and power lifters use anabolic steroids (Yesalis and Bahrke, 1995), and steroid use has been found to be prevalent even in high-school boys (Laure *et al.*, 2004). Clearly, steroid use is not restricted to athletes and sportsmen, but is found in other men who want to increase their muscularity (Hildebrandt *et al.*, 2006).

In work published in 2000 and 2001, we asked men and women bodybuilders to complete questionnaires on their motivation for steroid use. We found that 59 out of 135 (44 percent) bodybuilders who completed questionnaires that we placed in two bodybuilding magazines had used steroids. We applied content analysis to the responses and found that motivations to use steroids were complex and person specific (Wright *et al.*, 2000, 2001). However, there were some commonalities in the results. Wanting to get bigger/more muscular was the most frequent incentive for starting to use steroids (31 percent of steroid users), demonstrating the importance of the "look" produced by the drugs (as opposed to strength and endurance). Nonusers of steroids were more likely to be concerned about the negative physical side effects of steroid use (95 percent of nonusers versus 64 percent of users), and steroid users were significantly more likely to agree that steroids are necessary for effective bodybuilding, are necessary for competition, and maximize hard training. Steroid users were also significantly more likely to agree that only "ignorant people" criticized steroids, that steroids are not harmful in moderation, and that they are harmful only if used in excess. In a series of interviews conducted between 1997 and 2004, we asked six male steroid users about motivation for steroid use (Grogan *et al.*, 2006a). Men told consistent stories about their reasons for starting to use steroids. Most had tried steroids after becoming frustrated at lack of muscle gain through intensive weight training and a high-protein diet:

> I was training let's say 12 months, and, you know, I'd seen people looking bigger than me, and we got talking, and then I decided, you know, after a long time to take steroids. Really I needed, I felt I needed, to be bigger, and basically I thought steroids would do it. Literally I decided to take them because other people were kind of getting bigger than me, and they were taking them, so it was just like a knock-on effect. They do it, so, like, you do it.

All the men we interviewed cited pressures from images in bodybuilding magazines, and images from movies and television, as being influential in their decision to take steroids:

> The more I trained, the more magazines I looked at, the bigger I wanted to be . . . and there was a TV program, and when I watched these people, it made me feel really depressed, I didn't look as good as them, and it had a massive effect on my decision to take steroids. In fact, it was probably one of the biggest reasons why I did take them, seeing other people bigger than me.

Several respondents cited the bodybuilding gym culture as being influential in their decision to take steroids, because steroids were available and because people talked about them at the gym. For instance:

> In a hard-core bodybuilding gym you are going to see steroids readily available, you know, you are going to hear them talked about. You might see them, you know. So, yeah, people will talk to you about steroids, you know, different things you can take. So, yeah, if someone starts off at the gym intending just to train, they could be influenced by taking steroids because they can see, you know, they are in an atmosphere where people are taking steroids.

In terms of the effects of steroids on muscularity, reports were generally favorable (as might be expected). These men enjoyed the increased strength and muscularity that resulted from intensive training coupled with steroid intake, linking it with increased self-confidence:

> It made me look how I wanted to look, which was a lot more muscular . . . it made me feel a lot more confident and gave me more reassurance.

> I became more muscular, and, um, stronger, you know, a bigger look. It made me feel more confident in two ways. In the way with me being only quite short, it gave me a lot more confidence, you know, in general public, it made me feel better in myself.

However, the attention that large muscles attract was not always welcome. One bodybuilder described how he would hide his muscles when outside the gym:

> I used to wear clothes in the street to make me look smaller, you know like a black baggy jumper just to make me look smaller. It started to bother me after a bit, everybody staring at me. When I was 20 stone [280 lb], people in the street were staring back at me. It started to bother me after a bit.

The men we interviewed were keen to explode the myth that steroids alone would make someone muscular, and stressed the amount of work that goes into creating a well-muscled body, even when steroids are used as a catalyst:

> There's no drug makes a bodybuilder. People who talk about things like this are often people who have never trained a day in their life. They don't understand the first thing to do with bodybuilding. They just see a bodybuilder, and all they can see in their minds is the drugs that made that bodybuilder. They don't see how much hard dieting, how much hard training, how much real dedication has gone into it.

This may relate to the general cultural prejudice against artificiality in looks, as the prevailing aesthetic values a "natural" look. Gaines and Butler (1980) suggest that people do not value the bodies of bodybuilders because they are perceived as unnatural:

All those muscles somehow come out of a bottle . . . there is something as synthetic, unhealthy, useless and faintly sinful as plastic flowers about what they do and the way they look.

(Gaines and Butler, 1980: 76)

The steroid-using bodybuilders we interviewed were keen to show us how much work went into their physiques, representing themselves as creating natural muscle and only using the steroids as a catalyst. As such, they were emphasizing the fact that the muscles gained were not synthetic, not produced by the steroids, but produced through their own hard work. They wanted to take responsibility, to retain ownership of their bodies, resenting the impression of people outside bodybuilding who (they believed) thought of steroids as being a lazy way to achieve a muscular body. This links to Gaines and Butler's (1980) suggestion of a cultural belief that steroid-users' muscles are somehow "sinful" and "useless," since they are not the result of hard physical labor (which would not, presumably, be sinful or useless), but the result of pharmacological intervention. It is no surprise, then, that bodybuilders who used steroids felt it necessary to explain at length how hard they had to work to attain their body shape and size.

Steroid use presents particular tensions between the appearance of the body (the muscularity of the body implying strength and fitness) and the felt body (fitness/health as experienced by bodybuilders themselves who may feel weak and ill). One of the most important questions to be answered is how men who choose to use steroids make sense of the paradoxical relationship between the apparently healthy (muscled) external appearance and the (often) unhealthy internal state of their bodies. In our interviews (Grogan et al., 2006a), men reported that they had experienced serious health side effects (liver and kidney damage and hypertension), but saw these only as minor irritations and not significant disincentives for use. Side effects were linked with "abuse" (uninformed use involving overdose), and all users believed that steroids used in moderation presented no significant health risks. Participants argued that (taken in moderation) steroids served a useful function and are safe. For instance, one respondent argued that all drugs (including steroids) are potentially dangerous if taken in huge quantities, likening anabolic steroids to over-the-counter analgesics and alcohol, which (he argued) would be equally dangerous if taken in large quantities. Information from healthcare professionals tended to be mistrusted because it was not based on firsthand experience of use. Trusted sources of information on safe use were books written by those within the bodybuilding community ("steroid bibles"), websites run by steroid users, and word-of-mouth information from other users. Social support, especially from within the bodybuilding community, was an important motivator, and men believed that it would be impossible to compete in bodybuilding competitions without steroids. Clearly, any attempts to encourage safer steroid use, or steroid avoidance, need to be developed with the support of the bodybuilding community to be maximally effective.

## Cosmetic surgery

Men are increasingly likely to have cosmetic surgery to change the way they look. Surveys conducted since the 1990s have found reliably that more men are referred for cosmetic procedures than previously. For instance, the Harley Medical Group in Britain reported a significant increase in men requesting cosmetic surgery between 1983 and 1996 (Wilson, 1997). The most popular form of surgery was rhinoplasty, closely followed by breast augmentation to swell the pectoral muscles (the Harley Group reported performing at least two such operations on men each week) and liposuction on the waist. The Belvedere Clinic in Britain also reported that, in 1989, only 10 percent of its clients were male, whereas the proportion had risen to 40 percent by 1994 (Baker, 1994). Most men at the Belvedere Clinic in this time period requested the insertion of silicone pectorals or the removal of fat around the waist by liposuction or liposculpture. Figures from the USA are similar. The most prevalent operations internationally were liposuction and rhinoplasty. Harrison Pope and colleagues (2000) reported that men in the USA received 690,361 cosmetic procedures in 1996 alone.

In the 2000s, this trend has been maintained. For example, in 2004, 17 percent of cosmetic procedures in the USA were performed on men, over 32,000 men having liposuction and over 4,000 having abdominoplasty ("stomach" tuck), according to the American Society of Plastic Surgeons (2005). Statistics from 2006 show that 15 percent of liposuction and eyelid surgeries, and 24 percent of rhinoplasty operations were carried out on men in 2005 (Kennard, 2006). The most popular procedures on men in the USA in 2005 were nose reshaping, hair implants, eyelid surgery, liposuction, and breast reductions.

> Cosmetic surgery and related procedures in the United States have increased 32 per cent last year to 8.7 million, with Botox anti-wrinkle injection treatments being the most popular. The American Society of Plastic Surgeons said the number of surgical procedures

grew by 5 per cent, while minimally invasive procedures jumped 41 per cent as compared to 2002.

(Kennard, 2006: 1)

Clearly, a significant proportion of men are opting for the surgical fix to modify the look of their bodies, and accept the associated health problems and other risks. Body image is clearly sufficiently important to these men to make the risks worth taking and the costs worth paying. Social constructionist accounts attempt to make sense of this by developing an understanding of the social context of cosmetic surgery, bodybuilding, and steroid use. This will be addressed in the next section.

## Social construction of masculinity

Various social commentators have noted that there has been a radical change in social pressure on men to look slender and moderately muscular that started in the late 1980s. This has been linked with body dissatisfaction and the resulting body-fixing behaviors in men in Western cultures because of the positive social capital attached to having a slender and muscular body.

In the 1980s, Frank Mort argued that there had been a significant change in Western societies that meant an increased interest in the way that men look. He argued that men in the 1980s were being targeted by the advertising industry, and were becoming more aware than ever before of how they looked:

> Young men are being sold images which rupture traditional icons of masculinity. They are stimulated to look at themselves—and other men—as objects of consumer desire.
>
> (Mort, 1988: 194)

Mort argued that this change was significant, and required a rethinking of the meaning of "masculinity." Focusing on a 1980s advertisement for Levi's jeans, he showed how it used the standard technique for the sexual display of women, but pointed out that the target is now a man. Interestingly, one British newspaper also felt sufficiently uncomfortable about the follow-up Levi's TV commercial showing James Mardle in the bath in his Levi's to run a story stressing Mardle's heterosexuality. The move of male models from the gay press to the mainstream market obviously presented conflicts for some newspaper editors. Mort argued that changes in the acceptability of the visual display of the male body prompted men to look differently at themselves and other men, and to be generally more aware of the ways that their bodies looked, and of the ways that they dressed. However, he noted that this new awareness was not necessarily positive for women, arguing that although the "new man" may be more aware of his looks, this did not necessarily change the traditional codes of masculinity. Analyzing Levi's jeans advertisements, he shows how the hero is played off against stereotyped images of women (the sweetheart, the fat lady, the harassed mom, and the giggling girls). The "new man" image may just be another version of the old, macho image of the man going it alone, without/above women.

This theme was also taken up in the 1980s by Rowena Chapman (1988), who argued that the "new man" (nurturant and narcissistic) was largely the result of the British style culture of the early 1980s, promoted by the "style press" (music and fashion magazines aimed at a young and fashionable audience such as *i-D*, *The Face*, and *Arena*). The culture legitimized men's concern with their bodies and the consumerism necessary to adopt the role. The "new man," she argued, was not a major departure from the traditional, John Wayne-style, macho man, but was simply an adaptation of the role better suited to survive in a culture that rejected obvious machismo, largely due to the power of feminism.

> This leads me to the conclusion that the new man represents not so much a rebellion but an adaptation in masculinity. Men change, but only to hold on to power, not to relinquish it. The combination of feminism and social change may have produced a fragmentation in male identity by questioning its assumptions, but the effect of the emergence of the new man has been to reinforce the existing power structure, by producing a hybrid masculinity which is better able and more suited to retain control.
>
> (Chapman, 1988: 235)

Chapman noted the historic reticence in Western culture about male nudity, and the shift in the 1980s in the visibility of the male body. She argued that the dawning recognition of the marketability of the male body to women led to an increase in the representation of the male body on the cards, calendars, and posters produced by companies such as Athena, whose poster, *L'Enfant*, featuring a muscular man holding a baby, was its biggest seller in the late 1980s. However, she argued that women were still the objects of gaze more frequently and more completely than men, and that the objectification of the male body did nothing significant to reduce the power of men in society.

This trend continued in the 1990s. Harrison Pope and colleagues (2000) noted the increase in visibility of the male body, and that images of the male body had become increasingly muscular over the years. They commented on the increased visibility of the "supermale" (muscular) body in mainstream Western media:

> Look at television over the last several decades. The hard-bodied lifeguards in *Baywatch* are viewed by over 1 billion viewers in 142 countries—figures unmatched by any previous television series. Or look at the movies. Hollywood's most masculine men of the 1930s, 1940s and 1950s—John Wayne, Clark Gable, Gregory Peck —look like wimps in comparison to modern cinema's muscular action heroes—Arnold Schwarzenegger, Sylvester Stallone, or Jean-Claude van Damme. Today while growing up a young man is subjected to thousands of these supermale images.
>
> (Pope *et al.*, 2000: 12–13)

In the 2000s, the male body continues to be seen as a commodity used to increase sales. Lee Monaghan (2002) argues that we have seen the development in recent years of a "cult of male beauty" where slender, toned, and muscular male bodies have become eroticized and objectified. Kathy Davis (2002) has suggested that this has created a "dubious equality" between the sexes in which young men's bodies are now objectified in a similar way to women's. This will be discussed further in Chapter 6 in relation to impact of sexuality, age, social class, and ethnicity on body image.

## Summary

- The ideal male body shape in Western societies is slender and moderately muscular.
- Work on men's body satisfaction has suggested that a significant proportion of men are dissatisfied with some aspect of their body shape and weight.
- Men who are dissatisfied with their body shape are equally likely to want to be thinner or heavier (a different pattern from women, who mostly want to be slimmer).
- The main areas that produce dissatisfaction are the midtorso, biceps, shoulders, chest, and general muscle tone. Muscle tone and muscle mass are important to men.
- Men tend to use exercise (rather than diet) to try to change body shape.

- Interviews and questionnaires with bodybuilders demonstrate a strong social comparison effect, whereby bodybuilders compare their bodies to those of other men in the gym, encouraging them to train harder to try to develop more muscle.
- Some bodybuilders choose to take anabolic steroids to speed up the process of muscle development, despite unwanted side effects and the negative reactions of people outside the bodybuilding community.
- The incidence of cosmetic surgery procedures in men has increased since the 1990s and is being maintained.
- Since the late 1980s, there has been a significant increase in the visibility and marketability of the male body, and this is continuing into the 2000s.

# 5 Media effects

There is general agreement that pressures on women to be a particular shape and size are more pronounced than pressures on men. Studies that have investigated the portrayal of both genders have found that men and women are portrayed in markedly different ways in relation to body weight. Content analysis (where the frequency of portrayal of particular images is coded) has revealed that women are portrayed as abnormally slim in the media, whereas men tend to be portrayed as of standard weight. Linda Smolak (2004) notes that fashion models in the 2000s are thinner than 98 percent of US women, and Erin Strahan and colleagues (2006) argue that:

> Images of thin women are ubiquitous in the media, and women's magazines contain more messages about physical attractiveness than do men's magazines.
>
> (Strahan et al., 2006: 211)

Magazines aimed at girls and young women tend to present traditional slim images of attractiveness. In the 1990s, Eileen Guillen and Susan Barr investigated body image in *Seventeen* magazine between 1970 and 1990 and concluded that the magazine contributes to the current cultural milieu in which thinness is expected of women, be they adults or adolescents (Guillen and Barr, 1994). More recently, the US National Eating Disorders Association (2002) has noted that the average US model is 5 feet 11 inches tall and weighs 117 pounds, significantly taller and thinner than the average US woman, who weighs 140 pounds and is 5 feet 4 inches tall. Cultural norms for men's bodies are more flexible, and although there is a cultural preference for a slender but muscular body type (see Chapter 2), there is a greater range of media representations of attractive male bodies (Strahan et al., 2006). Digital manipulations of pictures of models' bodies mean that women in the 2000s are faced with even more idealized, and more slender bodies than in the 1990s (Bordo, 2003); and the thin, unrealistic proportions of Barbie dolls have been shown to reduce body esteem in 5–8-year-old British girls (Dittmar *et al.*, 2006).

Various authors have concluded that print media, particularly magazines aimed at young women, have powerful effects on their readers, serving to foster and maintain a "cult of femininity" and supplying definitions of what it means to be an attractive woman. Women's magazines are read by a large proportion of women (about half the adult female population of the UK) with each copy seen by many women (on average, each copy of *Vogue* is read by 16 women in Britain, since magazines are often shared among friends and are widely available in the waiting rooms of doctors, dentists, and hairdressers. In the 1980s, Marjorie Ferguson (1985) used content analysis to study a random selection of copies of *Woman's Own, Woman*, and *Woman's Weekly* between 1949 and 1974, and 1979 and 1980, looking for dominant themes, goals, and roles. She also interviewed 34 female magazine editors about their roles, beliefs, and professional practices, and about how they perceived the impact of social change upon their magazines and audiences; and 97 journalists, artists, publishers, and managers about their perceptions of the editorial process, publishing organizations, and the market context of women's periodical production. She interpreted her data in relation to the writings of Durkheim on the sociology of religion. She argued that there are interesting parallels between the practices promoted by women's magazines and the characteristic elements of the religious cult:

> I have argued that women's magazines collectively comprise a social institution which serves to foster and maintain a cult of femininity. In promoting a cult of femininity these journals are not merely reflecting the female role in society; they are also supplying one source of definitions of, and socialisation into, that role.
>
> (Ferguson, 1985: 184)

She saw the media as doing much more than simply reflecting current values. According to Ferguson, women's magazines may actually change a woman's view of herself by teaching her socially acceptable ways in which to behave. More recently, Maggie Wykes and Barrie Gunter (2005) have argued that popular print media still promote a narrow body ideal for women that is young, white, and slender, but that they do this in different and more subtle ways to appeal to a more knowing audience than in previous years. While critiquing the dieting industry, magazines and newspapers present very slender images and subtly derogate women who do not conform to a very slender ideal. Wykes and Gunter argued that women are expected to work on their bodies (through diet, exercise, and cosmetic surgery) to attain a socially acceptable body shape, and the underlying message is that if they do not achieve this look, they will not be attractive to men:

> The modern print media are perhaps more covert operators on the body than explicitly overt as they were suggested to be in these earlier content analyses. At the outset of the twenty-first century, there are of course publications like *Shape* which are explicitly engaged in reconstructing women's bodies, but the print media analysed here are not, and are even critical of the diet and slimming industries. Despite this, the stories that they do tell about femininity are insidiously, repetitively and systematically engaged in a very particular construction of femininity that is deeply body-conscious and embedded within a particular gendered narrative.
>
> (Wykes and Gunter, 2005: 95)

In the 1980s and 1990s, the male body became more "visible" in the popular media in both Britain and the USA. Frank Mort (1988) and Rowena Chapman (1988) noted the increasing prevalence of the well-muscled male body in British advertising. Marc Mishkind and colleagues (1986) argued that examination of US magazines and other media demonstrated that body image concern was strong for men. They suggested that media images of the young, lean, muscular male body represent changes in society's attitudes to the male body, as a result of which men are under increased pressure to look slender and muscular:

> Advertisements celebrate the young, lean, muscular male body, and men's fashions have undergone significant changes in style both to accommodate and to accentuate changes in men's physiques toward a more muscular and trim body.
>
> (Mishkind *et al.*, 1986: 545)

They went on to suggest that the pressures of society to conform to the slender, muscular male body ideal may be producing an increase in body dissatisfaction and low self-esteem in men. Stuart Elliot (1994) also documented this trend, describing how *Sports Illustrated* magazine opted to use male models to advertise swimwear for the first time in 1994, and Peter Baker (1994) noted the increased use of attractive men (young, handsome, and muscular) in advertisements and movies, and argued that this had led to an increase in men's self-consciousness about their bodies:

> Men's self-consciousness about their appearance is probably greater now than ever before. How could it be otherwise, given the massive exposure of men's bodies in the media?
>
> (Baker, 1994: 130)

More recently, this has been corroborated by Harrison Pope and colleagues (2000), who have shown that images of the muscular, V-shaped male ideal have become increasingly prevalent in the media, and that men's bodies are exposed more frequently and objectified more than in previous years (see also Rohlinger, 2002). Pope and colleagues have suggested that repeated exposure to idealized media images of men's bodies causes men to feel less secure about their bodies and increases their body dissatisfaction.

## Surveys relating media exposure to body image

Psychology researchers have conducted surveys to investigate the link between media exposure and body dissatisfaction by asking participants to complete questionnaires in which they report exposure to magazine and television and in which body image is also measured (usually through questionnaires assessing body dissatisfaction). Several studies have shown that girls and women who have higher levels of exposure to media imagery tend to be less satisfied with the way that they look than those with lower levels of exposure (Levine *et al.*, 1994; Botta, 1999; Harrison 2000; Anderson *et al.*, 2001). Botta (2000) found that magazine exposure (mediated by social comparison processes) was linked to body dissatisfaction in boys as well as girls, and in 2003 argued that:

> Magazine reading, social comparisons, and critical body image processing are important predictors of body image and eating disturbances in adolescent boys and girls.
>
> (Botta, 2003: 389)

There is also some evidence that exposure to particular kinds of television images may influence body satisfaction in girls. Although number of hours of television watched has not generally been found to correlate with body dissatisfaction, the content of what is watched has been found to predict body satisfaction and drive for thinness in girls. For instance, various authors have suggested that exposure to music videos predicts body dissatisfaction (e.g., Borzekowski *et al.*, 2000) and drive for thinness (e.g., Tiggemann and Pickering, 1996).

One of the problems with survey work that provides evidence of a correlation between exposure and body dissatisfaction is that it is impossible to tell whether the media exposure produced changes in satisfaction, or whether people who are less satisfied with their bodies gravitate toward particular kinds of media. In order to disentangle these effects, studies need either to investigate the direction of the relationship through prospective work in which media exposure and body image are both tested and then participants are followed up to look at changes in satisfaction, or to investigate experimentally the direct effects of media imagery on satisfaction.

Prospective studies are rare in the body image literature. However, Marika Tiggemann (2006) recently ran a prospective study of body image and media exposure with 214 Australian girls (mean age 14 years). At time 1, they completed questionnaire measures of media exposure (including both magazines and television), internalization of appearance ideals, appearance schemas, body dissatisfaction, and drive for thinness. One year later, at time 2, they completed the same measures. Tiggemann found that none of the media exposure measures at time 1 predicted body image at time 2. She also found that body image at time 1 did not predict change in media exposure. She reports:

> It was concluded that for this age group, media exposure and body image seem to co-occur but that either one is temporally antecedent to the other. Thus the study demonstrated no causal role for media exposure in the body image of adolescent girls.
>
> (Tiggemann, 2006: 523)

Clearly, mere exposure to media imagery may not be sufficient to modify body image. The meanings attached to the images (and the importance attached to the thin ideal), the extent to which the person compares his or her own body to the images, and the size and direction of any perceived gap between the idealized image and the self may all be crucial in determining the effect of exposure.

## Studies investigating direct effects of media images on body image

Rather than looking at associations between media exposure and body dissatisfaction, some authors have run experimental studies to investigate the effects of media imagery on body dissatisfaction in controlled laboratory situations. Most researchers have measured body satisfaction in women after (and sometimes before and after) observing slim fashion models, or magazine or television images. Most have found a decrease in body esteem after viewing (Groetz *et al.*, 2002), although some have found no change, and one study even found an increase in satisfaction.

In an early study, Thomas Cash *et al.* (1983) showed female students pictures of female models taken from magazines. One group saw pictures of women previously rated as physically attractive, one group saw pictures of physically attractive women whom they were told were professional models, and the third group saw pictures previously rated as not attractive. Women in the groups exposed to attractive models rated their own attractiveness less highly after viewing these images than those who had viewed the less attractive models. This was particularly the case in the condition where the attractive women were not labeled as models, suggesting that perceived similarity to viewed images is important, as suggested by social comparison theory (Major *et al.*, 1991: see below).

Lori Irving (1990) looked specifically at the effects of media images on women with "eating disorders." She investigated the impact of exposure to slides of thin, average, and oversized models on the self-evaluations of 162 women college students who exhibited a significant level of "bulimic symptoms" on the BULIT test, which is specifically designed to identify such symptoms (Smith and Thelen, 1984). Exposure to the thin models resulted in lowered self-esteem, although not to differences in weight satisfaction. However, the study was flawed in that no pre-exposure measurements of self-evaluation were taken (although the groups were checked for equivalence of bulimic symptoms and age). The post-exposure-test-only design leaves open the alternative hypothesis that the groups may have differed on weight satisfaction prior to exposure to the stimuli, and makes the data difficult to interpret with confidence.

Leslie Heinberg and Kevin Thompson (1995) investigated the effects of televised images on body satisfaction. A 10-minute tape of either appearance-related or non-appearance-related commercials was viewed by 139 women. Pre-test and post-test measures of body dissatisfaction revealed that participants who were high on "body image disturbance" (rated by Schulman *et al.*'s (1986) Bulimia Cognitive Distortions Scale; physical appearance subscale) and/or high on awareness or acceptance of societal attitudes to thinness and attractiveness (as measured by Heinberg and Thompson's Societal Attitudes Toward Appearance Questionnaire) were significantly less satisfied after viewing the appearance-related images. Participants below the median on body image disturbance showed no change or showed improved satisfaction. The authors suggested that, for certain susceptible individuals, media images of thinness are particularly salient, and that this group may use media models as social comparison targets when assessing their own physical attractiveness. Their data suggest that only a specific subsection of the population—those who agree with statements such as "being physically fit is a priority in today's society" (awareness of societal attitudes); "photographs of thin women make me wish that I were thin" (acceptance of societal attitudes); or "my value as a person is related to my weight" (cognitive distortions related to physical appearance)—are "at risk" from such images.

Philip Myers and Frank Biocca (1992) ran a fascinating study in which 76 female university students aged 18–24 viewed either body-image-oriented or neutral programming. The participants then completed questionnaires measuring mood, and estimated body size by the light-adjustment technique described in Chapter 3. They found that most of the young women overestimated their body size (in agreement with the research cited in Chapter 3). Watching a 30-minute tape of body-image-oriented advertisements and programming had a significant effect on body size estimation and mood levels. Surprisingly, the body-image-oriented material reduced body size overestimation and reduced depression levels. Myers and Biocca explain these surprising results by suggesting that the young women may have imagined themselves in the ideal body presented in the tape. They may have felt more in control, and may have seen the ideal as more attainable and within reach. They use these findings to suggest a two-stage process of building a distorted body image. In the first stage, young women "bond" with the models, visualizing themselves in the socially represented ideal body. At this stage, the "elastic" present body image moves toward the internalized ideal body, making the woman feel good about her body. The self-criticism that comes from a realization of the gap between the objective body and the internalized ideal body comes later. So the short-term effect is to make the woman feel that she is closer to her ideal (through identification with the models, and consequent change to her current body image). However, once the identification has "worn off," she will make unfavorable comparisons between her objective body and her internalized ideal, leading to dissatisfaction. Unfortunately, Myers and Biocca did not look at the longer-term effects of the images. Their argument on long-term effects would be more convincing if it were accompanied by evidence that this long-term shift does in fact take place. It would also have been useful to have measured body dissatisfaction directly, rather than inferring it through body size estimation and depression levels.

Jill Cattarin and colleagues (2000) showed television advertisements to female students. These either depicted slim, attractive models or were not appearance focused. Participants were told to compare themselves with the models in the advertisements, to focus on the product, or were given nonspecific instructions. They found that the group viewing the appearance-related advertisements that had been told to compare themselves with the models had the lowest body satisfaction after viewing the images. This explicit social comparison manipulation showed that women who are prompted to focus on the bodies of models are likely to become significantly less satisfied with their own looks after viewing. Other work has also shown that self-discrepancy moderates the influence of these social comparison processes. Gayle Bessenoff's (2006) study found that women with high levels of body image self-discrepancy were most likely to engage in social comparison with media images, as well as being more likely to experience negative consequences of such comparisons. In a recent meta-analysis of 25 studies conducted up until 2001, Groetz *et al.* (2002) concluded that young women feel worse after exposure to thin images than other types of images, with those with a history of body dissatisfaction being more negatively affected by these images than other women.

Work in this area has tended to focus on women. Some recent studies have considered effects on men. The issue of men's body esteem is of particular interest at present because of recent suggestions that Western cultural attitudes to the male body are in a state of change, and that men are becoming more and more concerned with body image (see Chapter 4). In a study conducted in 1995, we looked at the effects on both men and women of viewing same-gender, slim, conventionally attractive models. The study was designed to investigate these effects on body esteem. Body esteem scales were completed by 49 men and 45 women (aged 17–32) before and after viewing pictures of same-gender photographic models (experimental group) or landscapes (control group). Women scored significantly lower than men on the body esteem scale, irrespective of whether they were in the experimental or control group, showing that these women were generally less satisfied with their bodies than were the men. There were interesting differences between the experimental and control groups after seeing the photographs. Body esteem scores decreased significantly (and to a similar degree) in men and women after viewing the same-gender photographic models, whereas men and women in the control group (who viewed landscapes) showed no change (Grogan *et al.*, 1996).

This suggests that these men and women felt significantly less satisfied with their bodies after viewing attractive same-gender models. At least in the short term, these participants felt less good about the way that their bodies looked after comparison with those of well-toned, slender models. The data are particularly interesting since they show an equivalent shift in satisfaction for both men and women. The effect does not seem to be mediated by problematic relationships with food. Scores on the Eating Attitude Test (a measure of such relationships) did not correlate significantly with body esteem changes in the experimental groups, suggesting that the effect is independent of attitudes to eating. The effect is short term, and there is no way of knowing how long it will last. It is, nonetheless, interesting that a relatively brief encounter with pictures of attractive fashion models can have such an effect on body satisfaction, suggesting that body image is indeed "elastic," as suggested by Myers and Biocca (1992).

Ogden and Mundray (1996) present some interesting results from a study in which they exposed medical students (men and women) to images of either thin models or overweight individuals matched for gender. Measures of body satisfaction were taken before and after viewing. They found that participants showed significant decreases in satisfaction after viewing the thin models, and increased satisfaction after viewing the heavier models. This effect was not gender specific and was found in both men and women, although the effect was stronger for women. This study is one of the few in the existing literature that used pictures of overweight models, and shows that upward comparisons seem to have been made with the thin models, but downward comparisons with the plumper models. The study also supports the Grogan *et al.* (1996) study in showing that men are as likely to be affected by media models as women.

Studies that have shown men muscular images have found that men can be made to feel significantly less satisfied with their bodies after viewing muscular images. In one US study (Leit *et al.*, 2002), male students were shown pictures of muscular men taken from magazine advertisements. On average, these men reported greater dissatisfaction with their muscularity than men shown images of clothing advertisements. There was no effect on their satisfaction with their fat levels. Other work has also found that dissatisfaction is increased after viewing muscular images compared with thin, normal weight, and plump images (Lorenzen *et al.*, 2004). In a recent Canadian study, Kelly Arbour and Kathleen Martin-Ginis (2006) have investigated the effects of the degree of muscularity of images on men's body image, displayed in the realistic context of a nutrition and weight-training seminar. Seventy-four men completed body dissatisfaction and muscularity dissatisfaction measures before and after attending the seminar, in which either muscular or hypermuscular images were viewed. Men who had pre-existing muscularity dissatisfaction had increased body dissatisfaction after viewing the muscular, but not hypermuscular, images. The authors conclude that exposure to the lean, muscular ideal promoted in the media leads to increased body dissatisfaction in men with pre-existing muscularity concerns. Hypermuscular (bodybuilder) images did not have any significant effect, possibly because this was perceived as unattainable (and so not a relevant comparison), or because the moderately muscular images were perceived as more "ideal" than the hypermuscular images.

Studies of media effects have generally found that idealized images impact negatively on viewers' body images and that these effects are similar (although possibly less extreme) for men and women. Social comparison seems to mediate the process, and women who have internalized the thin ideal and who have a greater discrepancy between their actual body and their internalized ideal body seem most at risk of experiencing negative effects. In men, existing muscularity dissatisfaction may predispose to more negative effects of media images.

Authors of intervention studies tend to assume that results obtained in the laboratory can be generalized to real-life situations. However, results obtained in the somewhat sterile laboratory situation may not be generalizable to more realistic viewing situations for several reasons. Experiments carried out in university laboratories (as most of the above have been) place participants in a strange, unfamiliar situation, in which they are given something specific to observe (rather than choosing it themselves), they are (usually) observed while they view, and they are (usually) asked to pay attention to details of the material they view. None of these factors are likely to be common to participants' everyday life, so results obtained in the laboratory may be different from those that would be obtained if we observed the participants in their everyday environment. These studies are also open to demand characteristics (people respond as they think they should respond in that particular unfamiliar situation). Survey studies have the advantage of observing naturally occurring media exposure, but do not enable us to know enough about the causal direction of effects. An alternative and fruitful approach is to interview people about their experience of media exposure, to help us to understand more about the experience of viewing these images from the viewer's perspective. In our interviews with women reported in Chapter 3, participants did not accept uncritically the media images offered to them. They were highly critical of the fact that "skinny" models and actresses were represented as "normal" body shapes in magazines and on film. They saw fashion models as being too thin, representative of an unrealistic ideal. Data from these interviews will be discussed further in the section on body image role models later in this chapter. Other recent data also suggest that women are aware of the idealized nature of images presented to them in the media, and know how to criticize media imagery aimed at them (Engeln-Maddox, 2005). Further work is needed to examine how men see these kinds of images, although existing focus group work suggests that although they are aware of idealized images, they are mostly not highly motivated to emulate them (see below and Grogan and Richards, 2002).

## Theories of media influence

Psychologists have developed three main theories to explain how media images might affect body image, and who might be particularly vulnerable to these effects. The most influential psychological theories of media effects are adaptations of Festinger's (1954) social comparison theory, Higgins's (1987) self-discrepancy theory, and Markus's (1977) self-schema theory.

### Social comparison theory

In 1954, Leon Festinger published his landmark theory on social comparison processes. According to his social comparison theory, we desire accurate, objective evaluations of our abilities and attitudes. When unable to evaluate ourselves directly, we seek to satisfy this need for self-evaluation through comparison with other people. Unfavorable comparisons (where the other is judged to score higher in the target attribute than oneself) are known as "upward comparisons." Favorable comparisons (where the other is judged as lower on the target attribute) are known as "downward comparisons." This social comparison process may be unconscious, and may be outside volitional control (Miller, 1984). Most people are expected to prefer to make self-enhancing downward comparisons with others where possible (Wilson and Ross, 2000), although Rebecca Collins (1996) argues that some may choose to make upward comparisons in the hope of using the target to guide self-improvement (see also Strahan *et al.*, 2006).

Social comparison theory predicts that people might use images projected by the media as standards for comparison. Upward comparisons with models' bodies (slim and carefully arranged in the most flattering poses) would be expected to lead to unfavorable evaluation of the body of the perceiver, so long as participants considered models to be sufficiently similar to them on relevant dimensions and body image to be self-relevant (Major *et al.*, 1991). Even if images are not similar on all relevant dimensions, and if they are potentially damaging to self-esteem, they may still be chosen for comparison if the information they provide is high in perceived self-relevance. Renee Engeln-Maddox (2005) shows that even though comparisons with beautiful models may not seem logical for most women due to lack of similarity, and may be damaging due to potential to reduce body satisfaction, this needs to be understood within a context in which these images provide valuable information about social evaluation of one's own appearance, and may be seen as inspirational images and comparison targets for self-improvement (Halliwell and Dittmar, 2005).

Social comparison processes in body image have been demonstrated consistently by Kevin Thompson and colleagues in the USA (Heinberg and Thompson, 1992), and by others in the UK (Grogan *et al.*, 1996; Ogden and Mundray, 1996). Effects on body satisfaction are most marked if participants are encouraged to engage in overt comparison between their own bodies and those of the media models (Cattarin *et al.*, 2000). Some authors have suggested that men are less likely to make upward comparisons with images of men's bodies than are women because men's bodies have less sociocultural importance than women's (Wykes and Gunter, 2005). However, studies that have investigated the effects of viewing media images have shown that women and men show decreased body satisfaction when viewing, respectively, slender media models (Grogan *et al.*, 1996; Ogden and Mundray, 1996) and muscular models (Leit *et al.*, 2002; Lorenzen *et al.*, 2004; Arbour and Martin-Ginis, 2006).

### Self-schema theory

Self-schema theory was developed by Markus in 1977. A self-schema is a person's mental representation of those elements that make him/ her distinctive from others, those aspects that constitute a sense of "me." According to Markus, people develop their sense of self through reflecting on their own behaviors, from observing reactions of others to the self, and through processing social information about which aspects of the self are most valued. Self-schemas influence how new incoming information is processed through organizing and guiding processing of this new information (Hogg and Vaughan, 1995). Self-schema theory predicts that people who were schematic for appearance would be particularly sensitized to body-related media messages, and that information contained in media images would be incorporated into, and would affect, that person's concept of self (Markus *et al.*, 1987).

One of the key aspects of self-schema theory is that it leads to the prediction that particular people may be more sensitive than others to body-related imagery, and more likely to internalize the slender body ideal. According to Markus *et al.* (1987), body image can become a central defining feature of self-concept for some people, meaning that they become extremely sensitive to additional incoming information about weight, shape, and size (including media information and imagery). Cash and Labarge's (1996) Appearance Schema Inventory enables researchers to assess the degree of centrality of appearance to people's self-concepts, including items such as "What I look like is an important part of who I am." People who are high on appearance schematicity have been found to be particularly sensitive to media imagery relating to the body. Duane Hargreaves and Marika Tiggemann (2002) have also shown that adolescents high in schematicity were more negatively affected by exposure to appearance-related television advertisements than those lower in this trait.

### Self-discrepancy theory

Self-discrepancy theory (Higgins, 1987) proposes that people's emotional vulnerabilities and motivations result from discrepancies in their patterns of beliefs about themselves. In order to reduce distress and discomfort, individuals are motivated to match their perceived actual self with an ideal self (the person they would ideally like to be) and an ought self (the person they believe that they ought to be through obligation to others). Higgins proposes that a discrepancy between the actual and ideal/ought selves leads to discomfort and body dissatisfaction. Media imagery is conceptualized as part of the range of influences that can mold the ideal self, along with the influence of romantic partners, peers, parents, and other significant others in the person's social world (Cash and Szymanski, 1995; Tantleff-Dunn and Thompson, 1995).

The main focus of self-discrepancy theory is the emotional reaction caused by lack of match between a person's perceived actual self and what are known as self-guides (ideal and ought selves), and this theory has been related more frequently and successfully to studies of eating disorders than to body image per se (e.g., Higgins *et al.*, 1992). However, some studies have looked at body dissatisfaction within a self-discrepancy framework and have suggested that media imagery may form part of the information used to formulate the ideal self in relation to appearance, and that lack of match with this ideal may cause distress.

Altabe and Thompson (1996) have shown that media imagery can produce emotional reactions in people with greater perceived discrepancies between actual and ideal body image characteristics, and Dittmar and Howard (2004) have found that body-focused anxiety reactions to thin media images are conditional on having a thin ideal body. Other authors have found that actual–ideal discrepancies are correlated with body dissatisfaction as well as eating disorder symptoms (Strauman *et al.*, 1991; Forston and Stanton, 1992), and that women with high levels of body image self-discrepancy are most likely to engage in social comparison with media images (Bessenoff, 2006). There is growing evidence that internalization of the thin ideal predicts a negative response to media imagery in terms of body dissatisfaction and concern (Cattarin *et al.*, 2000; Halliwell and Dittmar, 2004; Yamamiya *et al.*, 2005).

Self-discrepancy theory is useful in helping us to understand how and why particular body-related media images may trigger emotional reactions such as distress and body concerns, and how this may in some cases lead to appearance-fixing behaviors to try to rectify the perceived disparity between people's perceived current bodies and their ideal.

## Body shape role models

After it has been shown that media images can result in a shift in body satisfaction, it is important to investigate the relative importance of media imagery compared to other sources of social influence. Clearly, the media are only one source of influence on body image, and other sources may be more or less salient at particular times, and to particular individuals, although media imagery appears to be a particularly salient influence for many women (Thompson *et al.*, 1999). Irving (1990), in a study of female college students scoring high on bulimic symptoms, asked her participants to rate the importance of different sources of social pressure. When she ordered their responses by rank, she found that the most powerful source of perceived social pressure for this group was "media," followed by "peers," followed by "family."

Heinberg and Thompson (1992) looked specifically at this issue of relevant body image comparison groups. They asked 297 women and men to rate the importance of six different groups. These ranged from particularistic (family and friends) to universalistic (celebrities and US citizens). Women and men put the comparison groups in the same order of importance. The most important group was friends; then came celebrities, classmates, and students; and then US citizens and family. So celebrities were rated as important as classmates and students. Women with "eating disorders" or body image disturbance were more likely to compare their appearance with celebrities. Heinberg and Thompson used these data to argue that media figures are most likely to be used for body image evaluation in women with body image disturbance.

In 1996, in a study reported in the previous edition of this book (Grogan, 1999), 200 US college students (and friends of college students) aged 16–48 were asked to nominate their body image role models ("Who would you like to look like?"). The sample was made up of equal numbers of men and women. Their responses were content analyzed and coded into four categories: actor, model, sports person, and family member. Participants were split into four age groups: 16–19, 20–29, 30–39, and 40–49. Of the men, 23 percent of 16–19-year-olds had role models who were actors (e.g., Arnold Schwarzenegger, Jean-Claude Van Damme), and 3 percent had role models who were sportsmen (e.g., Michael Jordan). The rest of the group reported having no role models for body shape. Of the 20–29-year-olds, 13 percent cited actors, 2 percent sportsmen, and 2 percent family members (brothers) as role models. In the 30–39-year-olds, 31 percent cited actors as role models, while the rest reported no body image role models. The older men (40–49) also reported that they had no particular body image role models. Some of the men reported wanting to look like well-muscled Hollywood actors and sportsmen with high media profiles (Arnold Schwarzenegger and Michael Jordan were those cited most frequently). Men in the 20–29-year-old age group differed from the other groups in proposing family members (usually their older brother, but in some cases their father) as models of how they would like to look.

Of the women, 10 percent of the 16–19-year-olds cited fashion models as role models (usually Claudia Schiffer, Cindy Crawford, Elle MacPherson, or Christy Turlington), 5 percent cited actresses (e.g., Halle Berry, Demi Moore, Alicia Silverstone), 3 percent cited sportswomen (e.g., Gail Devers), and 3 percent a family member (usually the mother). Of the women in their twenties, 9 percent had role models who were fashion models and 9 percent role models who were actresses, while 2 percent cited sports persons and 2 percent cited a friend they would like to look like. The actresses, models, and sportswomen chosen were the same as those of the younger women. For women in their thirties, actresses (Michelle Pfeiffer and Demi Moore) represented role models for 13 percent of the group, with 7 percent citing sportswomen and 7 percent a family member (mother or sister). Of the women in their forties, 17 percent cited a family member (mother or sister), and the remaining 83 percent cited no particular role model.

These results suggest that media figures (fashion models, actors/ actresses, and sports persons) provide body image role models for a significant proportion of men and women under 40. Well-muscled Hollywood actors such as Arnold Schwarzenegger and Jean-Claude Van Damme were the chosen model for many men under 40. More men in their thirties cited these actors as role models than in any other age group. For a significant proportion of women in their teens and twenties, fashion models represented how they would like to look. Women in their thirties chose actresses rather than fashion models. As the age of the participants increased, they were more likely to choose a family member, such as a sister or their mother, as their model, rather than a media figure. Clearly, media role models are more important to men and women in the younger age groups. It was also interesting that many participants in each age group did not cite any particular person that they would like to look like. Between 40 and 50 percent of each group gave "like myself" or "no one in particular" as their response to the question, "Who would you like to look like?" Perhaps there was some social desirability effect in operation here. It may be that participants wanted to appear satisfied with the way that they looked, with no need of a media role model. Perhaps they were concerned about not being seen to be unduly influenced by anyone else. Or perhaps they really had no particular physical role model to which they compared themselves.

In interview work, this issue was explored further. It is much easier to investigate such issues when people can be asked to detail the reasons for their choices. In interview, girls aged 8 and 13 reported that they thought that fashion models in magazines were too thin to be attractive (Grogan and Wainwright, 1996).

*Girl 1:*  They look horrible. They're ugly half the time.
*Girl 2:*  Yeah, they are.
*Girl 1:*  I think they do sometimes look too thin. They look anorexic.

For the 8-year-olds, competitors in the 1990s UK television show *Gladiators* represented how they would like to look. The women in this show were slender and moderately muscled. The 8-year-olds' favorite was Jet, although they thought that she was perhaps a bit too muscular. Muscles were seen as inappropriate for women by girls in both age groups.

Adult women expressed similar preferences and concerns to the two groups of girls. Women in our interviews in the USA and Britain cited the models Naomi Campbell and Claudia Schiffer as how they would like to look, although they said that they were too thin. For instance:

> They make me sick. They are too thin. But I would kill for one of their bodies.

In interviews, women aged 16–60 cited fashion models and actresses as their ideal (see Chapter 3). However, most women we have interviewed present complex views relating to the influence of media models (see Chapter 3). Clearly, they aspired to being slim and shapely, like the models Claudia Schiffer (Plate 12) and Cindy Crawford, who were often cited as the ideal. However, they generally felt that extreme thinness was inappropriate and unhealthy.

Kate Moss (Plate 6) was often cited as being too thin. In general, the women we have interviewed want "skinny curves," as one woman put it. They wanted to look slim but curvy. Still, they are pragmatic about the possibilities of achieving these "skinny curves," and some made an effort to explain that, while they would like to look like Cindy Crawford, they accepted that this was not a realistic possibility. For instance, in a discussion group with US women in their twenties carried out by Jacqueline Gardner for the previous edition of this book, one woman talked about Cindy Crawford:

> I don't know anyone who looks like her. I think she comes from another planet somewhere, and they placed her in our society so that we will all feel bad, and we'll all go on diets and make the diet industry rich [laughs]. She's really a Martian! It doesn't logically make sense, but it makes me feel better.

Models were generally thought to be too skinny, and even Cindy Crawford (who was not considered to be too thin) was felt to be unnaturally thin for her height:

*Woman 1:*    I look at some models and think "no."
*Woman 2:*    I do think that they can be too skinny.
*Woman 1:*    Cindy Crawford, she's not too thin. She's not sickly thin. She looks quite healthy.
*Woman 3:*    But she's thin.
*Woman 1:*    Yeah, and she is 6 foot tall. If I was 6 foot tall and weighed what I do, I'd be pretty cool too.

*Plate 12* Claudia Schiffer.

*Source*: © Retna UK

Similarly, talking about how Hollywood has unrealistic standards so that women who are really of average size are perceived as overweight simply because they are not unnaturally skinny:

> They had an interview with, you know, the mother on *Home Improvement* and they were saying she was "chunky." And it's like, her, chunky? I don't think she is chunky, but by Hollywood standards she is chunky.

These women were critical of media portrayal of skinny models, and wanted to see more realistic images of models with average-size bodies in magazines. They were particularly critical of what they saw as double standards projected by magazines, in which there would be articles saying that all body shapes are fine, but this would be contradicted by images of skinny models on other pages of the magazines:

> This is the image you are trying to attain, in every women's magazine. I get [a women's magazine] . . . and every month there is an article saying you should like the way that you look. It is OK. But then on the next page there is someone who weighs 120 lb and who is 6 feet tall, and that is not normal. Actually, they are the freaks of nature because that is not normal. And every single month they get all these letters, and they print a lot of them saying, "Why do we never see average-sized models?" Every month there is a letter like that.

They were critical of the fact that advertisements for "plus-size" (large-size) clothes were modeled by average-size women at the bottom end of the size range of clothes sold by those companies. There was agreement that these average-size women should be modeling regular clothes instead of the skinny models in the magazines.

*Woman 1:* I'll tell you what used to drive me mad. Working for [a plus-size clothing company] who were supposed to cater for larger women, 22, 24. . . . They always, on all the billboards they would have size 14 models. They would have models in the smallest size that they carried. I mean, here is a company which is specializing in making clothes for larger women. But what do they do? They still go to size 14. Because to larger women that size 14 looks good. It looks like a size 3.

*Woman 1:* The large-size models are the same size I am, and I'm a size 9. Christine, she is beautiful, she is a large-size model. She's not fat at all. But she is a large-size model. She should be modeling regular clothes because she is an average size. I'm not a plus size and she doesn't look like a plus size.

It was striking, when listening to women talking in interview about media representations of the female body, how angry and dissatisfied many were with the way that the female body is portrayed in the media. They perceived that the fashion industry tries to manipulate them into feeling insecure about the way that they look. We have found a similar pattern of dissatisfaction in women aged 16–60 in Britain and in the USA. Their experiences challenge conceptions of women as passive "victims" of a system of oppression. The women we have interviewed are aware that the images presented are unrealistic and unhealthy (although they still aspire to look like fashion models in magazines) and are often angry at what they see as the media manipulating them into feeling bad about the way that they look. In *Beauty Secrets* (1986), Wendy Chapkis argued that women need to accept themselves as they really are and reject the unrealistic ideals set up by the advertising industry, the communications media, and the cosmetic industry. Clearly, women (even the 13-year-olds we have interviewed) are critical of the unrealistic images portrayed to them. However, most women still aspire to a very slim ideal, leaving a wide gap between ideal and current body shape for most women. This ambivalence is clear in our interviews with women of all ages.

Boys aged 8 and 13 reported in interview (Grogan *et al.*, 1997) that they aspired to the bodies of muscular men on television and in movies—mainly competitors on *Gladiators*, Jean Claude Van Damme, and Arnold Schwarzenegger (Plate 13).

In interview and questionnaire work with male bodybuilders (see Chapter 4), we have also found that men often describe making unfavorable comparisons between the media images of highly muscled men on television and in bodybuilding magazines and their own bodies. In some cases, this was cited as a catalyst in the decision to take anabolic steroids:

> The more I trained, the more magazines I looked at, the bigger I wanted to be . . . and there was a TV program and when I watched these people it made me feel really depressed, I didn't look as good as them, and it had a massive effect on my decision to take steroids.

However, most adult men we have interviewed report a minimal effect

*Plate 13* Arnold Schwarzenegger.

Source: White Mountain Prods (Courtesy Kobal)

of media imagery on their body esteem (Grogan and Richards, 2002). Adults and 16-year-olds were more likely to report how they compared themselves with male friends and wanted to match those who were more muscular. An interesting difference between interviews with men and with women is that adult men tended to see media images as realistic goals. There was a general feeling that they could look like the media images if they wanted to, but that they did not care enough about the way they looked to spend time weight training. Spending time trying to look good was generally thought to be feminine—and therefore inappropriate—behavior (see Chapter 4). A similar pattern emerged from interviews with 16-year-old boys, who reported that they would like to look more muscular (like the Chippendales) but were insufficiently motivated. The implication again is that they could look like them if they chose to do so, but had more important things to do:

> I wouldn't mind looking like that. But I wouldn't put myself out to look like it, you know.

Data from interviews, when combined with questionnaire data, suggest that men and women do use media images as standards for comparison to evaluate their own body shape and size. However, women (even young girls) are critical of the limited range of images, and (usually) see them as unrealistic. Men may aspire to emulate the muscular form of men who represent their body shape ideal, but are unwilling to admit to putting their energies into trying to build a muscular physique. Bodybuilders (who are seen as inappropriately narcissistic by many) are exceptional in putting time, energy, and money (especially those who take anabolic steroids) into the quest for a well-muscled body that matches more closely the media ideal portrayed on television and in bodybuilding magazines. For both men and women, friends and family are also used as body image role models. In interview, they explicitly reported comparing themselves unfavorably to peers. For instance:

> I don't look at movie stars or anything like that. I look at the average person who is smaller than me. Even when I think, "She's really not that pretty," the first thing that hits me is, "She is little," and to me it is like, I would rather look like her. I don't even think she is pretty, but I just want to be slender.

> I would never not be friends with someone just because they are smaller than me, but when I am around somebody smaller than I am I feel that everyone is looking at her and then at me, and they are thinking, "Look how big she is."

Similar experiences were described by men, although this time they wanted to be at least as big as their friends:

> If you've got friends who are, like, quite big in build, you want to be the same as them. Although you might not be able to do anything about it, it's on your conscience all the time. You want to be that sort of size.

Our questionnaire work suggests that media models often become less important standards for comparison, and friends and family more important, as people reach their thirties and forties. Social comparison theory predicts that, in order to be effective standards for comparison, people must see the bodies of models and actors/actresses as in some way similar to their own (Major *et al.*, 1991). Since most fashion models are in their teens and twenties, they would be expected to be less influential on other women once those women are out of that age range. This is borne out by our questionnaire data, in which actresses (Michelle Pfeiffer and Demi Moore) in the thirties age range are seen as role models for women in their thirties. Once people are in the forties, family role models become more relevant. Similarly for men, actors (Schwarzenegger and Van Damme) in the thirties are most frequently used as role models by men in their thirties. Above that range, no particular role models for body shape are cited. These data suggest that media models are used as standards for comparison for both men and women, but usually only by those who identify in some way with the person whose body is portrayed.

## Recent developments

In the mid-1990s there was an interesting new trend for media to discuss their use of slender models. This reflects (or, possibly, has created) a cultural awareness of the potential dangers of presenting young women with images of very thin models. In 1996, the watch manufacturer Omega made headline news in Britain by withdrawing its advertising from *Vogue* magazine, complaining that the models used in the *Vogue* fashion pages (Trish Goff and Annie Morton) were so thin as to appear anorexic. *The Guardian* newspaper of 31 May 1996 quoted the brand manager at Omega as saying:

> I thought it was irresponsible for a leading magazine which should be setting an example to select models of anorexic proportions. It made every effort to accentuate their skeletal appearance. Since

*Vogue* presumably targets an audience which includes young and impressionable females, its creators must surely be aware that they will inevitably be influenced by what laughably passes for fashion in these pages.

(Boseley, 1996: 1)

This trend continued in 1998 when the US media pilloried Calista Flockhart and Sarah Jessica Parker for being what were termed "lollipops" (having heads that looked too large for their thin bodies), and in Britain, in 2000, Victoria Beckham was criticized for looking too thin to be healthy and promoting starvation diets in young women who wanted to look like her (Reid, 2000). This coincided with the Body Summit in Britain, set up to discuss the potential link between magazine images of slender women and eating disorders. Around this time, newspapers in Britain carried stories about the link between media images of slender women and eating disorders ("Thin stars on T.V. put pressure on the young," *Daily Telegraph*, 31 May 2000; "Thin end of the wedge," *The Guardian*, 21 June 2000). In 2001, various newspaper journalists were discussing the "new athleticism" exemplified by the toned bodies of Beyoncé Knowles, Kelly Rowland, and Michelle Williams of the singing group Destiny's Child, noting that there had been a significant change in the acceptability of the extremely thin body shape for women. It was reported that the new aesthetic favored the muscular, worked-out, strong-looking body rather than a waifish, weak-looking, very thin body. For instance, in Britain, Polly Vernon, wrote in *The Independent on Sunday* in June 2001:

> The lollipop silhouette long-favoured by the female stars of American sitcoms, which involves disproportionately large heads wobbling atop stick-thin bodies does not say rich and it doesn't say clever. It says take me to a clinic. The New Athleticism, however, sends out a rather different set of messages: strong, confident, independent woman.
>
> (Vernon, 2001: 1)

In spite of this rhetoric, most models and actresses in 2006 are still extremely thin (Strahan *et al.*, 2006), and those who do not conform to the thin ideal are still criticized as being overweight (Wykes and Gunter, 2005). Nothing significant has changed, and although some marketing campaigns have challenged the thin, youthful ideal (such as the British Campaign for Real Beauty sponsored by Dove) most magazines continue to use very thin and youthful-looking models (Bordo,

2003; Strahan *et al.*, 2006). Images of men are also as lean and muscular as in the 1980s and 1990s, and it has become normal and expected that men in glamorous roles in movies and music videos are toned and muscular (Olivardia, 2002; Agliata and Tantleff-Dunn, 2004). The disparity between levels of muscularity for male actors in James Bond films in the 1960s (Sean Connery in *Thunderball* and *Dr No*) and in the 2000s (Daniel Craig in *Casino Royale* in 2006) illustrates this point. Clearly, media portrayals of the slender (and muscular, for men) body reflect current cultural ideology of the body as well as promoting these ideals. However, since the portrayal of such imagery has been shown to reduce body satisfaction and create body concerns, this is surely sufficient reason for advertisers to opt for the use of models in a range of sizes. Although advertisers may argue that only thin models sell products, recent British evidence from a study by Emma Halliwell and Helga Dittmar demonstrates that it is attractiveness, rather than size of models, that is crucial in making associated products attractive to consumers (Halliwell and Dittmar, 2004).

## Reducing the effects of media imagery

Recently, psychologists have suggested that people can be made resistant to the negative effects of media imagery by changing the ways that they interpret incoming social information. For instance, Leslie Heinberg and Kevin Thompson (1995) suggest that we should concentrate on investigating the cognitive strategies that some people use when faced with idealized media images, so that these can be taught to other people who find that their body image is affected by images of slender media models. They argue that training in these resistance strategies may reduce distress when faced with media imagery. If we accept that social comparison theory is a valid explanation of the mechanism through which unfavorable comparisons are made, then some logical suggestions follow. Social comparison rests on self-relevance and similarity (Major *et al.*, 1991). If people are encouraged to question the self-relevance and similarity to themselves of media images, they would be unlikely to make upward comparisons, since the model would be an inappropriate target. Media literacy techniques aim to enable women (most studies have been conducted on women rather than men) to reject media images as appropriate targets for comparison. Unfortunately, with two notable exceptions (Posavac *et al.* 2001; Thompson and Stice, 2001), although such studies have generally been successful in training women to be skeptical about these images, they have mostly not been successful in reducing women's tendency to compare their bodies to those in the media or in reducing resulting body dissatisfaction (Irving and Beral, 2001), and some studies have found that women who engaged in more critical body image processing had increases in drive for thinness and body dissatisfaction, suggesting that increased attention to these images may make social comparison more rather than less likely (Botta, 2003; Engeln-Maddox, 2005). Since the interviews cited above have shown that most women know how to criticize media imagery, it is perhaps not surprising that media literacy interventions with adult women tend to be ineffective in reducing body dissatisfaction.

Renee Engeln-Maddox (2005) has suggested that since so many women make comparisons with media ideals, teaching women to focus on making downward comparisons with the parts of the body that are superior to those of the model's may be helpful. She notes that in her study of 202 female students, there were some aspects of the women's bodies that they felt were better than those of the models (one woman's elbows, another's navel) and argues that getting women to focus on these positives may be an effective way to counter the negative effects of upward comparisons. Emma Halliwell and Helga Dittmar (2005) have shown that women's motives when making upward comparisons are also crucial in determining their effect. If women are motivated to self-improve (rather than self-evaluate) then making upward comparisons with media models does not seem to increase body-focused anxiety as women may temporarily imagine themselves as the idealized image portrayed. The authors note that further work is necessary to establish how long-lasting this effect might be.

Researchers working within the cognitive-behavioral paradigm focus on the mental image that we have of our bodies. Rita Freedman (1990) suggests that cognitive-behavioral therapy (CBT) could be used on an individual level to train people how to resist media pressure, through challenging "faulty cognitions" and developing new ways of conceptualizing incoming information. She argues that the image that we have of our body is not static, but is continually in a state of flux, depending on our recent experiences (including those of media images) and how we make sense of them. She sees body image disturbance as an individual problem caused by faulty cognitions about the body, irrational thoughts, and unrealistic and faulty explanations. Using Beck's (1976) taxonomy of cognitive errors, she argues that techniques of CBT can be used to detect such errors, which can generate irrational thoughts about the body, and which lead to body image problems. Freedman's clients are taught how to become aware of their faulty cognitions and are taught techniques to make these thoughts more rational, more self-enhancing and less self-defeating. Although Freedman recognizes that social pressures to be slim and physically attractive may exacerbate body dissatisfaction, her main focus is at an individual level, in identifying individuals' "faulty cognitions and rectifying them." Her model does not attempt to deal with the social problem of unrealistic media imagery, but tries to give clients a way of countering its effect by training them to question the validity of their interpretation of the incoming information. The effectiveness of CBT will be investigated further in Chapter 7.

Media literacy and CBT approaches assume that changes need to be made at the level of the individual. An alternative view is taken by many feminist writers who believe that women (as a group) should reject traditional media conceptions of body image completely (Bordo, 2003) and challenge traditional conceptions of "slim as beautiful." Our interviews with women suggested that many women (who may not consider themselves radical or feminist) are dissatisfied with, and angry about, the narrow range of images portrayed in the popular media. Various activists and academics are also challenging media institutions to try to force change. The media are responding, albeit slowly, and although there is no significant trend toward more realistic photographic models yet, at least magazines are starting to carry stories about the harmfulness of dieting and the importance of accepting a range of body shapes. Television personalities such as Dawn French, Roseanne Barr, Jo Brand, Beth Ditto, and many others have shown how alternative images of beauty can be brought into the mainstream. Activist feminist artists such as the "Guerrilla Girls" in New York have attacked the traditional position of women within visual culture as objects of male gaze. Other women artists are also challenging accepted notions of how women's bodies are portrayed in the media, often using their own bodies as subjects in their photographs (such as Carolee Schneeman's performance art in the 1970s, and more recently the work of Cindy Sherman, Della Grace, and Marianne Muller) to create a counter-aesthetic of the female body (see Muller, 1998). However, it is important not to overestimate the extent of any change. In 1997, the model Sophie Dahl made headlines because she modeled designer fashion and she was a (British) size 14—the average size for British women. The fact that this was newsworthy shows that the fashion industry had a long way to go before it accepted models that represented realistic images of women's bodies. By 2004, Sophie Dahl had dieted down to a British size 10, apparently due to embarrassment at being known as the "fat model" (Kay, 2004), and no one of a similar, more healthy and realistic size has replaced her in the fashion industry.

**Summary**

* Western media present the male and female body quite differently. Men tend to be portrayed as standard weight (usually slender and muscular), whereas women tend to be portrayed as underweight.
* Data from studies of the effects of media images have tended to show that both women and men can feel less good about their bodies after viewing these idealized media images.
* Media figures (fashion models, actors, sports persons) provide role models for a significant proportion of men and women under 40. Young men's body shape role models tended to be well-muscled actors. Women's varied with age, with women in their teens and twenties choosing fashion models, and those in their thirties choosing actresses.
* Interview work suggests that women are critical of the narrow range of body shapes presented in the media (which are viewed as unrealistic and unhealthy), and angry at the ways in which they perceive that the media (and in particular the fashion industry) set up unrealistically thin ideals.
* Most men reported that they would not exercise or diet to try to emulate the bodies of slender, muscular actors. Men who body build were exceptional, reporting that unfavorable comparisons with media images of highly muscled men often resulted in increases in weight training as they try to become more like their role models.
* Existing data challenge images of the viewer as primarily passive. Viewers engage critically with media imagery, using it to inform body image.

# 6 Age, social class, ethnicity, and sexuality

Previous chapters have identified gender-related differences in body image, and specifically in body satisfaction. The participants in most studies have been groups of white, middle-class college students, aged 18–25, and of unspecified socioeconomic status and sexuality. Although most psychological research relies on this age group due to convenience for the academic investigator (Christensen, 1997), the results are necessarily limited in generalizability. This chapter focuses on studies that have compared groups differing in age, social class, ethnicity, and sexuality. First, there will be a review of evidence for changes in body dissatisfaction throughout the life span, to identify critical periods for dissatisfaction and to look at development and change in body dissatisfaction in both women and men. This will be followed by a discussion of the historical links between "slenderness" and the middle and upper classes, with a review of studies of social class differences in body dissatisfaction. Following this, work on the effects of ethnicity on body satisfaction will be evaluated, considering in particular the negative effects of white Western values on body image in black subcultures. Finally, the impact of sexuality on body image will be investigated, looking at differential pressures on men and women to be sexually attractive, and establishing links between heterosexual, gay, and lesbian subcultures and body image.

## Body image across the life span

### Preadolescence

Research from psychology, sociology, and gender studies has suggested that boys and girls become critical of their bodies before adolescence, that girls use similar discourses of embodiment to adult women, and that, given a free choice, girls from age 5 choose thinner ideal body sizes than their perceived current size. In her classic work on the "culture of slenderness," Kim Chernin (1983) reports that preadolescent girls imitate the discourse of older women, expressing body dissatisfaction and concern over weight gain. In a British study conducted in the 1990s, Nicola Wainwright and I found that girls as young as 8 reported body dissatisfaction (Grogan and Wainwright, 1996). We had been unable to find any study in the literature that asked girls and female adolescents to describe their experiences of dissatisfaction with their body shape and size. It seemed to us that this was the most valid way to try to understand how girls and female adolescents felt about their bodies. Our experience of talking with adult women had suggested that many women remembered feeling under pressure to be slim from primary school onward. We wanted to explore the issues of body image and food with young women who could share with us their experiences, rather than investigating memories of such experiences with adult women. In our study, we carried out two focus groups; one with a group of 8-year-olds, and one with a group of 13-year-olds. The results provided some interesting insights into these young women's experiences and beliefs about their bodies, dieting, exercise, and food.

The 8-year-olds agreed that they wanted to be thin, both now and when they grew up. When asked whether they worried about how they looked, they said that they worried about getting fat. When they were asked how they would like to look when they were older, they were quite clear that they wanted to be thin.

| | |
|---|---|
| *Interviewer:* | What do you worry about then? |
| *Girl 1:* | Being fat mostly. |
| *Girl 2:* | Being fat. |
| *Interviewer:* | How would you like your body to look when you are older? |
| *All:* | Thin! |
| *Girl 3:* | Not fat. Really thin. |
| *Girl 2:* | Not really thin. Thin like I am now. |
| *Girl 3:* | I would like to keep thin like I am now. |

All 8-year-olds cited contenders on the television show *Gladiators* (muscular and fit entertainers popular in the 1990s) as role models, although they said that they did not want to get too muscled. Interestingly, having muscle was seen as being attractive to men, and thus to be avoided because it would lead to an increase in male attention. For instance, when asked whether they would like a lot of muscle like Jet (a female contender on *Gladiators*):

| | |
|---|---|
| *All:* | No. |
| *Girl 1:* | No, 'cos men'd be all around you. |
| *Interviewer:* | Do you think men like women with muscles? |
| *Girl 2:* | Yeah. |
| *Girl 3:* | Yeah. |
| *Girl 1:* | Yeah, but I would like to be like Jet though. |
| *Girl 3:* | Yes, but I wouldn't want muscles. |

Muscles were clearly seen as inappropriate for women (in line with comments from adult women, as reported in Chapter 3). When asked about their satisfaction with their present body shape, two of the 8-year-old girls said that they felt thin (and were satisfied with their weight), and two felt fat (and were dissatisfied). When asked what they would change about their bodies, both the girls who expressed dissatisfaction said they would want to lose weight.

| | |
|---|---|
| *Interviewer:* | Is there anything you like to do to change your body shape? |
| *Girl 3:* | Lose weight. |
| *Interviewer:* | Would you like to lose weight? |
| *Girl 3:* | Yeah. |
| *Girl 1:* | Lose weight. |
| *Girl 3:* | You're thin enough. |
| *Girl 1:* | I'm fat. |
| *Girl 2:* | Look at your legs. |
| *Girl 1:* | They're fat. |

These results provided direct evidence that these young women were dissatisfied with their body shape and size, and showed that girls as young as 8 reported dissatisfaction with their body weight and shape and showed a preference for a socially acceptably slim body. Their accounts suggested that they objectified and criticized their bodies and suggested that girls from primary-school age onward are sensitive to cultural pressures to conform to a limited range of acceptable body shapes.

In work where girls have been asked to choose "ideal" and "current" figure choices from age-appropriate figure drawings, researchers based in Britain, Australia, and the USA have found that girls tend to choose thinner ideal than current figures. In one of the earliest studies looking at figural choices in preadolescent girls, Marika Tiggemann and Barbara Pennington (1990) produced evidence that girls as young as 9 preferred thinner figures than perceived current size. In this Australian study, girls aged 9 were shown age-relevant body silhouettes and were asked to choose those closest to their "current" and "ideal." They reliably chose "ideal" figures that were thinner than their "current" choices. Tiggemann and Pennington suggest that body dissatisfaction is the normal experience of girls in Western culture from age 9, and that the imagery surrounding fatness and slimness on television and in other media is very influential in determining children's beliefs concerning ideal body size. These results were supported by British work by Andy Hill and colleagues (1992), who concluded that girls from the age of 9 were dissatisfied with their body shape and size. Hill and colleagues argue that children "consume" adult beliefs, values, and prejudices about body shape and size, and adopt them as their own. In a more recent Australian study, Helen Truby and Susan Paxton (2002) produce evidence that 48 percent of preadolescent girls in their sample wanted to be thinner compared to only 10 percent who wanted to be larger, supporting earlier work.

It has been suggested recently that body dissatisfaction and preference for a thin body shape may start even younger. Williamson and Delin (2001) have presented evidence that girls as young as 5 show a significant tendency to prefer thinner figures than their current size, and to be significantly less satisfied with their body size than are 5-year-old boys, and there is growing evidence that 5-year-old girls are aware of calorie counting as a means to lose weight (Wheatley, 2006). There are some difficulties associated with measuring body satisfaction through figure preferences in children younger than 8, making it difficult to draw conclusions with confidence on children in the 5–8 age group. Many studies have failed to find the expected correlation between children's "current" figure choice and their objectively measured size, casting doubt on the validity of this task with children in this younger age range (Smolak, 2004), so, although figural rating scales produce good, reliable, and valid measures of girls' body satisfaction from age 8 (Truby and Paxton, 2002; Ricciardelli, McCabe, Mussap, and Holt, in press) work on younger girls is less convincing.

Historically, there have been fewer studies of body satisfaction in boys than in girls (Cohane and Pope, 2001). Where boys have been studied, they have usually been included as a reference group for a comparison group of girls who are the main focus for the study. It is important to get a picture of how boys experience their bodies, and who or what their influences are when they are evaluating their bodies and deciding to engage (or not to engage) in activities relating to body image. This is particularly relevant in the light of recent evidence of a cultural change in the representation of the male body in the media.

Recently, there has been an increase in work on boys, partly fueled by concern about increases in eating problems in men (Ricciardelli and McCabe, 2004), and potential health risks associated with the drive to become more muscular (Pope *et al.*, 2000; Cafri *et al.*, 2005). In a rare study of boys' body image published in the 1980s, Michael Maloney and colleagues (1989) at the University of Ohio carried out an interesting study on a large sample of US boys and girls. Of the boys, they found (based on questionnaire data) that 31 percent of 9-year-olds, 22 percent of 10-year-olds, 44 percent of 11-year-olds, and 41 percent of 12-year-olds wanted to be thinner. They found that 31 percent of boys had tried to lose weight (36 percent at the 9-year level), 14 percent had dieted (27 percent at the 9-year level), and 37 percent had exercised to try to lose weight (44 percent at the 9-year level). They concluded that, for many boys and girls, body shape concerns start before adolescence. This work has been supported by more recent work suggesting that dieting is common in boys as young as 8 (Robinson *et al.*, 2001).

The extent and direction of body dissatisfaction may be different in boys and girls. Although some boys may want to be thinner (following the same pattern as girls), some may want to be broader and more muscular. For instance, one recent study found that although 35.5 percent of boys wanted to be thinner, 19.4 percent wanted to be heavier (Schur *et al.*, 2000); and Andy Hill and colleagues in the 1990s reported that more boys selected a heavier ideal figure than selected a thinner one (Hill *et al.*, 1992). In a very clear and useful review of body image studies conducted with children aged 7–11, Lina Ricciardelli and Marita McCabe (2001) found that there is some variation in numbers of boys dissatisfied with their bodies, ranging from 30 percent to 78 percent, and that the majority wanted a larger body size. In a further review of literature published since 2001, Lina Ricciardelli and colleagues have reported that specific estimates of numbers of preadolescent boys who desire a thinner body range from 27 to 47 percent, while the number of boys who want to be larger ranges from 15 to 44 percent (Ricciardelli, MaCabe, Mussap, and Holt, in press). Ricciardelli *et al.* report that estimates of the numbers of boys desiring a larger body size were similar to those reported in their 2001 review, whereas a lower number of boys wanted to be thinner than in the earlier studies covered in their previous review.

Recent interview work has allowed us to explain in more detail which aspects of body shape and size provoke most concern. This work has demonstrated that young boys represent adult body shape ideals, and present negative accounts of overweight. In the late 1990s, Nicola Wainwright ran focus groups with boys aged 8 in which they were asked about their body shape ideals (Grogan *et al.*, 1997; see also Grogan and Richards, 2002). She found that the 8-year-old boys wanted to be muscular when they grew up, and had role models who were well-muscled:

| | |
|---|---|
| *Interviewer:* | When you are in your twenties, how would you like to look? |
| *All:* | Muscly! |
| *Interviewer:* | Can you think who you would like to look like? |
| *Boy 2:* | Hulk Hogan. |
| *Boy 1:* | Shadow from the *Gladiators*. |
| *Boy 3:* | Saracen. |
| *Interviewer:* | So you would like to be muscly? |
| *All:* | Yeah. |

This supports more recent survey work by Lina Ricciardelli and colleagues suggesting that boys are more likely than girls to attribute importance to muscles (Ricciardelli and McCabe, 2001; Holt and Ricciardelli, 2002). None of the boys had dieted, although they were clear what it meant to diet:

| | |
|---|---|
| *Interviewer:* | Do you know what it means to be on a diet? |
| *Boy 4:* | Yeah, you don't eat as much. |
| *Boy 2:* | And you don't eat any fat. |
| *Interviewer:* | Have any of you lot been on a diet? |
| *Boy 3:* | No way. |
| *Boy 2:* | No. |

They all exercised to some extent, and saw exercise as a way to avoid getting fat:

| | |
|---|---|
| *Interviewer:* | So do you exercise? |
| *Boy 1:* | Um, sometimes. |
| *Boy 3:* | A bit. |
| *Boy 4:* | I always do it. |
| *Interviewer:* | What sort of exercise do you do? |
| *Boy 3:* | I do press-ups. |
| *Boy 4:* | Running, biking. |
| *Interviewer:* | So, do you think it is important to exercise, then? |
| *Boy 1:* | Yeah. |
| *Boy 4:* | It burns all your fat off. |

These results suggest that these 8-year-old boys shared body shape ideals with teenagers and young men in their early twenties. They wanted to be slim (they were fearful of being fat) and muscular (but not too muscular). The focus groups supported suggestions that body shape concerns start before adolescence. None of the boys had dieted, but they would diet or exercise to lose weight should weight become a problem. Body shape role models for these boys were television and movie celebrities, rather than their friends (who presumably were still too young to sport the culturally favored, postpubertal muscular body).

In 2006, Vivienne Hopkins at Staffordshire University carried out individual interviews and focus groups with preadolescent and postadolescent boys, exploring body satisfaction, body idealization, attributional style, and sociocultural influences on body image (Hopkins, 2006). She found that the preadolescent boys are generally positive about being moderate sized (rather than plump or thin), and that muscularity is linked with being fit and "cool." Plump and skinny boys are perceived negatively. In one group, the most "uncool" boy in their class at school is described as "Overweight. He might not do as much sport because he is lazy and a bit overweight." In another group, the least "cool" boy is described as "very weedy" and lacking in muscles:

> Likes trying to show off his muscles when he really doesn't have any. Like his shoulders . . . he says, "Look at my shoulders" . . . and then they are like pancakes.

Clearly, muscularity is important to these preadolescent boys, supporting other work suggesting that boys in this age range idealize a muscular body shape (Grogan and Richards, 2002). However, there is a limit to the degree of muscularity that is acceptable, and extremely muscular body types are not idealized because of fears that these would make them look fat: "not too much though, or you will look like . . . fat." Body satisfaction is linked by these boys to body function and specifically to sporting ability, supporting suggestions from other authors that sport provides a socially appropriate context for boys to talk about their bodies (Ricciardelli *et al.*, 2006). For instance:

*Interviewer:*  So can you describe your bodies now?
*Boy A:*  Well, I am not exactly slim. I'm quite good at tackling. I'm not that good at playing rugby. I'm quite good at knocking people over, but I'm not overweight, but I. . . .
*Boy B:*  I'd say I was reasonably fit.

Taken together, results from preadolescent boys and girls suggest that both genders are fearful of becoming fat, and conform to the slender ideal (although girls want to avoid muscularity and boys aspire to a muscular ideal). Accounts from boys and girls are very similar to the accounts from adults reported in Chapters 3 and 4. Body shape ideals are similar, as are role models.

## Adolescence

There has been a lot of interest in body satisfaction in adolescence. Adolescent girls in Western societies are subject to powerful cultural pressures to be very thin (Nichter, 2000; Smolak, 2004), and many authors have argued that adolescence is a time when body image concern in young women is at its peak due to physical changes in shape that may move girls away from a slender ideal (Burgess *et al.*, 2006). Researchers working in this area have tended to infer body satisfaction from surveys of dieting or from discrepancy between current and ideal shape on age-relevant silhouette figures. It has been suggested that many adolescent girls say that they feel fat and want to lose weight. In the 1990s, Thomas Wadden and colleagues (1991) argued that adolescent girls are at odds with their bodies, and reported (on the basis of questionnaire data) that body concern is one of the most important worries in the lives of teenage girls. This has been reiterated more recently by authors such as Mimi Nichter (2000). Body dissatisfaction does not seem to motivate healthy weight management behaviors in adolescent girls, but has been linked with very unhealthy weight control behaviors and low levels of physical activity. Dianne Neumark-Sztainer and colleagues followed a group of 2,516 adolescents over a 5-year period, finding that, for young women, lower body satisfaction predicted higher levels of dieting, binge eating, lower levels of exercise, and very unhealthy weight control behaviors. When they had controlled for weight (BMI), they found that dieting, very unhealthy weight control practices, and low levels of exercise were still predicted by low body satisfaction (Neumark-Sztainer *et al.*, 2006).

In focus groups with adolescent girls (Grogan and Wainwright, 1996), we found that they expressed a desire to be of average size, neither too thin nor too fat:

*Adolescent girl 3:*  Not too fat.
*Adolescent girl 4:*  Not too thin.
*Adolescent girl 2:*  Normal.

They expressed a dislike for the body shape of models in magazines because they thought they were too thin:

*Adolescent girl 1:*  They look horrible. They're ugly half the time.
*Adolescent girl 2:*  Yeah, they are.
*Adolescent girl 1:*  I think they do sometimes look too thin, they look anorexic.

However, they were envious of those of their friends who were skinny (like the models) and who ate "fattening" foods like chocolate and did not put on weight. They shared stories about skinny people they knew who could eat anything they liked and about how they envied them:

*Adolescent girl 3:*  Well, my friend used to come round all the time, but she's a right fussy eater and she's right skinny, but she eats a right lot of chocolate bars and everything.
*Adolescent girl 2:*  I hate it when really skinny people say, "Oh, I'm fat." They just do it to annoy you.

The 13-year-old girls were dissatisfied with their "stomachs," which were perceived to be too fat.

*Adolescent girl 1:*  I'd maybe change my tummy.
*Adolescent girl 3:*  Yeah, I'd like to be a bit thinner.
*Adolescent girl 4:*  Yeah, just got a bit of a bulge on my tummy.

These 13-year-olds expressed a dislike for muscles, which they saw as inappropriate for women because they made women look too masculine:

*Adolescent girl 4:*  I don't like women bodybuilders 'cos they're right . . .
*Adolescent girl 1:*  Fat and uhhh.
*Adolescent girl 2:*  It's all right for them to have a few muscles, but not like . . .
*Adolescent girl 4:*  Be like a man.
*Adolescent girl 2:*  Just looks totally . . .
*Adolescent girl 1:*  Out of shape.

The findings suggest that these young women have learned about the acceptability of the slim body in Western society (and the unacceptability of the body that does not fit the slim ideal). What struck us most when reading the transcripts was the similarity between the accounts given by these 13-year-olds and those given by the adults in the interviews cited in Chapter 3. Adolescent women and girls may find it particularly difficult to challenge dominant cultural representations of femininity at a time when they are still learning about what it means to be a woman in Western society, and when they are experiencing changes in body shape and size as they move into womanhood. Of course, talking about being fat can be a mechanism for gaining social approval and reassurance among girls and adult women. In *Fat Talk*, Mimi Nichter (2000) reports results of interviews and focus groups carried out with 240 14–15-year-old girls in the USA as part of the Teen Lifestyle Project. She discusses patterns of talk in which the statement from one girl that she is fat can act as a bonding mechanism between adolescent girls, and also prompt reassurance from other girls that she is not fat.

> Participation in fat talk was a critical component of peer-group membership and made girls appear no better than their friends. By affirming that their friends were not fat, girls helped one another keep their self-effacing thoughts about their bodies in check.
>
> (Nichter, 2000: 183)

However, the existence of "fat talk" does not mean that the concerns expressed are not real concerns for these young women. Mimi Nichter (2000) reports that her young women respondents engaged in continual personal surveillance to check how they matched up to the cultural ideal, which had a significant impact on the rest of their lives:

> As a result of being preoccupied with their physical selves, particularly during early adolescence, girls often fail to understand that they are far more than how they look. The comparisons that they draw between themselves and imagined or real others direct their energy away from more meaningful pursuits.
>
> (Nichter, 2000: 183–4)

There has been less work on body image in adolescent boys, although there has been a significant increase in studies investigating body image in adolescent boys in the 2000s, linked with concerns about unhealthy body-change behaviors such as anabolic steroid use in adolescents (Pope *et al.*, 2000). Estimates of the percentage of boys who have used anabolic steroids range from 1 to 12 percent (Ricciardelli and McCabe, 2004) depending where and when the study was undertaken. As discussed in

Chapter 4, anabolic steroid use is linked with serious health problems (see also Cafri *et al.*, 2005, for a review). Most studies using figural choices have shown that about a third of boys want to be larger and about a third want to be thinner (Ricciardelli and McCabe, 2003). One of the problems with figural choice work is that it is not possible for boys to indicate whether they would like to be more muscular or to have more body fat (although the latter is rare). Harrison Pope's *et al.*'s (2000) somatomorphic matrix (see Chapter 4) has made it possible to differentiate between wanting to be plumper and wanting to be more muscular, and work thus far has shown that a significant proportion of boys want to be more muscular. In *The Adonis Complex*, Harrison Pope reports results of a study with 11–17-year-old boys at a summer camp in the USA. On average, boys of all ages chose an ideal with about 35 lb more muscle than their current body size as their ideal. Other work has also shown that many adolescent boys are dissatisfied with their muscle size, strength, shoulders, biceps, and chests, and generally desire more muscle in these areas while maintaining a generally lean physique (McCabe and Ricciardelli, 2001).

There is very little work on dieting in adolescent boys as an indicator of desire to be thinner. One exception is a British study of 11- and 13-year-old boys by Mark Conner and colleagues (1996). The study examined body esteem, current ideal body discrepancy, and dieting in 128 11-year-olds (61 boys, 67 girls) and 103 12–14-year-olds (52 boys, 51 girls). Although boys were generally more satisfied with their bodies than girls and were less likely to diet, there were significant age differences in body esteem within the boys' group. The 13-year-old boys were significantly less satisfied with their body shape and weight than the 11-year-olds. This suggests that boys going through the physical and mental changes associated with puberty are less satisfied with their bodies than are prepubertal 11-year-olds. However, it does not tell us why they are dissatisfied, or what they find unsatisfactory about their bodies.

In interviews with 13-year-old boys, we found that body shape ideals are very similar to adult men's ideals (Grogan *et al.*, 1997; Grogan and Richards, 2002). Thirteen-year-old boys said that their ideal body shape for a man was of average build and fairly muscular, bringing their ideal into line with that of the adult men whose accounts are reported in Chapter 4:

| | |
|---|---|
| *Interviewer:* | What is your ideal shape for a man, say, when you are in your twenties? |
| *Adolescent boy 1:* | Muscular legs. |

| | |
|---|---|
| *Adolescent boy 2:* | Muscular. |
| *Adolescent boy 3:* | Good tan like. |
| *Adolescent boy 4:* | Like a footballer. Just medium build. |
| *Adolescent boy 1:* | Not fat, not right thin, just medium. |
| *Interviewer:* | So how would you like to develop? |
| *Adolescent boy 3:* | Bodybuilder. |
| *Adolescent boy 1:* | Boxer. |
| *Adolescent boy 2:* | Just a bit muscular. |
| *Adolescent boy 4:* | Yeah. |
| *Interviewer:* | Where would you like the muscles? |
| *All:* | On my arms. |
| *Adolescent boy 4:* | Chest. |
| *Adolescent boy 3:* | Back, biceps, and triceps. |
| *Adolescent boy 4:* | All over. |
| *Adolescent boy 2:* | I wouldn't want any of them ones like that though [illustrates large neck muscles with hands]. |

Adolescent boys cited Jean-Claude Van Damme as the person who most resembled their ideal because he was fit rather than really muscular:

| | |
|---|---|
| *Interviewer:* | So, can you think of who you would like to look like when you get older? |
| *Adolescent boy 1:* | Arnie [Arnold Schwarzenegger], but not as much, oh, Van Damme. |
| *Adolescent boy 2:* | Yeah, like Van Damme. |
| *Adolescent boy 1:* | He's not right muscly, he's right fit. He can do like a thousand chin-ups and stuff. |
| *Adolescent boy 2:* | I'd rather be fit than muscly. |

They did not want to become too muscular because they believed that this could lead to getting fat in later life:

| | |
|---|---|
| *Adolescent boy 1:* | [Bodybuilders] will get fat anyway 'cos when you get older all muscles turn to fat. . . . If you have too much muscle, you're gonna be fat when you're older unless you can get rid of it. |

They believed that they would be happier if they became closer to their ideal shape:

| | |
|---|---|
| *Interviewer:* | So, if you had this ideal body shape, do you think you would be happier? |

*Adolescent boy 1:*    Yeah, 'cos if you were fat you'd be looking at yourself thinking you're right ugly.

Friends with muscular bodies were explicitly mentioned as a relevant comparison group, and unfavorable comparisons were said to lead to unhappiness. This suggests that body image is important for these young men's self-esteem:

*Adolescent boy 3:*    And if you're hanging around with a mate who is right muscular and stuff and he's got a right good body shape, all women are hanging round him, that would depress you a bit, that would.

None of them had tried dieting, although they knew about the different diets available, and three of them had family members who had dieted:

*Adolescent boy 1:*    My mum does this diet where you can't eat bread and can't eat carbohydrates with protein, summat like that.
*Adolescent boy 3:*    Yeah, my mum's been on a hip-and-thigh diet.
*Adolescent boy 2:*    My mum tried Slim-Fast.

If they became overweight, though, two of them would diet:

*Interviewer:*    So, would any of you do step-ups?
*Adolescent boy 2:*    Not unless I were right fat, about 20 stone [280 1b].
*Adolescent boy 1:*    I wouldn't exercise to lose weight then . . .
*Adolescent boy 2:*    I'd just diet.
*Adolescent boy 3:*    I wouldn't, I'd exercise.

These data suggest that adolescents present a slender, muscular ideal that is very similar to the adult male ideal, as suggested by Marita McCabe and Lina Ricciardelli (2001).They are fearful of becoming fat, and would diet or exercise to avoid becoming overweight. Looking good is linked with happiness, and adolescents explicitly compare their body shapes with those of their friends (who were one of their body shape comparison groups, along with well-muscled actors). Clearly, body image is important to young men as well as young women. These adolescents have a clear ideal that corresponds to the adult male ideal that we have identified in interview work with men (see Chapter 4). These boys resist representing men's bodies, including their own bodies, as objects of aesthetic interest by deflecting discussion of how bodies looked into discussion of what they can do (looking "athletic" or "fit"). They are generally reticent about talking about the ways that their bodies look and are much more comfortable when talking about what a fit-looking body can do. These findings are supported by interviews with Australian adolescent boys by Lina Ricciardelli and colleagues (2006), who suggest that sport provides a context for discussing body image, and that attributes that boys like about their bodies are synonymous with those they associate with being successful at sport (Ricciardelli *et al.*, 2006).

Vivienne Hopkins (2006) found that her adolescent respondents (mean age 14 years 7 months) described similar ideals to the young British men in the focus groups described above. They wanted to be muscular but not too muscular, and to reduce their body fat. For instance:

*Interviewer:*        Is there anything you would like to change?
*Adolescent boy 5:*  I'd like to lose a bit of fat and get more muscly. My legs aren't bad, but maybe lose something off my stomach. Get a six pack. Bigger legs and arms.

The degree of muscularity exemplified in bodybuilders was seen as too big and to be avoided:

*Adolescent boy 6:*  It looks completely unnatural even if they are about to pop out of his body. Looks, because I think there's like a balance, so, you know [the bodybuilder in picture] is too, um, muscly and overweight and everything.

Duane Hargreaves and Marika Tiggemann (2006) interviewed Australian boys aged 14–16, attempting to gain access to the boys' own ideas and terminology about their bodies and body image. Their participants reported that talking about the look of their bodies was seen as inappropriate for heterosexual boys. Young men are socialized into not talking about their bodies from an aesthetic point of view, as being concerned about the look of the body is often seen as feminine-appropriate in Western societies (Aoki, 1996), so this reluctance is perhaps not surprising. In our interviews with men described in Chapter 4, it was only bodybuilders, well-practiced in objectifying and criticizing their own and other men's bodies, who appeared to feel comfortable talking about the look of their bodies. This needs to be taken into account in future work in which young men are asked to talk about body image, as they may not feel able to express their concerns, leading to an overestimation of degree of satisfaction in young men compared with young women. Adolescent boys and girls share body shape ideals and discourses relating to body image with adults of the same gender. In adolescent girls, the ideal is slenderness (though not too thin), and, for boys, slender and muscular (but not too muscular). The boys generally want to be more muscular (though not so muscular as bodybuilders, whose muscularity is seen as artificial and unnatural), whereas the girls believe muscularity is inappropriately "masculine" and want to be slender. The area of the body that presents most concern to girls is the "stomach," whereas the boys want to be more muscular in general, and particularly in the upper body. Being fat is feared by both boys and girls, in line with adult concerns.

### Body image throughout adulthood

Most psychological research on body image in adults has focused on samples of women and men aged 18–25. This is partly because most work has used college students as research participants, and most work has been done in US universities or high schools, where students (who may be co-opted into research as part of a course requirement) are usually young adults and are a convenient participant sample.

Work that has looked at body image concerns in older adults has produced some interesting findings. The idealized slender body shape is generally associated with youth. Women in particular are expected to try to maintain a youthful appearance, since youthfulness for women is valued in Western societies. Diane Cepanec and Barbara Payne (2000) argue that there is significant social pressure on women to maintain a youthful look, a pressure that is not imposed on men to the same extent, and that this fuels the cosmetic surgery industry:

> As a woman ages, failure to replicate society's ideal becomes all the more apparent. Beauty and youth tend to be seen as synonymous in our society. In short, surgical alteration of the face and body is a procedure that women in many cultures undergo in order to improve and transform their bodies to meet the cultural requirements of youth and femininity.
>
> (Cepanec and Payne, 2000: 122)

Many researchers have noted a "double standard" of aging, whereby women are judged more harshly than men in terms of physical attractiveness as they show signs of aging. Signs of aging in men may be seen to make them look "distinguished," whereas in women (who are often judged in terms of physical attractiveness rather then in terms of abilities or experience) signs of aging may be seen negatively both by others and by themselves. Susan Bordo (2003) notes that for older actresses "facelifts are virtually routine" (Bordo, 2003: 25) as they attempt to make themselves acceptable to an audience critical of any signs of aging in women. Jane Ussher (1993) argues that women are culturally defined as useless when they reach the end of their reproductive years. She argues that women of all ages are encouraged to compare themselves to youthful, slender role models, and that the discrepancies between this image and reality become more and more apparent as women age.

This advent of ageing is experienced as a crisis by many women: a crisis which is not experienced in the same way by men. Within the discourses concerning women, looking young is seen to be one of our main preoccupations: our images of "ideal women," against whom all women are judged and against which we judge ourselves, are primarily of young, slim, able-bodied, heterosexual, attractive women.

(Ussher, 1993: 116)

Men in their forties and fifties are frequently portrayed on film as attractive and sexual, and as having sexual relationships with much younger women. It is easy to think of examples of Hollywood actors who still play "love interest" roles in their sixties (Robert Redford, Sean Connery, Jack Nicholson, and Clint Eastwood), and it is not uncommon for men to be portrayed as lovers of women 20 years younger than themselves. Studies of media portrayal of men over 65 have tended to find that they are rarely portrayed on television (on average, about 5 percent of characters on television fall into this age range), although older men are represented significantly more frequently than older women. When they are portrayed in films, they have historically been portrayed as incapacitated, incompetent, pathetic, and the subject of ridicule (Ward, 1983). Older men's or women's bodies are rarely seen on film, except when they are represented in roles where their bodies might be expected to be exposed (e.g., as hospital patients).

Researchers who have analyzed media representations of women have reliably found that the predominant image of "woman" in the media is of a young, conventionally attractive, usually white model. Maggie Wykes and Barrie Gunter (2005) argue that although equality in the workplace is portrayed in 2000s television comedy dramas such as *Friends* and *Sex and the City*, the women characters are portrayed by similar-looking, slender, young actresses and the underlying message is that women need to be thin and beautiful to be successful and happy. Older women are rarely portrayed in movies, and when they are, they are usually represented as without role (unless that of a doting or senile grandmother). Often they are portrayed as lonely and depressed (Gannon, 2000). Older women are hardly never portrayed as sexual, and sexual desire in older women is often a point of ridicule (Ussher, 1993). When older women are portrayed in sexual roles, they are usually women who have a youthful appearance (e.g., Susan Sarandon), and the director often avoids exposing the body of the actress by implying sexual activity rather than actually filming the actors naked, by using body doubles, or by filming from a distance. Susan Bordo (2003) notes that although some older women are presented sexually in film, these tend to be those who have had cosmetic surgery to make their bodies acceptable to a critical audience. She argues that cosmetic surgery has shifted cultural expectations of how women are expected to look in their forties, fifties, sixties, and beyond, to a more youthful-looking image, and that this is not positive:

> These actresses, whose images surround us on television and in videos and films, are changing cultural expectations of what women "should" look like at forty-five and fifty. This is touted in the popular culture as a liberating development for older women; in the nineties, it is declared, fifty is still sexy. But in fact, Cher, Jane Fonda, and others have not made the ageing female body sexually more acceptable. They have established a new norm—achievable only through continual cosmetic surgery—where the female body ceases to age physically as the body grows chronologically older.
>
> (Bordo, 2003: 25–6)

Given that it is normal and healthy to gain some weight as they age (Andres *et al.*, 1993), women over 30 might be expected to suffer from higher levels of body dissatisfaction than younger women, since they may be even further from the youthful, slim ideal than younger women. However, most research has found that there is no change with age in terms of body satisfaction in women, although older men may be less satisfied than younger men.

In our interviews with women (see Chapter 3), we found that women aged 16–63 represented similar levels of dissatisfaction. Areas of the body that presented cause for concern did not differ in relation to the age of the interviewees. Women reliably reported dissatisfaction with stomach, hips, and thighs, irrespective of their age. Most were motivated to lose weight, and represented an ideal that was tall and slim with firm breasts, irrespective of their age. The main motivator for women of all ages was being able to get into favorite clothes. Women of all ages were able to identify a part of their body that they would like to change, and almost all wished to be slimmer if possible.

Women in their twenties and early thirties who had recently given birth often felt that the changes associated with pregnancy had brought their body shapes further from their ideals. In particular, having a "flabby belly" was reported by several women who had recently given birth, and "droopy breasts" (which they believed had resulted from breast feeding) were mentioned as a specific cause of dissatisfaction. Fox and Yamaguchi (1997) gave questionnaires to 76 women who were having their first baby, asking how they felt about their bodies (all were at least 30 weeks into their pregnancy), both currently and prior to pregnancy. They found that women who were of normal weight prior to pregnancy were likely to experience negative body image changes during pregnancy, whereas those who were overweight prior to pregnancy were likely to have experienced a positive change in body image at 30 weeks' gestation. Women's weight prior to pregnancy may also have a significant effect on body image after they have given birth. Women who were of average weight (or below) may experience more negative effects after birth than those who were overweight before (Fox and Yamaguchi, 1997).

Patricia Pliner and colleagues (1990) compared concern with body weight, eating, and physical appearance between men and women aged 10–79. The women were more concerned about eating, body weight, and physical appearance, and had lower appearance self-esteem (i.e., felt less attractive and less pleased with their appearance). Scores on the "appearance self-esteem test" did not differ between age groups ranging from 10 to over 60. Women over 60 were just as concerned as adolescents and young adults. The authors concluded that social pressures to be slim and attractive affect women of all ages. This fascinating finding suggests that the body dissatisfaction observed in young adult women may be generalized to women of all ages. Similarly, there were no differences in men's appearance self-esteem across the age range. This suggests that older men are just as satisfied as younger men with their attractiveness, even though they (probably) move further away from the slender, muscled societal ideal as they become older. Pliner and colleagues did not ask specifically about discrepancy between current and ideal body shapes. Sue Lamb and colleagues (1993) administered silhouette scales to older and younger women and men. The older women and men (aged about 50) were objectively heavier and considered themselves to be heavier than the younger groups (aged about 20). Younger and older women, and older men, presented body ideals that were much thinner than their perceived size. Only the younger men were satisfied with their bodies. This study suggests that some middle-aged men may be dissatisfied with their bodies, and this may relate to the physiological processes associated with aging, in which both men and women become heavier, perhaps taking them further away from their ideal.

Researchers have tended to assume that older people (particularly women) have body shape ideals derived from the media and other sources of information that are similar to those of younger groups, producing a larger discrepancy between current and ideal body shapes, and resulting in feelings of inadequacy (see Ussher, 1993). However, Lamb and colleagues (1993) argue that older people have a heavier ideal body size, based on a more realistic, age-related body ideal. Since people gain weight as they get older, it is possible that they also modify body shape ideals. Of course, data are difficult to interpret because, in cross-sectional work such as this, the different age groups also differ in terms of their experience of cultural pressures on body image. People in their fifties in the 1990s and 2000s have lived through the era of Marilyn Monroe and Jayne Mansfield, in which a heavier, fuller body was idealized. Perhaps this result says more about historical changes in stereotypes of body attractiveness than about age differences in body weight ideals. Longitudinal work, in which body image is studied in the same group over a period of several decades, would help to answer this question.

In Chapter 5, some data on role models in different cohorts were described. Although these data are beset with the same kinds of problems as the Lamb *et al.* study, they provide some additional insight into the role models of people of different ages. In our samples of 100 men and women aged 16–49, we found that the younger groups (under 30) were most likely to cite actors, actresses, and models as body image role models. Older men reported no particular body image role models, and older women were likely to cite a family member, or no particular model. One of the interesting findings of this study was that role models tended to be age-appropriate. Youthful media models became less important standards for comparison as people became older. Each age group tended to cite role models that were similar in age to themselves. In the group over 40, friends and relations were more likely to be used to make body image comparisons. This is as would be expected from social comparison theory, which predicts that people choose body image models in some way similar to themselves, to draw realistic and relevant body image comparisons. This may in some way explain why Pliner *et al.* and Lamb *et al.* did not find that older women (in particular) were less satisfied with their body shape and size than younger women, as would have been predicted by Jane Ussher's assumption that women of all ages compare themselves to media images of young, slender models. If women pick age-appropriate role models, they would not necessarily be expected to become less satisfied with age. This raises the question of why men become less satisfied with age (according to the Lamb *et al.* study). Men over 40 did not cite any role models, although two older men did say, in response to the question, "Who would you like to look like?," "Like myself when I was younger." Perhaps men are more likely to compare themselves with how they used to look when they were younger. If so, then the drop in satisfaction (and the slimmer ideal reported by Lamb *et al.*, 1993) would be expected, since most men increase in weight as they age (Monaghan, 2005a).

In a useful review of relevant work in this area, Marika Tiggemann (2004) showed that women's body dissatisfaction does not differ with age until they become quite elderly. Aging, then, can become positive for women in terms of body image. Reviewing work in women over 60, she found increased body satisfaction in women in this older age group, with a shift in focus toward body function and health, and similar levels of body satisfaction to men in this age group. She also noted that the "invisibility" of older women described by feminist writers such as Jane Ussher (1993) can mean that the importance of body size and weight decreases with age for women, as they are able to relinquish the internalized observer's perspective on their bodies. This can result in lowered self-objectification, reduced body monitoring, and less appearance anxiety. This freedom from self-consciousness and pressure to aspire to the slender, youthful, sexually available ideal has been largely overlooked in previous work that has focused on body dissatisfaction and on the potential negative effects of youth-obsessed media imagery.

> As women (and perhaps men) age, they place less emphasis on the importance of the body's appearance. Physical appearance is no longer such a central part of who they are. This allows a greater acceptance of the otherwise socially undesirable and largely uncontrollable age-related body changes which, in turn, means that older women are somewhat able to protect their self-concept and self-esteem from their increasing deviation from the thin and youthful ideal.
>
> (Tiggemann, 2004: 38)

Current data suggest that women are likely to be more dissatisfied than men aged 18–60. There are no significant differences in satisfaction in different age groups of women, irrespective of how body satisfaction is measured, despite suggestions that media imagery focuses on the importance of youth. This may be because women choose age-appropriate models for body image comparisons as they age and/or because appearance becomes less important as they age. Women seem to be as satisfied as men over 60, when body function may become more important than body appearance for both men and women. Older men are generally less satisfied than younger men, generally wishing to be thinner. Future research in this area needs to look at the process of body change with age in longitudinal studies that follow the same cohort through the various ages, to control effectively for the effects of historical changes in body shape ideals on the development of both men's and women's body image.

## Ethnicity and body image

Some variations in preferred body size have been documented in people from different ethnic groups in Western countries. Most studies have focused on antifat prejudice, body satisfaction, and frequency of dieting in different ethnic groups, and most have concentrated on women. Research has found that body dissatisfaction is most frequent in British and US white women, and less frequent among African-Americans and women from the British Afro-Caribbean community. Although research published in the 1990s reported that Hispanic and Asian women are generally more satisfied with their bodies than white women, new evidence suggests that Hispanic and Asian women are becoming less satisfied in the 2000s, bringing them in line with white women in terms of dissatisfaction. This evidence is reviewed below. There is less work on ethnic differences in men's body image, although there is general agreement that African-American men report higher levels of satisfaction than white men, and have heavier body ideals for women and men than do white men.

Research conducted in the USA in the 1990s produced convincing evidence that obesity and overweight are viewed more positively in non-white groups. Harris *et al.* (1991) reported that African-American participants (both men and women) were more positive about overweight in women than white Americans. Black US men were more likely than white US men to want to date overweight women, and to consider them sexually attractive. Harris *et al.* also found that obese African-American women had a more positive body image than obese white US women, and were less likely to want to lose weight. These findings suggested less negative attitudes to overweight in the African-American community.

Another study investigated ethnic and gender differences in perceptions of ideal body size in 9-year-olds (Thompson *et al.*, 1997). In a random sample of 817 children, half white and half female, the researchers found that African-American children selected significantly heavier ideal body sizes than white children for the categories of self, male child, female child, adult male, and adult female. Black boys selected significantly heavier figures for ideal girl and ideal woman than the white boys. They concluded that, by age 9, ethnic differences in ideal body sizes are apparent, with black boys and girls selecting significantly heavier figures than white boys and girls.

These differences in body ideals were correlated with differences in body satisfaction and dieting in women and girls. Studies undertaken in the 1990s suggested that African-American, Asian, and Hispanic women were likely to report higher desired body weights, larger desired body shapes, and fewer weight concerns than white women (Harris, 1994; Crago *et al.*, 1996). Studies of girls and adolescents produced similar findings, showing that African-American girls reported less dieting than white US girls. For instance, Neff *et al.* (1997) looked at body size perceptions and weight management practices in both black and white adolescent women. They selected their sample through a randomized sampling procedure designed to ensure that the sample was statistically representative of high-school students in South Carolina. The resulting sample was made up of 1,824 black and 2,256 white girls aged 14–18. They found that significantly more (41 percent) white girls than black girls (28 percent) consider themselves overweight. White girls were six times more likely to use diet pills and vomiting to control weight, and four times more likely to diet or exercise as a way to manage their weight. The authors concluded that white adolescent girls were significantly more likely to consider themselves overweight, and were more likely to engage in unhealthy weight management practices than black girls of the same age.

Similar results were found in British work conducted in the 1990s. In one British study, Jane Wardle and Louise Marsland (1990) found that fewer Afro-Caribbean and Asian British girls than white girls wanted to lose weight. In another study, Jane Wardle *et al.* (1993) studied body image and dieting concerns in a sample of 274 white and Asian British women aged 14–22. The Asian women were less likely to describe themselves as too fat, less dissatisfied with their body size, less likely to want to lose weight, and less likely to diet. Some of these differences were the result of generally lower body weight in the Asian group. However, when the researchers controlled for the effects of body size, they found that white women rated their stomach, thighs, and buttocks as significantly larger than those of Asian women of the same size. The authors concluded that white women felt larger than Asian women of the same size, and suggested that these results may demonstrate cultural differences between the two groups, as body shape may be a less emotive issue for the Asian group and/or obesity may not be such a stigma as in the white group.

Other work has suggested that women from Asian and Hispanic communities may be becoming less satisfied with their bodies than suggested in previous studies. Thomas Robinson *et al.* (1996) administered questionnaires to almost 1,000 sixth- and seventh-grade girls (average age 12), which included questions relating to body satisfaction and desired body shape. They found (contrary to other studies) that, of the slimmer girls (the leanest 25 percent on the BMI), Hispanic and Asian girls reported greater body dissatisfaction than the white girls. They concluded that Hispanic and Asian girls may be at greater risk than had previously been recognized, and suggested that these data may reflect the fact that mainstream sociocultural pressures for thinness are starting to spread beyond white women. Work conducted in the 2000s has also found that Hispanic, Asian, and white adolescents do not differ significantly on body satisfaction (Nishina *et al.*, 2006), and the existence of differences between Hispanic, Asian, and white women has been questioned (Shaw *et al.*, 2004). Kathleen Kawamura (2002) argues that, although obesity has traditionally been seen to be an indicator of prosperity, good health, and beauty in Asian culture, it is no longer so regarded, and that Chinese and Japanese women show a similar desire to white women for a slender body size. Madeline Altabe and Keisha-Gaye O'Garo (2002) have also argued that Hispanic women are heavily exposed to idealized, slender media imagery, and have adopted a thin ideal. However, the exact meaning of the thin ideal in Hispanic cultures may be more complex than simply adopting the dominant US beauty ideal, and may relate to religious values of self-sacrifice and denial (Altabe and O'Garo, 2002).

Shelly Grabe and Janet Hyde (2006) have conducted a meta-analysis of 98 studies looking at body dissatisfaction in Asian-American, black, Hispanic, and white women. They found that white women were only marginally less satisfied than other groups, noting that:

> The findings directly challenge the belief that there are large differences in body dissatisfaction between White and all Non-White women and suggest that body dissatisfaction may not be the golden girl problem promoted in the literature.
>
> (Grabe and Hyde, 2006: 622)

Although Hispanic and Asian groups have been found to be similarly dissatisfied to white groups in the 2000s, African-American women and girls still seem to be marginally more satisfied than girls and women from other groups (Nishina *et al.*, 2006). These differences in body concern may relate to subcultural differences in pressures on women to be slender. In ethnic groups where overweight is not stigmatized, healthier, more satisfied attitudes to larger body shape and size may develop. African-American culture has privileged plumpness in women, representing the voluptuous female body as being sexual and powerful (Cachelin *et al.*, 1998). This is displayed in the writings of Alice Walker, Maya Angelou, and other black women writers, and in traditional African-American jazz, blues, and rap music, which have represented the full-figured female as a symbol of sexuality and power. This is in marked contrast to the negative images of plumpness in mainstream (white) media.

Subcultural pressures may be more important than mainstream media images in influencing the value attached to body size. There are many reasons why African-American and British Afro-Caribbean women might reject mainstream media images as being offensive or (at best) irrelevant. Positive images of black women's bodies are rare in mainstream Western media. Gen Doy (1996) and Linda Nochlin (1991) have both documented the history of the objectification and sensualization of the black body, which has continued to the present day in mainstream media images of black models and actors, which portray black women as "shameless, sensual and available" (Doy, 1996: 19). Chris Shilling (1993) has also argued that the bodies of black men have been constructed as objects of dread and fascination by white men. This is particularly the case in pornographic material, which tends to portray black men as sexual studs or as exotic Orientals, as in *Ajitto* by Robert Mapplethorpe, in which the black male body is reduced to a sexual stereotype. Advertising has also used images of black bodies as sensual and dangerous, in order to advertise products aimed at the white consumer. Anoop Nayak (1997) shows how a Häagen-Dazs ice cream advertisement uses a black male model to contrast the "purity" of the white ice cream daubed on his back with the sensuality implied by his black skin. The utilization of the contrast between black skin and white product was also represented in Naomi Campbell's advertisements for milk in the USA, and for Müller yogurt in Britain in the 1990s. Some authors have suggested that the negative portrayal of black bodies in mainstream media may lead to privileging paler skin color within the black community (Nayak, 1997), and to dissatisfaction with skin color and features that do not conform to a Eurocentric ideal (Lewis, 1996).

There is a noticeable absence of African-American and Afro-Caribbean models in cosmetics advertisements (although Tyra Banks for Cover-Girl and Veronica Webb for Revlon are notable exceptions). Naomi Campbell and Iman have been the only really successful black catwalk supermodels to date. The rarity of positive black images in mainstream media may alienate African-American and British Afro-Caribbean viewers. This (along with conflicting values attached to plumpness) may make it likely that black viewers will reject the underlying values implied by mainstream media images.

Rejection of white Western values in relation to the idealization of slenderness may lead to less prejudice against overweight in men and women who identify with other ethnic groups. The degree of adoption of white Western body shape ideals has been shown to influence body image, and it has been found that higher acculturation levels relate to increased body dissatisfaction and more negative attitudes to over-weight (Franco and Herrera, 1997; Cachelin *et al.*, 2006), although Angela Celio *et al.* (2002) argue that the exact role of ethnic identity in body image development is unknown due to some conflicting findings in this area and problems in defining and measuring ethnic identity in African-American groups.

Relatively few studies have considered ethnic differences in body image in boys and men. Studies that have investigated body image in African-American groups have tended to find that black men are more satisfied with their bodies than white men (e.g., Miller *et al.*, 2000; Aruguete *et al.*, 2004) and prefer a larger body size than white men (Welch *et al.*, 2004; Yates *et al.*, 2004), although some have failed to find differences between ethnic groups (Nishina *et al.*, 2006). Studies of Hispanics have tended to find no differences in body size preferences (e.g., Ericksen *et al.*, 2005) or body satisfaction (e.g., Miller *et al.*, 2000) from white groups. Studies with Asian men are inconsistent, with some authors reporting no differences in satisfaction (Franzoi and Chang, 2002) and some finding that Asian men are less satisfied than white men (Kowner, 2002; Neumark-Sztainer *et al.*, 2002). Clearly, there are complex relationships here, and the picture is further complicated in that although African-Americans are generally more satisfied with their bodies than white men, they also tend to place more importance on their bodies than white men and are more likely to engage in chronic dieting and use diet pills, laxatives and diuretics, and vomiting than white groups (Barry and Grilo, 2002). In an excellent review of the role of ethnicity and culture on men's body image, Ricciardelli, McCabe, Williams, and Thompson (in press) conclude that men from nonwhite ethnic groups engage in more extreme body change strategies than white men. They suggest that a number of factors are important in moderating and/or mediating the relationship between ethnicity and body image in men, including body build, level of acculturation, socioeconomic status, media exposure, and internalization of the lean body ideal.

To summarize, current data suggest that white women are currently at more risk of "feeling fat," and are more likely to diet, than British Afro-Caribbean and African-American women. There is some evidence of recent increases in dissatisfaction in Asian-American and Hispanic women and girls, bringing their concerns in line with white women, possibly as a result of the adoption of dominant white sociocultural values in relation to body image. Data for men are less consistent. However, African-American men have generally been found to have higher levels of satisfaction than white men, and to attach more importance to their bodies. Studies with Hispanic men have tended to find no differences from white men, and there is some indication that Asian men may be less satisfied than white men. Further work is needed to clarify these differences and their etiology, although the availability of alternative, more flexible subcultural body shape ideals seems to protect against body dissatisfaction for both women and men. Future studies need to go much further in differentiating between subcultural groups, particularly within the wide bands conventionally defined as "Asian" and "Hispanic," to recognize the potential importance of differences between subgroups within these communities. These subgroups are likely to vary in important ways in terms of ideology around the body, body build, religion (and its implications for diet and denial of food), socioeconomic status, and ethnic identity.

## Social class and body image

Differences in body satisfaction in people from different social classes have rarely been addressed in research. Most psychology researchers do not even indicate the social classes of participants in their studies. Those that do indicate the socioeconomic status (SES) of their participants do not usually analyze the effects of SES on body image, making it difficult to identify any relevant trends in relation to body image.

Researchers who have compared body satisfaction in participants from different social groups have produced mixed results. Some studies have found SES differences in body concern in women. For instance, Wardle and Marsland (1990) interviewed 846 girls, aged 11–18, of different socioeconomic background, about weight and eating. They found higher levels of weight concern in girls from schools catering for higher social class backgrounds. Dieting was also more common in girls from these schools. They concluded that there are social class differences in body concern, with higher levels of concern among girls from higher social class backgrounds. This was supported by Australian work showing that physical self-esteem was lowest among 6–19-year-old overweight girls of middle/upper SES, and highest in boys of lower SES, despite the latter being more likely to be overweight (O'Dea and Caputi, 2001). Other work with women of differing social classes has also found that those in the higher social class bands are more dissatisfied with their bodies (Striegel-Moore *et al.*, 1986).

However, many studies have failed to find social class differences in body dissatisfaction. A Spanish study by Josep Toro and colleagues (1989) compared body shape evaluation and eating attitudes in a group of 1,554 adolescent boys and girls aged 12–19. The participants were chosen so as to span upper, middle, and lower SES brackets, based on parental occupation (the authors did not say how they determined which occupations fitted into each bracket). Fifty percent came from the upper classes, 25 percent from the middle classes, and 21 percent from the working classes, while 4 percent had parents who were unemployed. They found that social class did not relate to eating attitudes or body shape dissatisfaction. They concluded that the results suggest cultural homogeneity at different socioeconomic levels, as far as body aesthetics and satisfaction are concerned, for both men and women. This result is supported by Robinson and colleagues (1996) in a US study concentrating on young women. They asked 939 girls aged 12–13 to complete scales including parental education levels (the authors' definition of SES) and body dissatisfaction. They found that parent education level did not correlate significantly with body dissatisfaction, and concluded that there is no link between SES and body concern among young women. They suggested that pressures to be thin are spreading beyond the upper and middle classes, producing increased levels of body concern among working-class girls, and that body concern is no longer associated with SES in women. This was supported by Story *et al.* (1995), who assessed dieting behaviors and body perceptions in adolescents of different socioeconomic subgroups and found greater weight satisfaction and lower rates of unhealthy weight control behaviors in boys and girls higher in SES.

Western cultures are becoming more homogeneous in terms of pressures to be thin (Bordo, 2003). Many recent social commentators have suggested that the popular media have created more similar cultural pressures on people of different social classes. Developments in mass communications in the twenty-first century mean that most people have access to the same body shape ideals via magazines, the Internet, and movies and television (Wykes and Gunter, 2005). Through this democratization of vision, people of all social classes are presented with the same kinds of pressures to conform to the idealized images presented in the media. Mike Featherstone and others have suggested that the fact that people of all classes watch the same television programes and the same movies, read similar magazines, and aspire to the same fashions in clothes (although marketed more cheaply to those in lower income groups) has produced shared body shape ideals that span class divides (Featherstone, 1991).

Psychology studies have tended to find that body shape ideals are very similar in people of different social classes in affluent Western cultures. This was so as far back as the 1960s. In one classic study on the effects of social class on body shape ideals, Wells and Siegel (1961) asked 120 adults categorized into three class bands ("lower," "middle," and "upper" class) to assign personality traits to adult male silhouettes that were either average, mesomorphic, ectomorphic, or endomorphic, using a forced-choice procedure. They found no social class differences in the assignment of traits. Men and women from all social classes rated the mesomorphic trait more positively, and there were no differences between the trait assignments of male and female raters. This early study suggested similar class ideals for men's body shape and size. We have also found similar body shape ideals in women of different class backgrounds in the interviews reported in Chapter 3. Similar ideal slender body shapes were presented by women who were (among others) university students, waitresses, managers of shops, schoolteachers, nurses, solicitors, gym owners, and office cleaners.

In one British study (Hodkinson, 1997), 10 men and 10 women from Occupational Class 2 (Intermediate: teachers, nurses, and managers) and Class 3 (shop assistants) on the Registrar General's scale were asked about body shape beliefs in relation to work. Participants (irrespective of their own occupational group) believed that overweight people were slow workers, that slim people did the most work, that employers preferred slim staff, that people had a better chance of getting a job if they were slim, that slim people were more successful at work, and that they would be more successful in their jobs if they were slimmer. These responses support suggestions that cultural prejudice against overweight leads to fewer college and job opportunities for overweight people (Crandall, 1995; Averett and Korenman, 1996). All groups associated positive characteristics (self-discipline, health, fitness, and being energetic) with slenderness, and all agreed that overweight people are kind and caring. Slimness was also associated with youthfulness by all occupational groups, and all groups (on average) believed that they would look younger if they became slimmer. Obviously, these data come from only a limited range of occupational groups. Nevertheless, they are interesting in demonstrating similarities in beliefs and preferences in people between these groups. In the distant past, body shape ideals varied between social classes.

The expectation of class differences in body concern is probably based on the historical fact that, until the twentieth century, body concern was mostly limited to the middle and upper classes; those who had the time and money to follow "fashion" in clothes (Orbach, 1993). People with economic power have always set the standards for what is fashionable. This usually means that only the wealthy can afford to buy into the ideal. When resources are scarce, wealth may be reflected in plumpness and clothes that show plumpness to best advantage (seen, for instance, in Britain in the mid-nineteenth century). When resources are plentiful, and there is little fear of starvation, the wealthy may aim for a slender ideal. The wealthier classes have also tended to set styles in clothes, which often require a particular body shape and size for them to look as the designer intended.

Susan Bordo (2003) notes how, until the nineteenth century, body size was an indication of social class: the middle classes opted to display their wealth ostentatiously by eating enough to attain a corpulent form, whereas the upper classes attempted to attain a slender form, rejecting the need for an outward show of wealth. Bordo shows how corpulence went out of fashion for the middle classes at the turn of the century, when social power became linked with the ability to control and manage the labor of others. A slender ideal in men and women started to be associated with success and willpower, and overweight with lack of self-control. Bordo argues that slenderness has retained some of its high-class associations, although the link has become weaker over the years. Overweight and being working-class are often associated (as in the television sitcom *Roseanne* in the USA and the Dingle family in the television series *Emmerdale* in Britain), and often the overweight person is represented as lazy and to blame for lack of upward mobility. Popular Western culture is full of symbols of upward mobility through mastery and control of the body (e.g., the *Rocky* films, in which Sylvester Stallone is shown to be enduring pain to build up his strength and become successful, and—of course—to become wealthy and attain the trappings of the middle classes).

To the degree that the question of class still operates in all this, it relates to the category of social mobility (or lack of it) rather than class location. So, for example, when associations of fat and lower class status exist, they are usually mediated by moral qualities— fat being perceived as indicative of laziness, lack of discipline, unwillingness to conform, and absence of all those "managerial" abilities that, according to the dominant ideology, confer upward mobility.

(Bordo, 2003: 195)

Susie Orbach (1993) shows how fashion trendsetters have generally come from the middle and upper social classes, because they had the economic means to experiment with different kinds of fashion images. This was particularly the case in 1960s Britain. Jean Shrimpton, the first model to be represented as angular and thin, came from the upper-middle class, and was photographed in magazines catering for the upper classes (*Vogue* and *Harper's Bazaar*) wearing clothes designed by upper-middle-class designers, whose message was that women should break out from the confines of convention. The so-called "Jet Set," the wealthy young, produced a trend representing freedom and adventure. Tied in with this new image was the idea of thinness, which came to signify freedom and the rejection of convention. Thinness was seen as the key to enable working-class women to transcend the barriers of class, and to emulate the "Jet-Set" life. The emergence of Twiggy, a working-class model who did not attempt to hide her background, signaled to other young women that freedom and elegance could be achieved through thinness. In the USA, thinness became part of the "American dream," apparently achievable by anyone.

This apparent democracy is an illusion because, as we have seen, for most people the attainment of a fashionable body image requires economic power. Fashion designers and those in the slimming and cosmetics industries ensure that the fashionable "look" is constantly changing, and that its achievement requires time and money. It is often costly to attain a fashionably slender but muscular body. Sufficient resources are not equally available to everyone, thus effectively keeping the ideal at arm's length for most people. There are well-documented social class differences in the incidence of obesity. Working-class women and men are more likely to fall into the "obese" category than those in the dominant classes (Campos, 2004; Monaghan, 2005a). The current slender, toned, and muscular Western ideal requires time and resources for most people (unless they have a job which requires heavy manual labor). April Fallon (1990) argues that this ideal is easier to attain for the rich, who have the resources to spend time in the gym (or to have cosmetic surgery) to become fashionably lean and fit. She proposes that the body itself (with or without clothes) has become a way of conspicuous distinction between the lower and the upper classes.

In addition to differences in the availability of resources for body maintenance, there may also be social class differences in motivation to treat the body as a "project" in need of change. Pierre Bourdieu (1984) argues that different social classes develop clearly identifiable relations to the body, resulting in physical differences. He suggests that the working classes tend to develop an instrumental, functional (rather than aesthetic) relation to the body. When sporting activities are engaged in, these are seen as a means to an end (weight training to build strength, or soccer for excitement/socializing). On the other hand, the dominant classes are more likely to treat the body as a project for improvement in its own right, which can be conceptualized either as making the body healthier or as making it more aesthetically pleasing. According to Bourdieu, the dominant social classes choose sporting activities with the aim of improving health and/or with improving the "look" of the body. Elsewhere, Bourdieu conceptualizes class differences in sport as a result of the ways in which the body is viewed, as well as being due to constraints on the amount of time and money available to invest in body maintenance which he also views as important (Bourdieu, 1986).

Research linking social class to body image suggests that social class is not related to body shape ideals, since people from different social classes present similar ideals. Studies comparing body shape ideals and body satisfaction between men and women of varying social class cast doubt on the now outmoded assumption that body dissatisfaction is a middle-class phenomenon. Social theorists have suggested that social class relates to the ways in which the body is conceptualized, the dominant classes being more likely to view the body on aesthetic (rather than functional) dimensions, and being more likely than the working classes to invest time and energy in sports activities as a means of changing the way the body looks. Much more work is needed in this area, looking specifically at income and class differentials in body image, to extend the current literature and to develop work on body satisfaction beyond the traditional middle-class student group that is usually chosen for study by psychologists.

## Body shape, sexual attractiveness, and sexuality

Most of this text has considered body image in terms of aesthetics rather than sexual attractiveness. Body shape and size have important implications for sexual attraction. Some researchers have focused on the relationship between body shape and size and perceived sexual attractiveness, and have produced some interesting findings. There is some debate in the literature as to the basis for opposite-sex attraction in body shape and size. Social psychologists and sociologists have generally argued that sexual preferences in body shape and size are largely learned, and are affected by the value that a particular culture attaches to that kind of body shape. They have stressed the cultural relativity of body shape features that signal sexual attractiveness, and have focused on same-sex, as well as opposite-sex, attraction. On the other hand, evolutionary psychologists have argued that people have an inherent preference for sexual partners who are biologically "fit" (healthy and able to reproduce), and that body shape features, such as being of normal weight and having a pronounced waist (in women), or no pronounced waist (in men), serve as biological indicators of "mate value" to the opposite sex. Here we will consider arguments from these two perspectives, evaluating the usefulness of each approach in explaining the available data in relation to body shape ideals and body satisfaction. For convenience, this section is divided into four sections, looking separately at the specific social pressures on heterosexual women, lesbians, gay men, and heterosexual men.

## *Heterosexual women*

Many researchers, particularly within the feminist tradition, have focused on the social pressures experienced by women to conform to a particular body shape in order to be attractive to men. Nickie Charles and Marilyn Kerr (1986), in interviews with 200 British women, found that sexual attractiveness was cited as one of the major reasons why women desired to conform to the slim ideal. For most of the women they spoke to, this was phrased in terms of the necessity of staying (or getting) slim to maintain their current (heterosexual) sexual relationship. Many women reported that their sexual partners monitored their "fatness" and told them when they needed to lose weight. Charles and Kerr concluded that body image is closely linked with sexual attractiveness, and that, particularly after childbirth, women feel pressure from their sexual partners to regain their figures and to be slender, in order to maintain their sexual relationship. They concluded that the unnaturally thin feminine ideal leads women to be constantly dissatisfied with their bodies, and that perceived pressure from sexual partners is a key factor in this dissatisfaction.

In our interviews with women (reported in Chapter 3), many women reported that they felt their sexual relationships had suffered because they were self-conscious about their bodies, usually feeling too fat. They were clear that they had more desire to be sexually active when they felt good about themselves (including good about their bodies). Ironically, many women reported that their sexual partners thought they were attractive and had not commented negatively on their bodies, yet they still felt fat. For instance, one 23-year-old woman said:

> I'm off [on vacation] for a week, and I want to wear little sexy things and all that, and my sex life is suffering because of my body image. There are a lot of times that I would like to and he would like to, but I just can't bring myself to undress. I don't want him to see how fat I am.

The relationship between body image and satisfaction with sexual relationships is well documented (see Wiederman and Pryor, 1997). Tom Cash and colleagues (2004) have reported that women low in body satisfaction experience fear of intimacy in sexual relationships, replicating other work suggesting that women low in body satisfaction report concerns about the appearance of their body in sexual interactions with their partners (e.g., Ackard *et al.*, 2000). Werlinger and colleagues (1997) reported a significant increase in sexual desire among US women who had lost weight and developed a more positive body image as a result. The reasons why such a relationship exists are complex, and seem to relate to increased self-esteem (which may result from, or produce, body satisfaction) resulting in positive impacts on all aspects of life, including sexual performance and desire.

Many of the women we interviewed reported that it was important that their male sexual partner should be heavier and generally bigger, to make them feel relatively small and slender, and they cited occasions when they were made to feel really good because they felt that their partner was much larger. For instance:

> I have to look for someone with a certain body image that will make me feel better, feel small. I had this boyfriend in college who was huge, he was 6 feet 4 and he was a tanker. And I would put his jacket on and the sleeves would fall over my hand and I loved it. I mean, I loved it.

> [My partner tried to get my jeans on] the other day, and he said, "Oh, I am going to have to lose some weight," and I'm like . . . it was funny, but it made me feel so good that he couldn't wear my jeans.

These experiences may be most relevant to women with traditional views of male–female relationships in terms of dependence–independence, who tend to be more concerned with body image than those with less traditional views (Cash *et al.*, 1997).

Some interesting work has compared women's perceptions of men's ideal body size for women with men's actual preferences. In a classic study conducted in the 1980s, April Fallon and Paul Rozin (1985) asked a group of 248 men and 227 women to indicate their current figure, their ideal figure, the figure that they felt would be most attractive to the opposite sex, and the opposite sex figure to which they were most attracted, using Stunckard and colleagues' (1983) figural rating scales (see Chapters 3 and 4). The authors did not ask the participants to indicate whether they were heterosexual. For women, the current figure was heavier than the ideal figure, with the figure expected to be most attractive to men coming between. For men, all three figures were almost identical across the group. Interestingly, it was found that both men and women erred in estimating what the opposite sex would find attractive. Men thought that women preferred a heavier figure than they actually chose, and women thought that men would like a thinner figure than they chose in reality. The authors concluded that men's perceptions serve to keep them satisfied with their bodies, whereas women's serve to keep them dissatisfied. Men's ideal was generally thinner than women's perceived current figure, showing that men generally preferred a more slender figure than women's perceived current size.

These findings were supported by another US study, in which Sue Lamb and colleagues (1993) found that women tended to believe that men preferred much thinner body shapes than the men themselves actually chose. They found that women's ideal was actually thinner than the size that they thought men preferred. It seems likely that women are sensitive to pressure from men to be thin, but also that they are sensitive to more general cultural pressures, from the dieting industry, for instance, which may set up an even slimmer ideal, and pressure from other women to conform to a thin ideal. Fallon and Rozin's (1985) results were also replicated by Gail Huon and colleagues (1990) on a group of Australian men and women. Forty men and 40 women in the first year of a psychology course at the University of New South Wales were asked to select a photograph showing their ideal female figure, their actual size (or, for men, the size of their best female friend), the one they thought most men would prefer, and the one that most women would prefer. The choice was from 12 projected photographs of two female models, adjusted to different sizes by a device that systematically varied the images about the vertical axis. The men were accurate in predicting women's preferred size.

The women's preferred female size was the thinnest, followed by what they believed to be men's preferred female size, followed by their own ideal, followed by their actual size. The authors concluded that women's body image is affected by general social pressure, from women as well as from men.

Most evolutionary psychologists suggest that there are biological reasons for body shape and size preferences in potential sexual partners. According to David Buss (1987, 1989), a woman's physical attractiveness is largely a reflection of her potential reproductive success. Reproductive success is defined as the optimum (for the environment) number of children surviving to reach sexual maturity and to become parents themselves. Buss believes that men (irrespective of culture) place more importance on body shape and size in women than women place on these factors in men. He suggests that there are cultural universals in desired body shape and size for man–woman sexual attraction, and that these derive from the division of labor between men and women during the course of evolution; males specializing in hunting and women in food gathering and child rearing. Natural selection is believed to have operated such that men and women whose bodies were best suited for these roles (normal weight, muscles for men, and fat layers around hips for women) were more attractive to potential mates and so were more likely to reproduce. According to evolutionary theorists (Buss, 1989; Kenrick, 1989), women's physical attractiveness is important because it gives male sexual partners reliable cues to their health and potential reproductive success.

Devendra Singh (1993) suggests that men's preferences for women's shapes are determined by the woman being of normal weight and having a waist-to-hip ratio (WHR) that signals fertility. At puberty, women typically gain weight around the waist and hips. Singh suggests that the curves created by this "reproductive fat" provide men with a gauge of reproductive potential. According to Singh, healthy, fertile women typically have WHR of 0.6–0.8, meaning that their waists are 60–80 percent the size of their hips, whatever their weight. When women go through the menopause, they generally become heavier in the waist, so that the WHR becomes similar to the male range of 0.85–0.95. He suggests that women with higher WHR report having their first child at a later age than women with lower WHR. He also argues that low WHR relates to better general health, as defined by the absence of major diseases such as diabetes, heart attack, and stroke, which are all less common when people carry more fat in the lower body (Singh, 1993: 295). He concluded that WHR reliably signals degree of sexual maturity, reproductive potential, and good health.

In a study of *Playboy* centerfolds and "Miss America" contest winners, Singh found that women whose bodies were considered appropriate in the 1980s were measurably leaner than the women chosen in previous decades, yet their WHRs stayed around 0.7. When he asked male volunteers to rate line drawings of female figures for attractiveness, sexiness, health, and fertility, the preferred figure (irrespective of the culture or age of the participants) was the figure with the 0.7 WHR (which was the figure with the lowest WHR that he presented; see Figure 6.1). Singh concluded that the distribution of body fat plays a crucial role in judgments of women's physical attractiveness, health, youth, and reproductive potential; and that, to be perceived as attractive by male judges, women must be of normal weight and have a low WHR—neither factor alone is sufficient to predict attractiveness, since being either underweight or overweight reduces perceived attractiveness and also perceived healthiness.

Singh suggested that WHR may be involved in the initial stages of physical attraction, when men may be more likely to initiate contact with women with low WHR, so that this would lead to a filtering out of women with high WHR. Then a second filter would take account of culturally defined standards of attractiveness for that particular culture (for instance, overall plumpness or slenderness, facial features, etc.). However, all societies (whether they generally preferred plumpness or slenderness) would favor women of low WHR, because of its association with fertility and health.

Singh did not offer his participants the choice of the full range of WHRs (i.e., including WHRs of less than 0.7). The range of figures that he used (0.7–1.0) gave participants a restricted choice, and did not allow an assessment of the effects of very low WRH on perceived sexual attractiveness. Presumably, there may be an optimum WHR below which men no longer find the figure attractive. Although very few women have WHR below 0.5, it would nevertheless have been interesting to see how figures of 0.6 and 0.5 were rated. Following Singh's logic, these should be perceived as more sexually attractive than the 0.7 figure, which was the lowest he presented. Indeed, the corset and bustle combination that he mentioned (Singh, 1993: 296) would have produced a WHR below 0.7 in many women, through constricting the rib cage to give a tiny waist in relation to the hips (see Brownmiller, 1984). Although Singh assumed that the female body with low WHR is more sexually attractive to men than one with high WHR, it would have been informative to have investigated the limits of this effect, in order to try to identify an optimum WHR (as he did for women's judgments of men).

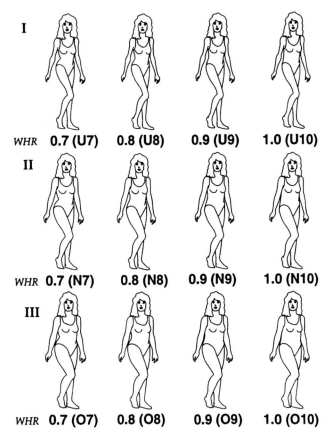

**I**

WHR  **0.7 (U7)    0.8 (U8)    0.9 (U9)    1.0 (U10)**

**II**

WHR  **0.7 (N7)    0.8 (N8)    0.9 (N9)    1.0 (N10)**

**III**

WHR  **0.7 (O7)    0.8 (O8)    0.9 (O9)    1.0 (O10)**

*Figure 6.1*  Female stimulus figures varying in WHR.

*Source*: Adapted from Singh (1993). Copyright patented 1993 by the American Psychological Association. Adapted with permission.

*Note*: Figures represent underweight (I), normal weight (II) and overweight (III), with waist-to-hip ratios (WHRs) shown under each figure in each weight category, along with a letter and number in brackets which identifies body weight category WHR.

Most evolutionary theorists (e.g., Buss, 1987) assume that attractiveness is intrinsically related to "mate value." However, Singh found that rankings of "reproductive ability" are independent of rankings of "health, youth, attractiveness and sexiness." These findings suggest that Singh's respondents rated women's attractiveness independently of their "mate value," probably on an aesthetic (rather than reproductive potential) dimension.

Although Singh investigated the consistency of the WHR effect in men of different ages, his biological argument would be more convincing if it were based on cross-cultural data. His participants were all US (white and Hispanic) males, so they were all likely to be experiencing similar cultural influences (television, magazines, etc.). It could be that he was observing a learned preference for a "slender but curvy" shape. Sixty-five percent of men rated normal weight figures most attractive, and 35 percent underweight ones. The "overweight" woman (irrespective of WHR) was not found "most attractive" by any man, despite the fact that she was not sufficiently overweight to represent a threat to reproductive status or health (the figure is designed to represent a 5 foot 5 inch tall woman weighing 150 lb, who is not obese as judged on the Metropolitan Life Insurance Tables). What strikes the reader is the fact that the 0.7 and 0.8 WHR bodies look very familiar on the page (i.e., they are similar to body shapes represented in the media), whereas the others do not. If, as Singh said, models tend to conform to the 0.7 WHR, then perhaps the findings reflect a familiarity effect; a learned preference for this kind of body shape. It would be interesting to show his line drawings to heterosexual women (or gay men), and to see which pictures are chosen as "most attractive." If the preferences he observed reflect learned social preferences rather than biological mate value, we would predict the same pattern of preferences in women as those seen in Singh's male participants. In Singh's study, the impact of men's sexuality was not reported.

In Chapter 3, we saw that the area of the body that presents most concern for women is the very area (hips and thighs) where women store the reproductive fat that is supposed to make them attractive to men. Nearly all the women we have interviewed, whatever their body type and weight, wanted to lose weight around their hips (i.e., to increase their WHR). This would not be predicted from Singh's model. Women generally also want to be slim (rather than of normal weight). There is clearly a conflict between the factors identified here as being high in "mate value" and women's desire to attain the slender, slim-hipped ideal. It seems likely that there may be a difference between heterosexual men's body shape preferences for women, and women's own preferences, which (according to interview data in Chapter 3) may relate more to fashion for a particular body type than to being sexually attractive to men, although this may be a secondary concern. Recent work has tended to find that BMI is a much better predictor of both men and women's attractiveness ratings for women's bodies than WHR (Tovee and Cornelissen, 2001: Swami *et al.*, 2006).

Social psychologists and evolutionary psychologists have generally been reticent about discussing the intersexual significance of breasts, even though there is no doubt that breast size and firmness are intimately tied to Western notions of heterosexual attractiveness in women. Evolutionary psychologists have generally argued that breast size is largely irrelevant to sexual attractiveness, since breast development does not reliably signal fertility. Women with adrenal tumors and true hermaphrodites have fully formed breasts, but they are infertile. Singh argues that these women have male-like WHR, making WHR a more reliable indicator of fertility. Desmond Morris (1985) even argues that the breasts evolved to mimic buttocks (to make women's front view more attractive to men), and have no sexual significance of their own. However, most social psychologists would agree that moderate-to-large breasts on a slender frame are men's cultural ideal in Western societies. A cursory perusal of popular men's magazines leaves the viewer in no doubt that the magazines' editors expect their readers will prefer women with firm, moderate-to-large breasts. In a study of *Playboy* centerfolds, Mazur (1986) notes that, although the women portrayed there have become thinner over the years, their breasts have remained relatively large.

Kevin Thompson and Stacey Tantleff (1992) ran an interesting study in which they asked US men and women to select schematic male and female figures differing in breast (see Figure 6.2) or chest size as current, ideal, and the size that they thought was the opposite sex's and their own sex's ideal. Overall, results indicated a preference for large breast/ chest sizes. Both sexes rated their own current size as smaller than ideal. Men's conception of ideal breast size was larger than women's. It was concluded that the findings explain the societal preoccupation with breasts, overall dissatisfaction with this area of the body in women, and the decision to seek cosmetic surgery for breast enlargement. Positive

*Figure 6.2* Female stimulus figures varying in breast size.

*Source*: Adapted from Thompson and Tantleff (1992) with permission.

adjectives were associated with large breasts (particularly confidence, popularity, and being likely to succeed) for both men and women judges. The only positive characteristics associated with small breasts were athleticism and intelligence.

Susan Brownmiller (1984) discusses the paradox for women of possession of breasts that are intensely private (usually hidden from view), yet very public (evaluated socially by men and by women themselves). She is particularly interested in the ways that men fetishize, and claim ownership of, women's breasts, leading women to be self-conscious about perceived inadequacies (too large, too small, or not firm enough).

No other part of the anatomy has such semi-public, intensely private status, and no other part of the body has such vaguely defined custodial rights. One learns to be selectively generous with breasts—this is the girl child's lesson—and through the breast iconography she sees all around her, she comes to understand that breasts belong to everybody, but especially to men. It is they who invent and refine their myths, who discuss breasts publicly, who criticise their failings as they extol their wonders, and who claim to have more need and intimate knowledge of them than a woman herself.

(Brownmiller, 1984: 24)

If men tend to prefer slenderness with largish breasts, this presents a conflict for women who wish to be attractive to men. Slenderness may be achieved through restriction of food intake. However, weight loss will also lead to breast shrinkage. Media images of women's bodies aimed at a male audience often present an unusual, slim-hipped, long-legged, large-breasted ideal (Pamela Anderson from the 1990s US television series *Baywatch* is a good example). This ideal is only possible for most women through a mixture of diet and exercise (to slenderize hips and thighs) and cosmetic surgery (to swell the breasts).

The popularity of cosmetic surgery to augment the breasts is increasing every year. Breast augmentations were first carried out in the 1950s in Japan, and by the 1960s silicone gel implants were being used more and more frequently to increase breast size, despite problems with rejection of the implants by the body's immune system (Meredith, 1988). By the 1990s, concern over silicone leakage led to a preference for saline implants, which, if they leak, cause less damage. Despite wide publicity about health risks, it is estimated that over a million women in the USA had had breast implants by the mid-1990s, and 6,000 implant operations were carried out each year in Britain in the early 1990s (Davis, 1995). In 2005, breast enlargement was the most common cosmetic procedure carried out in the UK (Department of Health, 2005). According to Kathy Davis, women tend to report that they have the operation for themselves, to rectify perceived inadequacies, to "take control of their lives," rather than being coerced by their partners. Katherine Viner (1997) critiques the argument that cosmetic surgery allows women to gain control over their bodies and their lives, showing that defending a woman's right to do what she wants with her body allows the potential for harm through (for instance) anorexia, bulimia, "cutting," and plastic surgery. She notes that cosmetic surgery reduces women to the sum of their parts, and is the result of a defeatist, "quick fix" mentality. Gillespie (1996) also argues that although collusion with restricted models of femininity may be a rational choice for some women at the individual level, such action goes against women's collective interests, and perpetuates social inequalities (see Chapter 3).

Heterosexual women are clearly under pressure to conform to a very slender ideal. Most studies have shown that women prefer a thinner ideal than do men. Social and evolutionary psychologists have suggested that individual Western men report preferences for "normal weight" (rather than very slender) women's bodies. However, women operate within a cultural context where a very thin ideal is promoted by the beauty industry, and these pressures (which Naomi Wolf, 1991, argues are controlled by male-dominated institutions) contribute to women's thin ideal. The recent increase in breast augmentations may also reflect perceived pressure from men. Although women tend to report that the decision to have cosmetic surgery was taken independently of pressure from sexual partners, it is difficult (or impossible) to separate women's choice in this matter from cultural influences (which include pressure from men).

*Lesbians*

There is very little research on the degree of pressure exerted on women who choose female sexual partners, although most authors tend to assume that lesbians are under significantly less pressure to be slender and large breasted from sexual partners than are heterosexual women. Laura Brown (1987) argues that lesbian culture downplays the importance of conventional physical attractiveness, leading to higher levels of body satisfaction among lesbians than heterosexual women, and lower levels of anorexia and bulimia. Interviews with bisexual women have also shown that women feel more pressure to conform to traditional beauty norms when in relationships with men than with women (Taub, 1999). However, Sari Dworkin (1988) argues that lesbians are socialized to conform to the same societal standards of physical attractiveness as heterosexual women, and must comply with socially accepted standards to be accepted within the lesbian community.

Most studies have failed to find differences in body image between lesbians and heterosexual women. A US study based on a small number of lesbian and heterosexual women concluded that the groups did not differ in degree of body dissatisfaction, although the lesbian group showed a lower frequency of dieting and had higher self-esteem (Striegel-Moore *et al.*, 1990). Similarly, Brand *et al.* (1992) found no differences in body satisfaction between lesbians and heterosexual women, concluding that gender was a better predictor of body dissatisfaction than sexuality. Strong *et al.* (2000) also found no significant differences in body dissatisfaction between lesbians and heterosexual women, although they suggest that body image may be less important to lesbians than to heterosexual women. In recent work conducted with British samples (Grogan *et al.*, 2006), we have failed to find differences in body-image-related motivations for exercise between lesbian and heterosexual women. We had predicted that heterosexual women would be more likely than lesbians to be motivated to exercise for appearance and weight management. In fact, there was no significant difference between the two groups, suggesting that exercise motivations did not differ between these groups of lesbians and heterosexual women. In another recent study, we also failed to find any significant difference between lesbians and heterosexual women on dieting (Conner *et al.*, 2004), concluding that both lesbians and heterosexual women are under mainstream social pressure to be thin, and that gender may be a better predictor of eating and exercise motives than sexuality in this context.

In a study that has identified differences, Michael Siever (1994) compared the importance placed on physical attractiveness in 53 lesbians, 62 heterosexual women, 59 gay men, and 63 heterosexual men. In a study at the University of Washington, Siever asked both men and women to complete a packet of self-report questionnaires, including the Franzoi and Shields (1984) Body Esteem Scale, the Cooper *et al.* (1987) Body Shape Questionnaire, and the Stunckard *et al.* silhouette drawings (see Chapters 3 and 4). He found that the lesbians who took part in his study placed significantly less emphasis on physical attractiveness in their sexual partners than did heterosexual women, and reported that their partners placed significantly less emphasis on physical attractiveness than did all other groups. Lesbians were also more satisfied with their bodies than were heterosexual women (although this difference was not statistically significant on most measures). Some of the lesbian group indicated that they had suffered from body dissatisfaction and disordered eating before they "came out." Siever suggests that the lesbian subculture may have a protective function in relation to body dissatisfaction, in that lesbians may become more satisfied with their bodies as they become assimilated into the subculture. He proposes that the lesbian subculture places less emphasis on youth and beauty, and does not promote the unrealistic ideals seen in mainstream heterosexual culture, leading to less objectification and higher body satisfaction. Siever's work has been highly influential, but in fact has been supported by very few studies, but most notably by Share and Mintz (2002), who found some evidence of more positive body image in lesbians than heterosexual women.

In a recent meta-analysis of existing literature, Melanie Morrison and colleagues (2004) conclude that across studies there is some evidence that when samples are well matched, lesbians may be slightly more satisfied than heterosexual samples, although the size of this difference is not statistically significant and does not approximate to the difference between gay and heterosexual men. They argue that the low magnitude of this difference suggests that "the norms of lesbian subculture may be insufficient to counteract the types of messages that bombard all women from childhood onward" (136), citing evidence that lesbians internalize societal standards of thinness, albeit not to the same extent as heterosexual women.

There are many unanswered questions in the existing literature on body image in lesbians. Studies have generally ignored the butch/femme gender style of participants. This is particularly important for studies of body image, where it could be expected that style of presentation could be salient in determining satisfaction with the body. It is possible that there is more social pressure for women presenting as "femme" to conform to prevailing social mores of slenderness (from their sexual partners, from lesbian subculture, and/or from mainstream culture). Initial work suggests that lesbians and bisexual women who present as "femme" may be lower in body satisfaction than those who present as masculine or androgenous (Ludwig and Brownell, 1999). This is a question requiring further research, and should be addressed through in-depth interviews with lesbians presenting as butch/femme to clarify the factors at work here.

The political climate within which lesbianism exists is also important in understanding lesbian body image. There is widespread cultural prejudice among the heterosexual population against homosexuality in general and lesbianism in particular (Kitzinger, 1987). Judith Butler (1991) argues that lesbians are oppressed through nonrecognition:

Lesbianism is not explicitly prohibited in part because it has not even made its way into the thinkable, the imaginable, that grid of cultural intelligibility that regulates the real and the nameable. How then to "be" a lesbian in a political context in which the lesbian does not exist? That is, in a political discourse that wages its violence against lesbianism in part by excluding lesbianism from discourse itself?

(Butler, 1991: 20)

Celia Kitzinger (1987) reiterates Butler's experiences of oppression, conceptualizing lesbianism as a political movement. In this context, rejection of male-dominated, mainstream cultural representations of how women should look, and the forging of a woman-centered aesthetic among lesbians, might be predicted. Prejudice from mainstream culture could be expected to strengthen group identification and social support from within radical feminist subculture, and a woman-centered philosophy may enable lesbians to forge more positive body images than heterosexual women. Certainly, feminist writers (e.g., Wolf, 1991) suggest that a woman-loving philosophy (among heterosexual women and lesbians) would be likely to promote more positive and accepting images of the female body. Some lesbians present accounts that reject lesbianism as a political decision (Kitzinger, 1987). It might be expected that these women might be more affected by mainstream cultural pressures to be slender than other lesbians who are more politically motivated (and better supported through radical feminist subculture). French *et al.* (1996) have argued that more positive attitudes to the body develop along with increased sociopolitical awareness as women age, so older lesbian and heterosexual women would be expected to differ more significantly on body satisfaction from younger groups. Since most existing literature has studied young women, any advantages conferred through greater sociopolitical awareness may have been missed. Future research needs to address these issues through asking women of a range of ages for accounts of social support, political beliefs, and body image.

In a review of relevant literature, Esther Rothblum (2002) discusses the diverse social pressures that may be experienced by lesbians and gay men, where they are first socialized by mainstream culture and then by the lesbian and gay communities. She suggests that lesbians may be "torn between their beliefs and their interactions with mainstream media, families of origin, and the work setting" (263), arguing that the experience of biculturality may explain the conflicting findings in the literature on lesbian body image. Clearly, there is some debate within the literature on the role of sexuality in women's body image, although there is some evidence that women who have sexual relationships with other women may suffer less body dissatisfaction (Morrison *et al.*, 2004). Further work is needed to investigate sources of social support, the influence of aging, and the effects of gender-style presentation and political orientation on body image in lesbians.

## Gay men

Gay men may be under more extreme social pressure than heterosexual men in relation to body image, in a context in which they are the objects of male gaze (Atkins, 1998). It is generally agreed that gay male subculture places an elevated importance on the appearance of the body (Lakoff and Scherr, 1984; Signorile, 1997). Rotello (1997) talks about the "powerful, even merciless system of rewards and penalties based on body image" (254) of gay male culture, and other authors such as Michelangelo Signorile deem the culture body fascistic in placing inordinate emphasis on attainment of the muscular mesomorphic ideal (Signorile, 1997).

Jamie Gough, writing in the late 1980s, noted a significant change in gay male culture that took place between the 1970s and the end of the 1980s, whereby having a male athletic body became important in developing the fashionable muscular, toned look. He notes that this change was most marked among gay men whose social life is centered on the "gay scene" (clubbing, drinking in "gay" venues, etc.), and in big cities more than in small towns. He is interested in this shift because it challenges traditional ideologies of gay men as effeminate (see Marshall, 1981). He argues that the masculinization of the "gay scene," in which the body must be toned and muscular, is oppressive to men (Gough, 1989).

> Masculinity as a sexual fetish is, therefore, oppressive not simply for dictating a certain norm, but for demanding something that cannot be achieved. The new style of sexual attractiveness is all the more tyrannous in that, as we have seen, it prescribes not only social behaviour but also physiology.
>
> (Gough, 1989: 121–2)

Studies of body satisfaction in gay men have generally suggested that they tend to show higher levels of body concern than heterosexual men. In a sample of both heterosexual and gay men, Marc Mishkind *et al.* (1986) found that the gay men expressed greater dissatisfaction with body shape, waist, biceps, arms, and stomach. They also indicated a greater discrepancy between their actual and ideal body shapes than did heterosexual men, and were more preoccupied with their weight and diet. The study was flawed, in that the sample of "heterosexual" men was drawn from a group of undergraduate men in an introductory psychology class who were assumed to be heterosexual. However, the study presents some interesting findings in relation to differences in pressures from the gay male subculture to conform to the male body ideal.

Mishkind *et al.*'s findings were replicated by a recent study with Yale University undergraduate students. Beren *et al.* (1996) found that their sample of 58 gay men reported significantly higher levels of body dissatisfaction than 58 heterosexual men. Using self-report measures, they were able to measure level of affiliation with the gay community. They expected that those who were more strongly affiliated with the gay community would indicate more body dissatisfaction, due to the emphasis placed on body appearance in the gay community. They supported this hypothesis, finding that those who identified most strongly with the gay community were least satisfied with their bodies. They concluded that aspects of the gay community increase vulnerability to body dissatisfaction. Perhaps these data should be interpreted more cautiously, since what they have actually demonstrated is merely an association between the two variables, meaning that the causal link may run in the opposite direction (so that men who are more satisfied with the way they look feel a closer link with the body-conscious gay culture). Still, the demonstration of a link is interesting and suggestive of social pressure within this community to have a "good" body.

Michael Siever (1994) noted that many researchers have proposed that gay male subculture imposes pressure on gay men to be physically attractive, and that empirical data suggest that gay men generally value physical appearance more than heterosexual men do. He found that gay men and heterosexual women showed the highest levels of body dissatisfaction. Gay men were significantly more dissatisfied with their bodies than heterosexual men. In fact, in this study, gay men were less satisfied with their bodies than were heterosexual women. Siever suggested that this may be because gay men have the potential to be dissatisfied with their bodies on two dimensions. Like heterosexual men, they may worry that their bodies are inadequate in terms of athletic prowess and, like heterosexual women, they may rate themselves on an aesthetic dimension. Siever concluded that sexual objectification results in increased emphasis on physical attractiveness and body dissatisfaction in the recipients of the objectification, be they men or women. He argues that assimilation into the gay subculture may lead to gay men becoming less satisfied with their bodies, within a context where slenderness and muscularity are prized.

Other studies have supported Siever's suggestion that gay men have more appearance concerns than heterosexual men. Christine Yelland and Marika Tiggemann (2003) investigated body concerns in a community sample of Australian participants: 52 gay men, 51 heterosexual men, and 55 heterosexual women. They found that gay men scored higher than heterosexual men and women on drive for muscularity, and higher than heterosexual men on drive for thinness. They did not differ from heterosexual men on body esteem, both groups of men scoring significantly above the sample of women. The authors concluded that gay men experience more body concern and disordered eating than heterosexual men, and that although gay men may not experience the same degree of body dissatisfaction as women, they experience a similar level of drive to reach their ideal body shape. In recent British studies on eating and exercise motives, we have found that gay men are more likely to diet (Conner *et al.*, 2004) and more likely to exercise for appearance reasons (Grogan *et al.*, 2006) than heterosexual men. In both studies, gay men's behavior and motivations did not differ from those of heterosexual women. In focus groups with a community-based sample of gay and heterosexual Australian men aged 18–52, Helen Fawkner (2004) also found that negative affect and behavior change as a result of self–ideal comparison were more prevalent in gay than heterosexual men, and in questionnaire work with 106 gay men and 244 heterosexual men, that the gay men were less satisfied with their appearance and more preoccupied with overweight. Maurice Levesque and David Vichesky (2006) have also produced evidence that gay men in their sample expressed high levels of body dissatisfaction and weight concern, and were primarily concerned with developing bigger muscles. In a meta-analysis of existing relevant literature, Melanie Morrison and colleagues (2004) conclude that existing evidence suggests that gay men are less satisfied with their bodies than heterosexual men, in parallel with increased pressure from the gay community to be slender and muscular.

It is important to place pressure from the gay community in its social context. Body-image-related pressures from the gay "scene" do not exist in a vacuum. They exist within mainstream culture, in which young men generally have significant spending power, making them an attractive market for consumer goods (Mort, 1988). The 1990s and 2000s have seen an opening of young men's markets generally, and particularly that of young gay men (O'Kelly, 1994; Pope *et al.*, 2000). It is clearly in the interests of purveyors of clothes, cosmetics, and other body-related consumer goods to encourage body consciousness in the gay community and to capitalize on the resulting demand, and the spending power of affluent gay men. In the late 1980s, Frank Mort noted that gay men were taking up a variety of different styles (high camp, biker imagery, and retro) that all involved consumerism, to the advantage of advertisers and marketers (Mort, 1988). Cultural pressure from the "gay scene" to be physically attractive is actively encouraged and supported by advertisers and others with a financial interest in gay men's spending power, who promote aspirational images of the muscular, attractive gay man through the media to encourage consumerism (O'Kelly, 1994).

In addition to pressures from within the gay community to be attractive, gay men are also faced with the cultural stereotype that "gay men look after their bodies" and are "physically fit." Duane Hargreaves and Marika Tiggemann (2006) found that the Australian male adolescents who took part in their study were reticent about talking about their bodies and body image, as they perceived this to be a "gay issue." Mainstream media are full of examples of gay men's bodies being represented as attractive and "fit." For instance, in an *Independent on Sunday* article discussing the reasons why women were not buying the new soft-pornography magazines aimed at them, one of the "problems" identified by the journalist was that magazines aimed at heterosexual women tended to use gay male models, since "gay men are the ones who tend to look after their bodies" (Forna, 1996: 3). Even feminist writers fall into the trap of objectifying gay men and expecting them to conform to the "fit gay" stereotype:

> Many gay men, as straight women often observe, are very attractive. There's a lot to be said for tight pants on a good body in excellent condition.
>
> (Brownmiller, 1984: 71)

As when women's and black men's bodies are objectified, the objectification of gay men's bodies is a way of disempowering the group. In a culture where the quest for beauty has been used for hundreds of years to control women's energies (Wolf, 1991), the expectation that gay men should be attractive can be conceptualized as a form of social control. Diana Fuss (1989) argues that gay men (and lesbians) are seen as a threat to public safety, and believes that gay men are persecuted by the state apparatus. The "gay man as fit body" stereotype is a potential source of social control, especially in a context where "heterosexism" is validated by the supposed risk of the spread of AIDS. Many authors have documented the rampant heterosexism that emerged in the 1980s with awareness of AIDS in both Britain (Kitzinger, 1987; Ellis and Heritage, 1989) and the USA (Yingling, 1991). External "fitness" can reassure the fearful both within and outside the gay community that the gay man (and his behavior) does not represent a risk.

Most studies have found that gay men are less satisfied with their bodies than heterosexual men. This may relate to pressures from the gay community to have an acceptably muscular body, within a mainstream cultural context where gay men are more "embodied" than heterosexual men, and where there is a cultural expectation of body consciousness in gay men from within and without the gay community. More work is needed in this area to compare men of different ages (since most work has focused on men under 30), and to compare men involved in the "gay scene" with others who are not. Choosing samples from venues attended by gay men (as most researchers have done) may overestimate the extent of body dissatisfaction by producing a sample who identify most strongly with the "scene." As Beren *et al.* (1996) have shown, men who are more highly involved in the "scene" may show higher levels of concern than those who have gay relationships but would not identify themselves with that subculture. At present, though, it seems likely that men who have sexual relationships with men are generally more concerned about their bodies, and less satisfied with them, than heterosexual men.

### Heterosexual men

Despite recent media interest in the social pressure on heterosexual men to conform to the well-muscled slender ideal, there is little evidence that most heterosexual men are responding to pressure from women by trying to attain a well-muscled look. In two studies (Fallon and Rozin, 1985; Rozin and Fallon, 1988), men's current and ideal sizes, and the size that they believed was attractive to women, were very similar, leading the authors to conclude that men's perceptions serve to keep them satisfied with their bodies. Although many heterosexual men report some dissatisfaction with the way that they look (Pope *et al.*, 2000), their levels of body concern are reliably lower than those reported for women (Cash, 2002) and for gay men (Morrison *et al.*, 2004). Heterosexual men are also less likely to be motivated to engage in appearance-fixing behaviors such as dieting, or to exercise for reasons relating to appearance than gay men or women (Conner *et al.*, 2004; Grogan *et al.*, 2006).

Interview work with heterosexual men suggests that men believe that women prefer them to be toned and muscular, and are aware of media pressure to be muscular, but are mostly not motivated to try to achieve this look through exercise or diet. In focus groups, men reported that most pressure came from male peers (rather than women), who criticized body shape and size especially if a man was considered to be overweight (Grogan and Richards, 2002). Some of the bodybuilders we interviewed have commented that the primary motivation to start to body build was to be more sexually attractive to women. However, once they had started to body build, competition with other men became a more important motivator. None of the men who were using steroids cited pressure from female partners as a motivator. Pressure from media models and other men training at the gym was a more significant factor here (see Chapter 4).

Michael Siever (1994) found that gay men, heterosexual women, and heterosexual men did not differ significantly on belief as to the degree to which their body mattered to potential sexual partners. Similarly, when asked about the importance of physical appearance to their own potential sexual partners, no significant differences in importance between heterosexual women, heterosexual men, and gay men were cited. These data are important since they show that (according to their own reports) heterosexual men and gay men do not place a higher premium on physical attractiveness in their partners than heterosexual women. Taken at face value, these findings might suggest that heterosexual men are under equivalent pressure to gay men and to heterosexual women to attain a slender and (in the case of men) muscled appearance to attract female sexual partners. However, although heterosexual men may receive, and perceive, pressure from women to look slender and muscular, existing data suggest that this is unlikely to motivate body change strategies (Grogan and Richards, 2002; Fawkner, 2004; Hargreaves and Tiggemann, 2006). This may be because pressure to look toned and muscular is to some extent counterbalanced by a general cultural attitude that attributes other than physical attractiveness are important in heterosexual men (Bordo, 2003), and because they function within a mainstream culture that does not openly sanction objectification of heterosexual men (Davis *et al.*, 2001; Morrison *et al.*, 2004).

Evolutionary psychologists have generally failed to consider what women find attractive in men, largely because of their assumption that what women are looking for in a man is his ability to defend and support her financially. However, even Charles Darwin argued that women would choose men for the way they look (rather than for their abilities to support her financially, or for personality factors):

> Both sexes, if the females as well as the males were permitted
> to exert any choice, would choose their partners not for mental

charms, or property, or social position, but almost solely from external appearance.

(Darwin, 1871, cited in Singh, 1995: 1089)

Devendra Singh (1995) has recently suggested that body shape may be important in determining how attractive women rate men to be. He suggests that body fat distribution is important in determining which men are judged sexually attractive by women. After puberty, men tend to lose fat from lower body parts, and deposit fat on upper body parts (shoulders, nape of neck, and abdomen). From an analysis of data from the US National Aeronautics and Space Administration, sampling from European, Asian, African, and Latin American men, Singh argues that most men, irrespective of culture, have a WHR of between 0.8 and 0.87. He argues that men with WHR in this range are healthier than other men, and are likely to be of reproductive age. In a series of studies, he found that white and Hispanic women of different ages found men with WHR in the average range most attractive when presented with male body shapes varying in WHR (see Figure 6.3). This effect was maximized if the males were of higher financial status. Singh suggests that physical appearance is important in determining women's choice of sexual partner because it relates to health:

> Women may select mates who are healthy to ensure that their offspring inherit a predisposition for good health and that the man would be able to provide good quality parental care.
>
> (Singh, 1995: 1099)

There are similar problems associated with these arguments to those relating to the data on men's preferences for women's body types. Although these results could be affected by biological factors, they may also be influenced by learned preferences. Data come from US (white and Hispanic) women who share similar cultural influences. The results would be more convincing if they came from different cultures. He shows that women tend to prefer men who fall into the average (i.e., most familiar) range. He does not examine waist-to-shoulder ratios or waist-to-chest ratios, which may be more telling in terms of women's preferences for male body types.

Kevin Thompson and Stacey Tantleff (1992) found that women showed a preference for large chest sizes for men when presented with male figures varying in chest size (Figure 6.4). Most men rated their current chest size as smaller than ideal on this scale. Women associated adjectives such as assertive, athletic, sexually active, confident, and

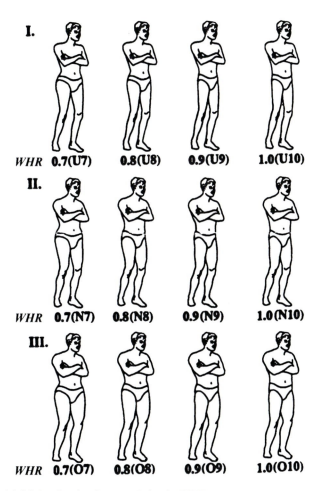

*Figure 6.3* Male stimulus figures varying in WHR.

*Source*: Adapted from Singh (1995). Copyright patented 1995 by the American Psychological Association. Adapted with permission.

*Note*: Figures represent underweight (I), normal weight (II) and overweight (III), with waist-to-hip ratios (WHRs) shown under each figure in each weight category, along with a letter and number in brackets which identifies body weight category WHR.

popular with large chest sizes for men. Thompson and Tantleff concluded that women (and the men themselves) show a distinct preference for large chest sizes.

Evolutionary psychologists have also argued that body symmetry is

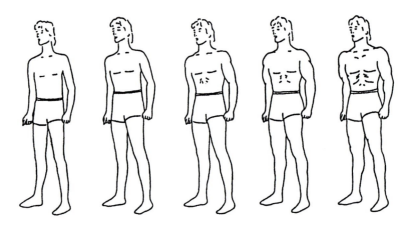

*Figure 6.4* Male stimulus figures varying in chest size.

*Source:* Adapted from Thompson and Tantleff (1992) with permission.

important in intersex attraction. Randy Thornhill and Steven Gangestad (1994) have suggested that having a symmetrical body may be extremely important in intersex physical attraction. Thornhill, a biologist, became interested in the effects of symmetry when he found that scorpion flies that had more symmetrical wings fared better in the competition for food and mates. Working with the psychologist Gangestad, he started to look at symmetry in humans. They measured body symmetry in hundreds of male and female college students. Through adding up the right–left differences in seven measurements (breadth of feet, ankles, hands, wrists, elbows, and breadth and length of ears), they were able to produce a score indicating degree of asymmetry for each person. For men and women, greater symmetry predicted larger numbers of sexual partners. Thornhill and Gangestad suggest that symmetry predicts other features with "mate value" including muscularity, health, and athleticism. Although symmetry may relate to health, it is also possible that it is a culturally determined preference. The data presented by Thornhill and Gangestad (1994) show that such a preference may exist, but the authors do not present a convincing argument that this preference has any biological basis.

   One of the problems with evolutionary arguments is that they are mostly post hoc explanations of existing social effects based on parallels with data derived from animals. Although they may be valid, they are usually open to the criticism that the same results may be explicable through recourse to cultural explanations. Bob Connell (1987) argues that sociobiological arguments are really pseudobiological, as they do not rest on serious biological investigation of human social life. He suggests that, despite their claim to scientific explanation, they cannot adequately substantiate the mechanisms through which sexual selection is supposed to operate. He suggests that sociobiology starts with an interpretation of social behavior (an interpretation which may be factually incorrect and is often sexist and ethnocentric) and projects this back upon a mythical history of human society, using this to posit processes of natural selection which justify the current social arrangements. This argument is supported by Chris Shilling (1993), who sees sociobiology as providing an incomplete view of human mating behavior, since it focuses on strategies for maximizing the chances that genes will be passed on to future generations, to the exclusion of social factors:

> Individuals are like robots controlled by forces beyond their reach. Human behaviour and social interaction is explained in terms of the costs, benefits, and even strategies of genes engaged in a competitive struggle for survival. Put simply, there is no need to look to social structures as determinants of human behaviour as there is no such thing as emergent social structures.
>
> (Shilling, 1993: 50)

April Fallon (1990) also argues against the biological determinist view. She demonstrates that some biological characteristics associated with reproduction, such as menstruation, pregnancy, and lactation, are rarely valued in terms of attractiveness. Similarly, male physical characteristics representing maturity and social dominance (for instance, baldness) are rarely considered attractive. She suggests that cultural diversity demonstrates that cultural influences are important in determining what is considered attractive, pointing to the fact that many cultures consider obesity attractive, and citing examples of plump women being considered to have greater sex appeal and to be more sexually satisfying than thin women.

To summarize, data linking sexuality and body image suggest that heterosexual women and gay men may have higher levels of body concern and dissatisfaction than heterosexual men, in relation to social pressure to be slender and muscular. Heterosexual women and gay men may also perceive the most pressure from actual or potential sexual partners to conform to a particular body shape and size, although heterosexual women are likely to perceive the male ideal as slimmer than it is according to men's reports. Heterosexual men perceive some pressure from sexual partners, but expect that their current body shape and size are close to women's ideal, and are less likely than other groups to be motivated to exercise and diet to make themselves more attractive to potential sexual partners. Lesbians may be slightly more satisfied with their bodies than heterosexual women. Arguments from evolutionary psychologists suggest that women and men in heterosexual relationships look for characteristics in their partners indicating "fitness" (low WHR in women and average WHR and body symmetry in men). However, these effects are open to alternative, sociocultural interpretations. Evolutionary psychologists have failed to demonstrate convincingly that preferences for particular body shapes are biologically based, and their work has many critics. Demonstration of cross-cultural similarities in the effects of WHR would lend more credibility to arguments presented by researchers working within this paradigm. Current data suggest that body satisfaction is largely determined by social factors, and is intimately tied to sexuality.

## Summary

- This chapter has reviewed data from a variety of sources looking at the mediating effects of age, ethnicity, social class, and sexuality on body image.
- Body dissatisfaction is evident from 8 years of age and possibly even earlier. Boys and girls express similar concerns to those voiced by adults in relation to their "fear of fat," and describe similar body shape ideals to those described by adults (slender for girls and slender but muscular for boys). Looking at body satisfaction throughout the life span, studies have found that women of all ages are less satisfied than men. Women do not appear to become less satisfied with age, and there is some indication that women's ideals may become heavier (in line with actual body size) as they become older. There is some evidence that men become less satisfied as they become older, although the gender differential is maintained throughout the life span until people are over 60, when the gender difference may decrease.
- Data in relation to ethnicity show that African-American and Afro-Caribbean British women have heavier body shape ideals, and are less dissatisfied than white US or white British women. Recent work suggests that Hispanic and Asian women may be becoming less satisfied as a result of the spread of mainstream, white cultural prejudice against overweight beyond the white community and are unlikely to differ from white women. Data from men are mixed,

although African-American men may be more satisfied than white men and have heavier ideals for both men and women, and Hispanic men do not seem to differ from white men.

- Studies of sexuality and body image have shown that heterosexual women and gay men may be most dissatisfied with their bodies, and heterosexual men most satisfied, due in part to differences in cultural pressures in relation to body shape and size. Lesbian subculture may be protective against body dissatisfaction in women, although research results are mixed.
- Data in relation to body image in people of differing age, class, ethnic group, and sexuality emphasize the crucial importance of understanding sociocultural pressures on group members in order to make sense of variations in body image.

# 7 Promoting positive body image

The preceding chapters have summarized existing work on men's and women's body image, and have painted a picture of body image in the average Western man or woman. From what we know about the impact of the effects of membership of particular cultural groups (gender, class, ethnicity, sexuality, and age), being white and being heterosexual are likely to predict body dissatisfaction in women. Age or social class are unlikely to have a significant impact, although there is some evidence that women over 60 may become more satisfied with the look of their bodies and focus more on body function and health. Men are likely to be more satisfied in general, and younger, heterosexual men may be expected to be most satisfied. The average woman could be expected to have dieted to try to lose weight, and the average man is probably not highly motivated to diet or exercise even if he perceives a mismatch between his current body and his ideal body image. If he does change his behavior, he will probably exercise. Women are likely to feel dissatisfaction with hips, thighs, "stomachs," and breasts; men are more likely to be dissatisfied with "stomachs" and muscularity. Most women want to lose weight, whereas men are equally likely to want to be heavier or lighter, and are most likely to want to be more muscular.

Dissatisfaction exists in a context where body image is subjective and socially determined. The social relativity of body satisfaction has been demonstrated by illustrating how satisfaction varies by culture and subculture. Data from different social groups have shown that the same body shape may be perceived more or less positively depending on the gender and culture of the person doing the perceiving. A person's body satisfaction is easier to predict from what we know about that person's subjective evaluation of what it means to have that particular kind of body within that particular subculture than from actual body size as determined by BMI (Tiggemann, 1992; 2005; Furnham and Greaves, 1994). This has led researchers from a range of disciplines to argue that body image is subjective, and open to change through social influences.

Most existing literature focuses on factors predicting dissatisfaction with the body rather than satisfaction, probably because work in this area has its roots in clinical work with people experiencing eating problems (Grogan, 2006). A shift in focus is timely. There is a general trend in psychology in favor of moving away from the traditional focus on problems and pathology toward positive psychology (Seligman and Csikszentmihalyi, 2000) focusing on factors predicting health and well-being (Cash, 2002). In order to develop strategies to help people feel better about their bodies it is informative to consider how some individuals manage to maintain body satisfaction in societies where the ideal is slender/muscular and their bodies do not correspond to this ideal. It is important to promote body satisfaction, as even relatively minor body concerns may lead to exercise avoidance (Choi, 2000a); use of anabolic steroids and other drugs to increase muscularity (Pope *et al.*, 2000; Wright *et al.*, 2000); unhealthy eating behaviors, such as binge eating, restrictive dieting, and self-induced vomiting (Levine and Piran, 2004; Stice and Shaw, 2004); inability to quit smoking (King *et al.*, 2005); and desire for cosmetic surgery with its associated health risks (Davis, 1995; von Soest *et al.*, 2006). This may be a particular problem with vulnerable groups such as adolescents. On the basis of the results of a large-scale prospective study of body image and health-related behaviors, Diane Neumarck-Sztainer and colleagues (2006) argue that body dissatisfaction puts adolescents at significant risk of weight gain and overall poor health. By identifying factors that predict satisfaction, we may be able to produce useful ideas for encouraging a more positive image of the body in those who are dissatisfied, to improve health and well-being.

## Psychological factors predicting positive body image

Psychologists have suggested various psychological factors that predict positive body image. The most important of these are self-esteem, resistance to internalization of the thin ideal, and beliefs about personal control and mastery over the body, all of which are linked with each other. Here we will examine the proposed link between these psychological variables and body satisfaction, and look specifically at how this psychological knowledge can be useful in trying to improve body satisfaction in women and men.

## Self-esteem

People higher in self-esteem in general tend to be more satisfied with their bodies. This is the case for both men and women (Mintz and Betz, 1986; Furnham and Greaves, 1994), although it has been suggested that there is a closer association of these two variables for women than for men (Mintz and Betz, 1986; Avsec, 2006; Connors and Casey, 2006), probably because body satisfaction is generally more central to women's sense of self than to men's (Tiggemann, 2005). Interview work has also supported the link between self-esteem and body image in both women and men. In interviews with women carried out by Charles and Kerr (1986), and by others on women and men of different ages (Grogan and Wainwright, 1986; Grogan and Richards, 2002; Grogan *et al.*, 2004), positive body image has been linked with positive feelings about the self, and feelings of self-confidence and power in social situations. Although most authors have assumed that high self-esteem leads to high body satisfaction rather than the reverse (e.g., Button *et al.*, 1996), recent evidence suggests that, at least for adolescent girls and late adolescent boys, body dissatisfaction may precede low self-esteem (Tiggemann, 2005; Paxton *et al.*, 2006). Work is needed to investigate further these links in men and in older women. Although body dissatisfaction may precede changes in self-esteem in girls in the critical adolescent years, there may be life-course changes that mean that at some points self-esteem predicts changes in body dissatisfaction (for instance, it is possible that women with higher self-esteem could find the physical changes associated with pregnancy and aging easier to cope with and less damaging to body satisfaction than other women). Further work will enable a fuller understanding of the time course links between these two variables, and the ways that this link is gendered.

Research in Australia and the USA has shown that programs designed to raise body esteem in adolescents (O'Dea and Abraham, 2000) and adults (Springer *et al.*, 1999) can be effective in improving body image. The idea behind these programs is that once self-esteem has improved, body image will also improve as a byproduct of the self-esteem intervention. Jenny O'Dea (2004) and Susan Paxton (1993) have both argued that interventions that focus directly on body image may inadvertently raise body concerns. The advantage of programs that do not focus directly on body image is that they may avoid increasing body focus in vulnerable people, and this may be particularly important in children who had not considered body image problematic prior to the intervention. More work is needed in this area to determine the effectiveness of programs that aim to build self-esteem and resiliency as an indirect method of improving body image, although existing US and Australian work with children and adolescents is producing very positive results (O'Dea, 1995; O'Dea and Abraham, 2000; Steese *et al.*, 2006).

## Resistance to internalization of the thin/muscular ideal

Women and men who reject the mainstream thin/muscular ideal may be less sensitive to thin-ideal media cues and less vulnerable to dissatisfaction caused by self-ideal discrepancies (e.g., Jones, 2004; Ahern and Hetherington, 2006). Yuko Yamamiya *et al.* (2005) have shown that body dissatisfaction can be increased by as little as 5 minutes of exposure to thin-and-beautiful images in women high in thin-ideal internalization, showing that social comparison with media ideals can produce particular risks for this group of women. Most studies in this area use Heinberg *et al.*'s (1995) Sociocultural Attitudes to Appearance Questionnaire, which measures the degree of internalization and awareness of the thin ideal seen in mainstream media. Studies using this scale find that women who score lower on internalization of the thin ideal are more satisfied with their bodies (e.g., Engeln-Maddox, 2005), and that men scoring lower on internalization of the slender and muscular ideal score significantly higher on body satisfaction (e.g., Jones, 2004). This raises the question of how some people resist internalizing the thin/muscular ideal. Internalization of this ideal, rather than awareness that it exists, is crucial in determining body dissatisfaction (Cusumano and Thompson, 1997).

Most work on internalization of cultural ideals has been conducted with women, although Harrison Pope *et al.* (2000) focus on ways that individual men can challenge the muscular ideal through an understanding of the ways that unrealistic images portrayed in the media are produced. A popular approach to resisting internalization of the thin ideal is to use psychoeducational interventions to teach women about the unrealistic standards set up in Western societies. These techniques are based on the sociocultural model of body image, which suggests that women are under significant pressure to be slender, mediated by media imagery and pressure from peers and family (Thompson *et al.*, 1999). These programs stress the cultural relativity of slenderness ideals, and usually involve explanations of the variety of photographic techniques that can be used to bring pictures of models closer to the cultural ideal (this is known as media literacy training). The effectiveness of these programs with nonclinical groups has been mixed. Although some authors have found that such programs are effective in reducing internalization of the thin ideal, most studies have not shown a significant reduction in body dissatisfaction (Levine and Smolak, 2002). There are some exceptions. In a study with female college students, Stormer and Thompson (1995) found that their psychoeducational media literacy program that educated women about media techniques to create idealized images and taught techniques for rejecting these images produced decreased weight concerns and lowered body anxiety. Other body image measures were not affected by the intervention. Interesting recent US work has suggested that women high in internalization given psychoeducational media literacy information directly before seeing idealized media images show less weight concern later than controls (Yamamiya *et al.*, 2005). Clearly, there is more work to be done in this area.

Another approach that has enabled people to challenge unrealistic cultural messages and to rethink unrealistic body standards is cognitive-behavioral therapy (CBT). CBT is based on the idea that negative thoughts, feelings, behaviors, and perceptions about the body are learned and can be unlearned. CBT interventions tend to include cognitive restructuring and self-monitoring to change body-related thoughts; behavioral techniques such as desensitization to change body-dissatisfaction-linked behaviors, such as avoidance of situations where the body might be exposed; and size estimation accuracy training to reduce size over- or underestimation (Jarry and Ip, 2005). CBT has been reported to be extremely effective in promoting positive body image in non-clinical populations (Cash and Strachan, 2002; Cash and Hrabosky, 2004). Recent reviews of the characteristics and effectiveness of body image interventions have concluded that CBT is a highly effective body image treatment producing long-term changes in body image (Jarry and Beraldi, 2004), and that interventions addressing the attitudinal, behavioral, and perceptual components of body image were more effective than those that address only attitude and behavior (Jarry and Ip, 2005).

Another factor that seems protective against internalization by women is having a personal feminist ideology. Research has shown that women who hold feminist attitudes relating to body image are more satisfied than those who do not identify with feminist values (Dionne *et al.*, 1995; Snyder and Hansbrouck, 1996). This has led some researchers to look at the effectiveness of incorporating feminist theory in the prevention of body dissatisfaction programs. Feminist theories such as those outlined in Chapter 3 have been applied in intervention programs to enable women to change the ways that they interpret cultural messages through recognizing and challenging unhealthy female body ideals and practices (e.g., Piran, 1996; Piran *et al.*, 2004). Work by Niva Piran and colleagues is informative in taking girls' and women's experiences as their starting point, enabling participants to evaluate critically the lived experience of being a female in a culture than idealizes extreme slenderness, and develop alternative conceptions that challenge the thin ideal. In a recent study, Rachel Peterson and colleagues (2006) have also investigated whether exposure to feminist perspectives increases women's body satisfaction through increasing feminist identity. Peterson and colleagues suggest that a feminist schema may operate as a buffer through which societal messages may be filtered, to enable women to resist internalization of the thin ideal. Women in the feminist theory intervention condition (focusing on feminist theories of body image and eating disturbance, and delineation of feminist theories), were more likely to increase their identification as a feminist relative to those in the psychoeducation intervention condition (where women were exposed to a media literacy program) or a control group who were not exposed to an intervention. Feminist identity predicted higher body satisfaction after the intervention. This study suggests that exposure to feminist theories may serve as an effective intervention to improve body image, at least in educated, university undergraduate samples similar to the women who took part in this study.

### Body mastery and control

Other work has suggested that those who feel greater mastery and personal control over their bodies are likely to be more satisfied, and to feel hopeful and positive about attaining their ideal body shape (Furnham and Greaves, 1994). This link has been supported in a survey (Furnham and Greaves, 1994) in which women and men were interviewed about their body image (Grogan, 1999). Women bodybuilders interviewed in our study (Grogan *et al.*, 2004) discussed in Chapter 3 indicated that bodybuilding had enabled them to take control of their bodies, and this had impacted positively on their body satisfaction, self-esteem, and feeling of mastery over their all aspects of their lives. Stressing control and mastery over the body is a traditional feminine discourse, drawing on notions of restraint and control of the female body (Bordo, 2003), although in this case women were talking about increasing rather than reducing the size of their bodies.

Gail Huon (1994) suggests that engagement in group discussion about practical strategies for improving body satisfaction stressing "taking control" may lead to improved body image. She investigated the extent to which it is possible to change young women's attitudes to their body and to reduce dieting intentions. Twenty-four women aged 18–25 were assigned to four discussion groups. Discussions focused on ideas for helping others to give up dieting, and to develop a more positive body image. She found that discussion of strategies for development of a more positive body image and for giving up dieting was sufficient to produce highly significant changes in the women's body satisfaction scores. Discussions of barriers to developing a positive body image produced no significant effects. Informal conversation after the interviews revealed that the women experienced the two kinds of discussion quite differently. Discussion of strategies to improve body satisfaction (taking up sports, identifying goals, and learning to value individuality) was experienced as positive and motivating, because the women felt that they had some control over these things. Discussion of factors over which they felt that they had no control (barriers such as media promotion of the thin image, and social attitudes to weight and shape, which are covered in media literacy programs) was experienced as demotivating because of perception of low control over these factors.

Other work on assertiveness training has also reported positive effects on women's body image through a focus on self-efficacy. Alan Blair *et al.* (1992) sent leaflets to 50 women. The leaflets were designed to facilitate improvement in self-efficacy and self-esteem, and to enable success in weight loss for those who want to lose weight. The "Personal Effectiveness" leaflet addressed general assertiveness, and also assertiveness in response to offers of food and comments regarding body shape from others. The "Social Pressure on Women" leaflet focused on societal attitudes that influence women's self-value, particularly as they relate to physical appearance, in an attempt to persuade women to reconsider their level of satisfaction with their present body size. They found significant reductions in emotional eating, and nonsignificant improvements in perceptions of body size, self-esteem, and self-efficacy.

### Exercise interventions

Although there is some evidence that participants in "lean sports" (where thinness is an advantage for performance) are more preoccupied with weight than the general population (Petrie, 1996; Smolak *et al.*, 2000), there is a growing body of evidence that moderate exercise, focusing on mastery rather than aesthetics, can improve perceptions of control, self-esteem, and satisfaction with the body, as well as improvements in health and fitness. Exercise improves mood, well-being, and perception of control, at least in the short term (Brown and Lawton, 1986), and there is a large body of evidence that exercise improves body satisfaction (see Martin and Lichtenberger, 2002, for an excellent review).

In one of the earliest studies of the link between exercise and body satisfaction in women, Snyder and Kivlin (1975) showed that female exercisers had higher body satisfaction than did controls. Other work has also found that exercisers rate themselves as more attractive, confident, healthy, and popular, and have significantly higher body satisfaction scores, than nonexercisers (Furnham *et al.*, 1994). Studies that have looked at differences in body satisfaction in women before and after exercise have also produced positive results. In a study conducted in the USA (Koff and Bauman, 1997), 140 college women participating in one of three types of physical education classes (wellness, fitness, and sports skills) responded to questions about body image, body–self relations, and lifestyle behaviors at the onset and conclusion of a 6-week program. The wellness and fitness classes both produced increased satisfaction with the body and physical appearance, although there was no change in these variables in the sports skills classes. The authors suggested that participation in wellness and fitness classes empowers participants, making them feel more positive toward their health and general well-being, including their body image. These results are convincing, because they study changes within individuals before and after exercise, rather than comparing exercisers with nonexercisers (who may differ on other psychological variables).

Other intervention studies where women have been randomly allocated to exercise and nonexercise conditions have also shown that exercise programs are effective in improving body image (see Martin and Lichtenberger, 2002). For instance, Gillian Burgess and colleagues (2006) investigated the effects on body satisfaction and physical self-perception of a 6-week aerobic dance program with 50 British female adolescents aged 13–14 years who were initially dissatisfied with their bodies. Results revealed that participation in the aerobic dance program significantly reduced body dissatisfaction and enhanced physical self-perception, and the authors conclude:

> These data present a particularly strong case for the positive benefits of aerobic dance for female adolescents with a poor image of themselves.
>
> (Burgess *et al.*, 2006: 63)

In a recent Canadian study by Kathleen Martin-Ginis and colleagues (2005), 28 men and 16 women completed a 12-week, 5-day-a-week strength training program. Significant improvements in body image were found for both men and women. The authors conclude that both men and women benefit from subjective perceptions of their body composition and strength, and that women also appear to benefit from objective improvements in strength. These results support our interview work conducted with women bodybuilders (Grogan *et al.*, 2004). It seems likely that exercise enhances self-esteem and body image in women by producing a firmer and stronger body, by giving a sense of competence, and by focusing on body mastery and function rather than on aesthetics. Kathleen Martin and Catherine Lichtenberger (2002) note that increases in measurable physical fitness do not need to be produced by an intervention in order for the intervention to improve body image. What is crucial is that the person feels subjectively fitter and higher in self-efficacy. According to Sonstroem and Morgan's (1989) exercise and self-esteem model, exercise-related changes in physical self-efficacy are the vital element in exercise-related changes in body image.

Evidence for positive effects of exercise on men's body image is less clear, although several authors have reported that men who exercise are significantly more satisfied than those who avoid exercise (Davis *et al.*, 1991; Huddy and Cash, 1997). In a Canadian study by Caroline Davis and colleagues (1991), 103 male college students aged 18–34 and 88 regularly exercising men aged 16–64 completed self-report surveys, including the Eysenck Personality Inventory (EPI), physical activity, body dissatisfaction, and weight satisfaction scales. Exercisers engaged in more than double the physical activity engaged in by the college sample. The exercisers were also significantly more satisfied with their bodies. In regression analysis, physical activity predicted about 11 percent of the variance in body dissatisfaction, showing that frequency and duration of exercise are a significant predictor of satisfaction with the body. The authors concluded that men who are physically active are more satisfied with their bodies, suggesting that men's body satisfaction may be influenced by the extent that they perceive themselves to be physically fit rather than by the extent that they conform to a subjective weight ideal. Other studies have reported that men who exercise are less satisfied (Kiernan *et al.*, 1992). However, in these survey studies, men who are exercisers are self-selected and may be engaging in exercise because they are dissatisfied with their bodies, and/or to control weight (Drewnowski and Yee, 1987; Pope *et al.*, 2000). In experimental studies in which men are randomly allocated to groups, the effects of exercise are very positive. Although there are relatively few studies in this area, those that have been conducted have produced positive results showing that participation in exercise and strength training programs leads to significant improvements in body satisfaction (Melnick and Mookerjee, 1991; Martin and Lichtenberger, 2002; Martin-Ginnis *et al.*, 2005).

These positive effects of exercise on mental health and well-being, and especially on body satisfaction, suggest that people, and particularly women, should be encouraged to undertake exercise as a way of improving self-esteem and body image. In fact, recent estimates of frequency of exercise have tended to find that relatively few people in Britain (particularly in the older age groups) undertake regular exercise, despite the physical and mental health benefits. According to the 2002–3 General Household Survey in Britain, participation in sport and physical activity had reduced compared to estimates from the 1980s and 1990s (Office of National Statistics, 2005). In the 4 weeks prior to interview, 51 percent of men and 36 percent of women had taken part in any sport or physical activity, excluding walking. When walking was entered, 65 percent of men and 53 percent of women had engaged in any sport or physical activity. For both men and women, walking was the most frequent activity at 36 percent for men and 43 percent for women. Most frequent for men were then snooker/pool/billiards (15 percent), cycling (12 percent), swimming (12 percent), soccer (10 percent), golf (9 percent), and weight training (9 percent). For women, these were keep fit/yoga (16 percent), swimming (15 percent), cycling (6 percent), snooker/pool/billiards (4 percent), and weight training, running, and tenpin bowling/skittles (3 percent). Activity levels decreased significantly with age, as might be expected, and although walking was the most popular activity for women at all ages, soccer was the most popular for men aged 16–19 at 45 percent participation. Men overall had higher participation rates at all ages, and gender differences were most marked in the 16–19 and 20–29 age groups.

Similar results have been found in studies with children. In the Avon Longitudinal Study conducted in Britain in 2005, only 10 percent of 4,500 11-year-olds were exercising one hour a day or more, and rates were particularly low for girls, despite the British government's Physical Education School Sports and Club Links Strategy, which was intended to increase the amount of physical exercise and sports in and out of school (*The Observer*, 29 May 2005). The Health Behaviour of School-Aged Children survey (Turtle *et al.*, 1997) randomly sampled pupils aged 11, 13, and 15 from each of 75 schools in England, producing a final sample size of 6,372, who completed all parts of the questionnaire. One in five young people played games or sports that made them out of breath or sweaty in their free time every day. One-third of the group engaged in strenuous exercise only once a week or less. Boys were more likely to engage in strenuous exercise than girls (one in four boys reported aerobic exercise once a day compared to one in 10 girls). As children became older, they engaged in less and less exercise. By age 15, one in 10 never got out of breath playing sports in their free time. Recent data suggest that inactivity relates to increasing levels of child obesity, which has tripled between 1995 and 2006 (Economic and Social Research Council, 2006). Given the relatively low levels of exercise being currently undertaken by adults and children, it is important to know what barriers to exercise are perceived by men and women. Myers and Roth (1997) administered questionnaires to 432 college students, asking them about current exercise, perceived benefits of and barriers to exercise, and intention to become more active. The participants perceived many benefits of exercise (including benefits to body image), but found it hard to motivate themselves to take exercise due to perceived lack of time and social responsibilities. Whitehead (1988) notes that another major barrier to taking exercise is cost. Making exercise facilities at sports centers cheaper or free may be one way to encourage people to exercise more. Recent British data suggest that people on low incomes are significantly less likely to exercise than those on higher incomes, unemployed men and women showing the highest rates of physical inactivity at 64 percent and 69 percent, respectively, and professional groups being more likely to have taken exercise in the 4 weeks prior to the interview than other groups (Office of National Statistics, 2005). Although other body-image-relevant social-class factors are confounded with income (see Chapter 6), cost may be one factor influencing uptake of exercise in people on low incomes.

Shifting the focus of exercise from competition to enjoyment (as the Sport for All initiative in Britain tried to do) may also encourage those who were alienated from sport, perhaps through early experiences of physical education at school. This is particularly important for groups who may feel alienated from the competitive "sports culture," including women and people of either gender over 40 (Cox *et al.*, 1993). A group that may feel particularly alienated is overweight people (or those who "feel fat"). Shelley Bovey, in *Being Fat Is Not a Sin* (1989), says that exercise may be made less enjoyable for people who are overweight by other people's reaction to them. Compliance with exercise regimes depends on enjoyment, which is difficult for obese people, who may be ridiculed, and may find that equipment and sports clothes are not suitable for their weight. Encouragement of enjoyment (rather than competition or appearance focus) in sports and exercise may improve motivation to exercise and frequency of exercise (Burgess *et al.*, 2006; Grogan *et al.*, 2006b). There is now sufficient evidence of the potentially beneficial effects of exercise to encourage a regular regime of exercise in everyone, to improve self-esteem and body image and to counteract stress. When Gail Huon (1988) asked young women to identify strategies for developing a more positive body image, one of their suggestions was to encourage girls and young women to take up enjoyable exercise activities in their leisure time. Studies reviewed in this chapter suggest that moderate exercise, along with improvement in self-esteem and perceptions of control, is likely to be an effective way to improve body image.

## General conclusions

This book presents an account of current research on body image in men, women, and children. It has been necessarily selective. Most of the research that is cited comes from the realm of psychology, since most empirical work on body image has been carried out by psychologists. Where possible, data from other social sciences have been presented. The result is a comprehensive, wide-ranging, but necessarily partial review of the variety of influences on men's and women's body image, and the behavioral effects of these influences. People most at risk of body dissatisfaction are those who belong to identified at-risk groups (white heterosexual women and gay men), those who have low self-esteem, those who perceive a lack of control over their bodies, and those who have internalized the thin/muscular ideal. Media representations of the slender ideal (slender and muscular for men) may lead to unfavorable social comparisons, and may result in dissatisfaction, particularly in women who have internalized societal ideals and men low in muscularity satisfaction. However, interview work suggests that women in particular are cynical about media portrayal of the "ideal body," and want to see more realistic images of women in the media. Media role models may differ depending on the age of the viewer, with viewers making active choices as to comparison groups. Older women are not more dissatisfied with their bodies than young women, in spite of media preferences for very young models, probably because they choose age-relevant targets for body image comparisons. There is some evidence that older men are more dissatisfied than younger men (although still more satisfied than women until women are over 60), probably because they compare body size with themselves at a younger (and usually more slender) age. Children from age 8 present similar discourses of body shape, and similar levels of body concern, to adults. It seems that some body dissatisfaction is the common experience of many people raised in Western cultures.

There are still many questions to be answered through further research. We need to know much more about the development of body dissatisfaction, especially in children under 8 years of age. We also need to know whether cultural homogenization in body satisfaction, in relation to social class and ethnic group in the early 2000s, is a reliable trend. More research with nonwhite, non-middle-class groups would help to answer this question. We also need to know more about the strategies used by those who are satisfied with their bodies to maintain a positive body image and to resist cultural pressure. Clearly, there is scope for future investigation.

Based on what we do know about men's and women's body image, we can conclude that the way forward in terms of developing positive body image must be a reduction in the objectification of the body (both male and female) and the development of body ideals based on function as well as aesthetics. In particular, acceptance in mainstream Western cultures of the wide variety of body shapes and sizes that represent the normal range, and the destigmatization of overweight, may help to reduce dissatisfaction. Cultural factors are important in determining people's experience of their bodies, and current evidence from cultural groups that do not stigmatize obesity suggests that acceptance of diversity may be expected to lead to a reduction in body dissatisfaction. Belonging to a cultural group that supports alternative body images may enable women to resist social pressures to be slender. There is evidence that women who body build at physique level, attaining a highly muscled physique, are supported in this by the bodybuilding community (other bodybuilders and competition judges), enabling these women to feel physically and mentally strong, and raising their self-esteem and self-confidence. Other groups of women who forge an alternative body ideal also seem to be more satisfied with the way that they look. Various authors have argued that lesbian subculture de-emphasizes the slim beauty ideal and has a broader range of acceptable body types (Brown, 1987), and recent reviews have concluded that lesbians tend to be marginally more satisfied on average than heterosexual women (Morrison *et al.*, 2004). Black women also tend to be more satisfied with their bodies than white women, and it has been argued that they are supported through African-American and Afro-Caribbean cultures that have more flexible and less thin body-shape ideals for women than white subcultures (see Chapter 6).

A recurrent theme in the body image literature is the importance of gender in determining body satisfaction. Irrespective of age, ethnicity, and class, women (in general) are less satisfied with their bodies than are men. Clearly, future work needs to do more to clarify this gender imbalance, and to present potential solutions for improving women's body image. Feminist authors, such as Naomi Wolf (1991), have suggested ways forward in terms of reclaiming the ways that "beauty" for women is represented in the popular media and in the culture as a whole. Wolf suggests that women need to regain control of their bodies, to resist the objectification of the female body, and to build a model of female beauty that allows individual women freedom for adornment, expressed sexuality, and time spent grooming their bodies, within a context that does not judge women on the basis of the extent to which they conform to the established cultural ideal:

> Costumes and disguises will be light-hearted and fun when women are granted rock-solid identities. Clothing that highlights women's sexuality will be casual wear when women's sexuality is under our own control. . . . Women will be able thoughtlessly to adorn ourselves with pretty objects when there is no question that we are not objects. Women will be free of the beauty myth when we can choose to use our faces and our clothes as simply one form of self-expression out of a full range of others.
>
> (Wolf, 1991: 273–4)

Wolf argues that Western culture (through the media in particular) sets up women in competition with each other in relation to their bodies, and that this harms all women. In our interviews with women and girls (Chapters 3 and 6), we found that women compared their bodies explicitly with those of other women (models, friends, and family members) and often found their bodies wanting, leading to lowered body satisfaction. Naomi Wolf argues that competition between women on the basis of their bodies is actively encouraged by the beauty industry, which has a vested interest in women's dissatisfaction. She says that women need to resist cultural pressures to compete on the basis of their bodies, and to support each other's beauty choices and body types, to build women's body satisfaction. She sees male-dominated institutions (rather than individual men) as the biggest challenge to the development of a radical new approach to beauty for women. She argues that women must reject models of beauty promoted by self-interested institutions, and develop a women-oriented ideal to put in their place that allows women to experiment and play with images of the body, and to accept the variations in bodies of women of different ages as acceptable and beautiful, rather than trying to conform to the unrealistic ideals promoted by advertisers and the fashion and diet industries. In her vision of the "new women's beauty," she suggests:

> A woman loving definition of beauty supplants desperation with

play, narcissism with self-love, dismemberment with wholeness, absence with presence, stillness with animation.

(Wolf, 1991: 291)

The recent move toward the objectification of the male body was discussed in Chapter 4. It cannot be in the interests of women if cultural objectification of the body is expanded to include men's bodies as well as women's. Objectification of the body needs to be challenged whether the targets are women or men. This is particularly the case for young gay men, whose bodies are generally more objectified than those of heterosexual men, in association with higher levels of appearance concern.

The 2000s are doubtless a time of increased concern with the body. Scientific developments in fields such as cosmetic surgery and pharmacology have given people in Western cultures the potential to change the ways that their bodies look. The representation of a narrow range of body shapes in the mass media leaves viewers in no doubt as to how they are expected to look, and ideals are becoming culturally homogeneous in the 2000s. The diet and cosmetic surgery industries benefit from this dissatisfaction by offering apparent solutions that can be bought by the body-dissatisfied consumer. A reduction in cultural objectification of the body, a shift in body aesthetics to encompass a variety of body shapes and sizes in the long term, and social support for alternative body types to the prevailing aesthetic in the short term would be expected to result in increased body satisfaction and improved quality of life for a significant proportion of the population, and particularly for women.

## Summary

- The social relativity of body satisfaction has been demonstrated by illustrating how satisfaction varies by social group. Data from different social groups have shown that the same body shape may be perceived more or less positively depending on the gender and social group of the person doing the perceiving. Being white and being heterosexual are likely to predict body dissatisfaction in women. Men are likely to be more satisfied in general, although older, white, and gay men may be expected to be most dissatisfied.
- The average woman could be expected to have dieted to try to lose weight, and the average man is probably not highly motivated to diet or exercise even if he perceives a mismatch between current body image and ideal body image. If he does change his behavior, he will probably exercise.

- High self-esteem, resistance to internalization of the thin ideal, and perceptions of body mastery and control predict body satisfaction. Interventions designed to promote satisfaction seem to be promising, especially those stressing body mastery and control and positive physical self-perception. Moderate exercise, focusing on body mastery and enjoyment rather than appearance and weight, may also be an effective strategy for improving body satisfaction.

- Cultural changes in the acceptability of a variety of body types for both men and women, and a focus on body function rather than aesthetics, would be likely to improve body satisfaction for both women and men.

# Bibliography

Ackard, D.M., Kearney-Cooke, A. and Peterson, C.B. (2000) 'Effect of body image and self-image on women's sexual behaviours,' *International Journal of Eating Disorders*, 28: 422–9.

Adams, G., Turner, H. and Bucks, R. (2005) 'The experience of body dissatisfaction in men,' *Body Image: An International Journal of Research*, 2: 271–84.

Agliata, D. and Tantleff-Dunn, S. (2004) 'The impact of media exposure on males' body image,' *Journal of Social and Clinical Psychology*, 23: 7–22.

Ahern, A.L. and Hetherington, M.M. (2006) 'The thin ideal and body image: An experimental study of implicit attitudes,' *Psychology of Addictive Behaviours*, 20(3): 338–42.

Alley, T. and Scully, K. (1994) 'The impact of actual and perceived changes in body weight on women's physical attractiveness,' *Basic and Applied Social Psychology*, 15(4): 535–42.

Altabe, M. and Thompson, J.K. (1996) 'Body image: A cognitive self-schema construct?,' *Cognitive Therapy and Research*, 20: 171–93.

Altabe, M. and O'Garo, K.-G. (2002) 'Hispanic body images,' in T.F. Cash and T. Pruzinsky (eds) *Body image. A handbook of theory, research, and clinical practice* (250–6), New York: Guilford Press.

American Society of Plastic Surgeons (ASPS) (2005) *National plastic surgery statistics: 2005 report of the 2004 patient statistics*, Arlington Heights, IL: ASPS.

Anderson, D.R., Huston, A.C., Schmitt, K.L., Linebarger, D.L. and Wright, J.C. (2001) 'Early childhood television viewing and adolescent behaviour: The recontact study,' *Monographs of the Society for Research in Child Development*, 66: 1–146.

Andres, R., Muller, D. and Sorkin, J. (1993) 'Long-term effects of change in body weight on all-cause mortality: A review,' *Annals of Internal Medicine*, 119: 737–43.

Aoki, D. (1996) 'Sex and muscle: The female bodybuilder meets Lacan,' *Body and Society*, 2(4): 45–57.

Arbour, K.P. and Martin-Ginis, K. (2006) 'Effects of exposure of muscular and hypermuscular images on young men's muscularity dissatisfaction and body dissatisfaction,' *Body Image: An International Journal of Research*, 3: 153–62.

Armstrong, M.L. and Fell, P.R. (2000) 'Body art: Regulatory issues and the NEHA body art model code,' *Environmental Health*, 62(9): 25–30.

Armstrong, S. (1996) 'Cast against type,' *The Guardian*, 3 June: 15.

Aruguete, M.S., Nickleberry, L.D. and Yates, A. (2004) 'Acculturation, body image, and eating attitudes among black and white college students,' *North American Journal of Psychology*, 6: 393–404.

Atkins, D. (ed.) (1998) *Looking queer: Body image and identity in lesbian, bisexual, gay and transgender communities*, New York: Harrington Park Press.

Atkinson, M. (2004) 'Tattooing and civilizing processes: Body modification as self-control,' *Canadian Review of Sociology and Anthropology*, 41(2): 125–46.

Averett, S. and Korenman, S. (1996) 'The economic reality of the beauty myth,' *Journal of Human Resources*, 31(2): 304–30.

Avsec, A. (2006) 'Gender differences in the structure of self-concept: Are the self-conceptions about physical attractiveness really more important for women's self-esteem?,' *Studia Psychologica*, 48(1): 31–43.

Baker, P. (1994) 'Under pressure: What the media is doing to men,' *Cosmopolitan*, November: 129–32.

Bardwell, M.D. and Choudury, I.Y. (2000) 'Body dissatisfaction and eating attitudes in slimming and fitness gyms in London and Lahore: A cross-cultural study,' *European Eating Disorders Review*, 8(3): 217–24.

Barry, D.T. and Grilo, C.M. (2002) Eating and body image disturbances in adolescent psychiatric inpatients: Gender and ethnicity patterns', *International Journal of Eating Disorders*, 32: 335–43.

Bartky, S. (1990) *Femininity and domination: Studies in the phenomenology of oppression*, New York: Routledge.

Beck, A.T. (1976) *Cognitive therapy and the emotional disorders*, New York: International Universities Press.

Becker, A.E. (ed.) (1995) *Body, self, and society*, Philadelphia: University of Philadelphia Press.

Becker, A. (2004) 'Television, disordered eating, and young women in Fiji: Negotiating body image and identity during rapid social change,' *Culture Medicine and Psychiatry*, 28(4): 533–59.

Bee, P. (2006) 'The BMI myth,' *The Guardian*, 28 November: 18.

Bennett, W. and Gurin, J. (1982) *The dieter's dilemma*, New York: Basic Books.

Ben-Tovim, D. and Walker, K. (1991) 'Women's body attitudes: A review of measurement techniques,' *International Journal of Eating Disorders*, 10(2): 155–67.

Beren, S., Hayden, H., Wilfley, D. and Grilo, C. (1996) 'The influence of sexual orientation on body dissatisfaction in adult men and women,' *International Journal of Eating Disorders*, 2: 135–41.

Bergstron, E., Stenlund, H. and Svedjehall, B. (2000) 'Assessment of body perception among Swedish adolescents and young adults,' *Journal of Eating Disorders*, 6: 385–91.

Berscheid, E., Walster, E. and Bornstedt, G. (1973) 'The happy American body: A survey report,' *Psychology Today*, 7: 119–31.

Bessenoff, G. (2006) 'Can the media affect us? Social comparison, self-discrepancy, and the thin ideal,' *Psychology of Women Quarterly*, 30(3): 239–51.

Bordo, S. (2003) *Unbearable weight: Feminism, Western culture, and the body* (10th anniversary edn), Berkeley, CA: University of California Press.

Borzekowski, D.L., Robinson, T.N. and Killen, J.D. (2000) 'Does the camera add 10 pounds? Media use, perceived importance of appearance and weight concerns among teenage girls,' *Journal of Adolescent Health*, 26(1): 36–41.

Boseley, S. (1996) ' "Anorexic" models cost "Vogue" ads,' *The Guardian*, 31 May: 1.

Botta, R.A. (1999) 'Television images and adolescent girls' body image disturbance,' *Journal of Communication*, 49: 22–41.

—— (2000) 'The mirror of television: A comparison of black and white adolescents' body image,' *Journal of Communication*, 50: 144–59.

—— (2003) 'For your health? The relationship between magazine reading and adolescents' body image and eating disturbances,' *Sex Roles*, 48: 389–99.

Bourdieu, P. (1984) *Distinction: A social critique of the judgement of taste*, London: Routledge.

Bovey, S. (1989) *Being fat is not a sin*, London: Pandora Press.

Bradley, P. (1982) 'Is obesity an advantageous adaptation?,' *International Journal of Obesity*, 6: 43–52.

Brand, P., Rothblum, E. and Soloman, L. (1992) 'A comparison of lesbians, gay men, and heterosexuals on weight and restricted eating,' *International Journal of Eating Disorders*, 11: 253–9.

Bray, G.A. (1986) 'Effects of obesity on health and happiness,' in K.D. Brownell and J.P. Foreyt (eds) *Handbook of eating disorders: Physiology, psychology and treatment of obesity, anorexia, and bulimia* (3–44), New York: Basic Books.

British Heart Foundation (1994) *Coronary heart disease statistics*, London: British Heart Foundation.

—— (2003) *Coronary heart disease statistics*, London: British Heart Foundation.

Brown, J. and Lawton, M. (1986) 'Stress and well-being in adolescence: The moderating role of physical exercise,' *Journal of Human Stress*, 12: 125–31.

Brown, L. (1987) 'Lesbians, weight and eating: New analyses and perspectives,' in Boston Lesbian Psychologies Collective (eds) *Lesbian psychologies* (294–309), Urbana, IL: University of Illinois Press.

Brownell, K.D. and Wadden, T. (1992) 'Etiology and treatment of obesity: Understanding a serious, prevalent, and refractory disorder,' *Journal of Counselling and Clinical Psychology*, 60: 505–17.

Brownell, K.D. and Rodin, J.R. (1994) 'The dieting maelstrom: Is it possible and advisable to lose weight?,' *American Psychologist*, 49: 781–91.

Brownell, K.D., Greenwood, M., Stellar, E. and Shrager, E. (1986) 'The effects of repeated cycles of weight loss and regain in rats,' *Physiology and Behaviour*, 38: 459–64.

Brownell, K.D., Rodin, J.R. and Wilmore, J. (1992) *Eating, body weight, and performance in athletes: Disorders of modern society*, Philadelphia: Lea and Febiger.

Brownmiller, S. (1984) *Femininity*, New York: Linden Press.

Bruch, H. (1962) 'Perceptual and conceptual disturbances in anorexia nervosa,' *Psychological Medicine*, 24: 187–94.

—— (1973) *Eating disorders: obesity, anorexia nervosa, and the person within*, New York: Basic Books.

Burgess, G., Grogan, S. and Burwitz, L. (2006) 'Effects of a 6-week aerobic dance intervention on body image and physical self-perceptions in adolescent girls,' *Body Image: An International Journal of Research*, 3: 57–67.

Buss, D. (1987) 'Sex differences in human mate selection criteria: An evolutionary perspective,' in C. Crawford, M. Smith and D. Krebs (eds) *Sociobiology and psychology: Ideas, issues, and application* (335–51), Hillsdale, NJ: Erlbaum.

—— (1989) 'Sex differences in human mate preference: Evolutionary hypothesis tested in 37 cultures,' *Behavioral and Brain Sciences*, 12: 1–49.

Butler, J. (1991) 'Imitation and gender insubordination,' in D. Fuss (ed.) *Inside out: Lesbian theories, gay theories* (13–32), New York: Routledge.

Button, E. (1993) *Eating disorders: Personal construct therapy and change*, Chichester, UK: Wiley.

Button, E., Sonuga-Barke, E., Davies, J. and Thompson, M. (1996) 'A prospective study of self-esteem in the prediction of eating problems in adolescent schoolgirls: Questionnaire findings,' *British Journal of Clinical Psychology*, 35: 193–203.

Cachelin, F.M., Striegel-Moore, R.H. and Elder, K.A. (1998) 'Realistic weight perception and body size assessment in a racially diverse community sample of dieters,' *Obesity Research*, 6: 62–8.

Cachelin, F.M., Monreal, T.K. and Juarez, L.C. (2006) 'Body image and size perceptions of Mexican-American women,' *Body Image: An International Journal of Research*, 3: 67–76.

Cafri, G. and Thompson, J.K. (2004) 'Measuring male body image: A review of the current methodology,' *Psychology of Men and Masculinity*, 5: 18–29.

Cafri, G., Thompson, J.K., Ricciardelli, L., McCabe, M., Smolak, L. and Yesalis, C. (2005) 'Pursuit of the muscular ideal: Physical and psychological consequences and putative risk factors,' *Clinical Psychology Review*, 25: 215–39.

Caitlin, D. and Hatton, C. (1991) 'Use and abuse of anabolic and other drugs for athletic enhancement,' *Advances in Internal Medicine*, 36: 399–424.

Caldwell, D. (1981) *And all was revealed: Ladies' underwear 1907–1980*, New York: St. Martin's Press.

Campbell, J. (2006) 'Cosmetic surgery: Women's experiences,' unpublished MSc Health Psychology dissertation, Staffordshire University.

Campos, P. (2004) *The obesity myth: Why America's obsession with weight is hazardous to your health*, New York: Gotham Books.

Carruth, B. and Goldberg, D. (1990) 'Nutritional issues of adolescents: Athletics and the body image mania,' *Journal of Early Adolescence*, 10: 122–40.

Cash, T.F. (1990) 'The psychology of physical appearance: Aesthetics, attributes, and images,' in T. Cash and T. Pruzinsky (eds) *Body images: Development, deviance and change* (51–79), New York: Guilford Press.

—— (2000) *Users manual for the Multidimensional Body–Self Relations Questionnaire*. Available from the author on http://www.body-images.com.

—— (2002) 'Cognitive-behavioural perspectives on body image,' in T.F. Cash and T. Pruzinsky (eds) *Body image: A handbook of theory, research, and clinical practice* (38–46), New York: Guilford.

—— (2004) 'Body image: Past, present and future,' *Body Image: An International Journal of Research*, 1: 1–5.

Cash, T. and Pruzinsky, T. (eds) (1990) *Body images: Development, deviance and change*, New York: Guilford Press.

Cash, T.F., and Szymanski, M.L. (1995) 'The development and validation of the Body-Ideals Questionnaire,' *Journal of Personality Assessment*, 64: 466–77.

Cash, T.F. and Labarge, A.S. (1996) 'Development of the Appearance Schemas Inventory: A new cognitive body-image assessment,' *Cognitive Therapy and Research*, 20: 37–50.

Cash, T.F. and Strachan, M.T. (2002) 'Cognitive-behavioral approaches to changing body image,' in T.F. Cash and T. Pruzinsky (eds), *Body image. A handbook of theory, research, and clinical practice* (478–86), New York: Guilford Press.

Cash, T.F. and Hrabosky, J.I. (2004) 'The effects of psycho-education and self-monitoring in a cognitive-behavioral program for body-image improvement,' *Eating Disorders*, 11: 255–70.

Cash, T., Winstead, B. and Janda, L. (1986) 'The great American shape-up: Body image survey report,' *Psychology Today*, 20(4): 30–7.

Cash, T.F., Cash, D.W. and Butters, J.W. (1983) 'Mirror, mirror on the wall . . .? Contrast effects and self-evaluations of physical attractiveness,' *Personality and Social Psychology*, 9: 359–64.

Cash, T., Ancis, J. and Strachan, M. (1997) 'Gender attitudes, feminist identity, and body images among college women,' *Sex Roles*, 36: 433–47.

Cash, T.F., Theriault, J. and Annis, N.M. (2004) 'Body image in an interpersonal context: Adult attachment, fear of intimacy, and social anxiety,' *Journal of Social and Clinical Psychology*, 23(1): 89–103.

Cattarin, J., Thompson, J.K., Thomas, C.M. and Williams, R. (2000) 'Body image, mood and televised images of attractiveness: the role of social comparison,' *Journal of Social and Clinical Psychology*, 19(2): 220–39.

Celio, A.A., Zabinski, M.F. and Wilfley, D.E. (2002) 'African-American body images,' in T.F. Cash and T. Pruzinsky (eds), *Body image. A handbook of theory, research, and clinical practice* (234–42), New York: Guilford Press.

Cepanec, D. and Payne, B. (2000) ' "Old bags" under the knife: Facial cosmetic surgery among women,' in B. Miedema, J.M. Stoppard and V. Anderson (eds) *Women's bodies, women's lives* (121–41), Toronto: Sumach Press.

Chapkis, W. (1986) *Beauty secrets*, London: Women's Press.

Chapman, R. (1988) 'The great pretender: Variations on the new man theme,' in R. Chapman and J. Rutherford (eds) *Male order: Unwrapping masculinity* (225–48), London: Lawrence and Wishart.

Charles, N. and Kerr, M. (1986) 'Food for feminist thought,' *Sociological Review*, 34: 537–72.

Chaudhary, V. (1996) 'The state we're in,' *The Guardian*, 11 June: 14.

Chernin, K. (1983) *Womansize: The tyranny of slenderness*, London: Women's Press.

Chesters, L. (1994) 'Women's talk: Food, weight and body image,' *Feminism and Psychology*, 4(3): 449–57.

Choi, P.Y.L. (2000a) 'Looking good and feeling good: Why do fewer women than men exercise?,' in J. Ussher (ed.) *Women's health* (372–9), Leicester: BPS Books.

Choi, P.Y.L. (2000b) *Femininity and the physically active woman*, London: Routledge.

Choi, P.Y.L. and Mutrie, N. (1997) 'The psychological benefits of physical exercise for women: Improving employee quality of life,' in J. Kerr, A. Griffiths and T. Cox (eds) *Workplace health: Employee fitness and exercise*, London: Taylor & Francis.

Christensen, L. (1997) *Experimental methodology* (7th edn), London: Allyn and Bacon.

Cohane, G.H. and Pope, H.J. (2001) 'Body image in boys: A review of the literature,' *International Journal of Eating Disorders*, 29(4): 373–9.

Collins, R. (1996) 'For better of worse: The impact of upward social comparison on self-evaluations,' *Psychological Bulletin*, 119(1): 51–69.

Connell, R. (1987) *Gender and power*, Cambridge: Polity Press.

Conner, M., Martin, E., Silverdale, N. and Grogan, S. (1996) 'Dieting in adolescence: An application of the theory of planned behaviour,' *British Journal of Health Psychology*, 1: 315–25.

Conner, M., Johnson, C. and Grogan, S. (2004) 'Gender, sexuality, body image and eating behaviours,' *Journal of Health Psychology*, 9(4): 505–15.

Connors, J. and Casey, P. (2006) 'Sex, body-esteem and self-esteem,' *Psychological Reports*, 98: 699–704.

Cooper, P., Taylor, M., Cooper, Z. and Fairburn, C. (1987) 'The development and validation of the Body Shape Questionnaire,' *International Journal of Eating Disorders*, 6: 485–94.

Cororve-Fingeret, M., Gleaves, D.H. and Pearson, C.A. (2004) 'On the methodology of body image assessment: The use of figural scales to evaluate body dissatisfaction and the ideal body standards of women,' *Body Image: An International Journal of Research*, 1: 207–12.

Cox, B.D., Huppert, F.A. and Whichelow, M.J. (eds) (1993) *The Health and Lifestyle Survey: Seven years on*, Aldershot, UK: Dartmouth.

Crago, M., Shisslak, C.M. and Estes, L.S. (1996) 'Eating disturbances among American minority groups: A review,' *International Journal of Eating Disorders*, 19: 239–48.

Crandall, C. (1995) 'Do parents discriminate against their heavyweight daughters?,' *Personality and Social Psychology Bulletin*, 21: 724–35.

Crandall, C. and Martinez, R. (1996) 'Culture, ideology, and anti-fat attitudes,' *Personality and Social Psychology Bulletin*, 22: 1165–76.

Cusumano, D.L. and Thompson, J.K. (1997) 'Body image and body shape ideals in magazines: Exposure, awareness and internalisation,' *Sex Roles*, 37: 701–21.

Darling-Wolf, F. (2000) 'From air-brushing to liposuction: The technological reconstruction of the female body,' in B. Miedema, J.M. Stoppard and V. Anderson (eds) *Women's bodies, women's lives* (277–93), Toronto: Sumach Press.

Davis, C. (1990) 'Body image and weight preoccupation: A comparison between exercising and non-exercising women,' *Appetite*, 15: 13–21.

Davis, C. and Dionne, M. (1990) 'Weight preoccupation and exercise: A structural equation analysis,' paper presented at the Fourth International Conference on Eating Disorders, New York, April 1990.

Davis, C., Elliot, S., Dionne, M. and Mitchell, I. (1991) 'The relationship of personality factors and physical activity to body satisfaction in men,' *Personality and Individual Differences*, 12: 689–94.

Davis, C., Fox, J., Brewer, H. and Ratusny, D. (1995) 'Motivations to exercise as a function of personality characteristics, age, and gender,' *Personality and Individual Differences*, 19: 165–74.

Davis, C., Dionne, M. and Schuster, B. (2001) 'Physical and psychological correlates of appearance orientation,' *Personality and Individual Differences*, 30: 21–30.

Davis, K. (1995) *Reshaping the female body: The dilemma of cosmetic surgery*, London: Routledge.

—— (2002) 'A dubious equality': Men and women in cosmetic surgery,' *Body and Society*, 8(1): 49–65.

DeMello, M. (2000) *Bodies of inscription: A cultural history of the modern tattoo community*, Durham, NC: Duke University Press.

Department of Health (1993) *The health of the nation*, London: HMSO.

—— (2002) *Breast implants: Information for women considering breast implants*, London: Department of Health.

Dewberry, C. and Ussher, J. (1995) 'Restraint and perception of body weight among British adults,' *Journal of Social Psychology*, 134: 609–19.

Dion, K., Berscheid, E. and Walster, E. (1972) 'What is beautiful is good,' *Journal of Personality and Social Psychology*, 24: 285–90.

Dionne, M., Davis, C., Fox, J. and Gurevich, M. (1995) 'Feminist ideology as a predictor of body dissatisfaction in women,' *Sex Roles*, 33(3/4): 277–87.

Dittmar, H. and Howard, S. (2004) 'Thin-ideal internalisation and social comparison tendency as moderators of media models' impact on women's body-focused anxiety,' *Journal of Social and Clinical Psychology*, 23: 768–91.

Dittmar, H., Halliwell, E. and Ive, S. (2006) 'Does Barbie make girls want to be thin? The effect of experimental exposure to images of dolls on the body image of 5- to 8-year-old girls,' *Developmental Psychology*, 42: 283–92.

Dolan, B.M., Birchnell, S.A. and Lacey, J.H. (1987) 'Body image distortion in non-eating disordered men and women,' *Journal of Psychosomatic Research*, 1: 513–20.

Donaldson, C. (1996) 'A study of male body image and the effects of the media,' unpublished BSc dissertation, Manchester Metropolitan University.

Doy, G. (1996) 'Out of Africa: Orientalism, "race", and the female body,' *Body and Society*, 2: 17–44.

Drewnowski, A. and Yee, D.K. (1987) 'Men and body image: Are males satisfied with their body weight?,' *Psychosomatic Medicine*, 49: 626–34.

Dworkin, A. (1988) 'Not in man's image: Lesbians and the cultural oppression of body image,' *Women and Therapy*, 8: 27–39.

Eagley, A., Ashmore, R., Makhijani, M. and Longo, L. (1991) 'What is beautiful is good but . . .: A meta-analytic review of research on the physical attractiveness stereotype,' *Psychological Bulletin*, 110: 109–28.

Economic and Social Science Research Council (2006) *ESRC Society Today – Diet and obesity in the UK* [*http://www.esrc.ac.uk/ESRCInfoCentre/facts/UK/index55.aspx?ComponentId=12741&SourcePageId=14975*] accessed 17 January 2007.

Elliot, S. (1994) 'Hunks in trunks hit a gap in the sports market,' *The Guardian*, 17 February: 14.

Ellis, S. and Heritage, P. (1989) 'AIDS and the cultural response: The normal heart and we all fall down,' in S. Shephard and M. Wallis (eds) *Coming on strong: Gay politics and culture* (39–53), London: Unwin Hyman.

Emery, J., Benson, P., Cohen-Tovee, E. and Tovee, M. (1995) 'A computerised measure of body image and body shape,' personal communication.

Engeln-Maddox, R. (2005) 'Cognitive responses to idealized media images of women: The relationship of social comparison and critical processing to body image disturbance in college women,' *Journal of Social and Clinical Psychology*, 24(8): 1114–38.

Epperley, T. (1993) 'Drugs and sports,' in W. Lillegard and K.S. Rucker (eds) *Handbook of sports medicine* (249–58), Stoneham, MA: Andover.

Ericksen, A.J., Markey, C.N. and Tinsley, B.J. (2005) 'Familial influences on Mexican-American and Euro-American preadolescent boys' and girls' body dissatisfaction,' *Eating Behaviours*, 4: 245–55.

Evans, C. and Dolan, B. (1992) 'Body Shape Questionnaire: Derivation of shortened "alternate forms" ,' *International Journal of Eating Disorders*, 13: 315–32.

Evans-Young, M. (1995) *Diet breaking: Having it all without having to die*, London: Hodder & Stoughton.

Ewing, W.A. (1994) *The body: Photoworks of the human form*, London: Thames and Hudson.

Fallon, A. (1990) 'Culture in the mirror: Sociocultural determinants of body image,' in T. Cash and T. Pruzinsky (eds) *Body images: Development, deviance and change* (80–109), New York: Guilford Press.

Fallon, A. and Rozin, P. (1985) 'Sex differences in perceptions of desirable body shape,' *Journal of Abnormal Psychology*, 94(1): 102–5.

Fawkner, H. (2004) 'Body image attitudes in men: An examination of the ante-cedents and consequent adjustive strategies and behaviors,' unpublished PhD thesis, University of Melbourne.

Featherstone, M. (1991) 'The body in consumer culture,' in M. Featherstone, M. Hepworth and B.S. Turner (eds) *The body: Social processes and cultural theory* (170–96), London: Sage.

——(1999) 'Body modification: An introduction.' *Body and Society*, 5(2–3): 1–4.

Ferguson, M. (1985) *Forever feminine: Women's magazines and the cult of femininity*, Aldershot, UK: Gower.

Festinger, L. (1954) 'A theory of social comparison processes,' *Human Relations*, 7: 117–40.

Fisher, S. (1990) 'The evolution of psychological concepts about the body,' in T. Cash and T. Pruzinsky (eds) *Body images: Development, deviance and change* (3–20), New York: Guilford Press.

Flegal, K.M., Graubard, B.I., Williamson, D.F. and Gail, M.H. (2005) 'Excess deaths associated with underweight, overweight, and obesity,' *Journal of the American Medical Association*, 293: 1861–7.

Forna, A. (1996) 'For women, or for men only?,' *The Independent on Sunday*, 28 April.

Forston, M.T. and Stanton, A.L. (1992) 'Self-discrepancy theory as a frame-work for understanding bulimic symptomatology and associated distress,' *Journal of Social and Clinical Psychology*, 11(2): 103–18.

Fox, P. and Yamaguchi, C. (1997) 'Body image change in pregnancy: A com-parison of normal weight and overweight primagravidas,' *Birth Issues in Perinatal Care*, 24: 35–40.

Francis, B. (1989) *Bev Francis' power bodybuilding*, New York: Stirling.

Franco, D.L. and Herrera, I. (1997) 'Body image differences in Guatemalan-American and white college women,' *Eating Disorders*, 5: 119–27.

Frankel, S. (1998) 'The fashion of destruction,' *The Guardian*, 7 February: 5.

Franzoi, S. and Shields, S. (1984) 'The body esteem scale: Multidimensional structure and sex differences in a college population,' *Journal of Personality Assessment*, 448: 173–8.

Franzoi, S.L. and Chang, Z. (2002) 'The body esteem of Hmong and Causasian young adults,' *Psychology of Women Quarterly*, 26: 89–91.

Frederick, D.A., Fessler, D.M.T. and Haselton, M.G. (2005) 'Do representa-tions of male muscularity differ in men's and women's magazines?,' *Body Image: An International Journal of Research*, 2: 81–6.

Frederickson, B.L. and Roberts, T. (1997) 'Objectification theory: Towards understanding women's lived experience and mental health risks,' *Psychology of Women Quarterly*, 21: 173–206.

Frederickson, B.L., Roberts, T., Noll, S.M., Quinn, D.M. and Twenge, J.M. (1998) 'That swimsuit becomes you: Sex differences in self-objectification, restrained eating and math performance,' *Journal of Personality and Social Psychology*, 75: 269–84.

Freedman, R. (1986) *Beauty bound*, Lexington, MA: Lexington Books.

—— (1990) 'Cognitive-behavioral perspectives on body image change,' in T. Cash and T. Pruzinsky (eds) *Body images: Development, deviance and change* (272–95), New York: Guilford Press.

Freeman, H. (2007) 'Celebrity fit club,' *The Guardian*, 23 January: 17–19.

French, S.A., Story M., Remafedi, G. and Resnik, M.D. (1996) 'Sexual orientation and prevalence of body dissatisfaction and eating disordered behaviors: A population-based study of adolescents,' *International Journal of Eating Disorders*, 19: 119–26.

Furnham, A. and Alibhai, N. (1983) 'Cross cultural differences in the perception of male and female body shapes,' *Psychological Medicine*, 13: 829–37.

Furnham, A. and Greaves, N. (1994) 'Gender and locus of control correlates of body image dissatisfaction,' *European Journal of Personality*, 8: 183–200.

Furnham, A., Titman, P. and Sleeman, E. (1994) 'Perception of female body shapes as a function of exercise,' *Journal of Social Behaviour and Personality*, 9: 335–52.

Fuss, D. (1989) *Essentially speaking: Feminism, nature and difference*, New York and London: Routledge.

Gaesser, G. (2002) *Big fat lies: The truth about your weight and your health*, Carlsbad, CA: Gurze Books.

Gaines, C. and Butler, G. (1980) *Pumping iron: The art and sport of bodybuilding*, London: Sphere.

Gannon, L. (2000) 'Psychological well-being in aging women,' in J. Ussher (ed.) *Women's health: Contemporary international perspectives* (476–85), Leicester, UK: BPS Books.

Gardner, R.M. and Moncrieff, C. (1988) 'Body image distortion in anorexics as a non-sensory phenomenon: A signal detection approach,' *Journal of Clinical Psychology*, 44: 101–7.

Garner, D.M. (1997) 'The 1997 body image survey results,' *Psychology Today*, 30(1): 30–48.

Garner, D., Garfinkel, P., Schwartz, D. and Thompson, M. (1980) 'Cultural expectations of thinness in women,' *Psychological Reports*, 47: 483–91.

Garner, D., Olmsted, M. and Garfinkel, P. (1983a) 'Does anorexia nervosa occur on a continuum?,' *International Journal of Eating Disorders*, 2: 11–20.

Garner, D., Olmsted, M. and Polivy, J. (1983b) 'Development and validation of a multidimensional eating disorder inventory for anorexia nervosa and bulimia,' *International Journal of Eating Disorders*, 2: 15–34.

Gillespie, R. (1996) 'Women, the body, and brand extension of medicine: Cosmetic surgery and the paradox of choice,' *Women and Health*, 24: 69–85.

Gittelson, J., Harris, S., Thorne-Lyman, A., Hanley, A., Barnie, A. and Zinman, B. (1996) 'Body image concepts differ by age and sex in an Ojibway-Cree community in Canada,' *Journal of Nutrition*, 126: 2990–3000.

Gordon, R. (1990) *Anorexia and bulimia: Anatomy of a social epidemic*, Oxford: Blackwell.

Gough, B. (2007) ' "Real men don't diet": An analysis of contemporary newspaper representations of men, food and health,' *Social Science and Medicine*, 64: 326–37.

Gough, J. (1989) 'Theories of sexual identity and the masculinisation of the gay man,' in S. Shepherd and M. Wallis (eds) *Coming on strong: Gay politics and culture* (119–35), London: Unwin Hyman.

Grabe, S. and Hyde, J. (2006) 'Ethnicity and body dissatisfaction among women in the United States: A meta-analysis,' *Psychological Bulletin*, 132(4): 622–40.

Greenleaf, C., Starks, M., Gomez, L., Chambliss, H. and Martin, S. (2004) 'Weight-related words associated with figure silhouettes,' *Body Image: An International Journal of Research*, 1: 373–85.

Greil, H. (1990) 'Sex differences in body build and their relationship to sex-specific processes of ageing,' *Collegium Anthropologicum*, 14: 247–53.

Groetz, L.M., Levine, M.P. and Murnen, S.K. (2002) 'The effect of experimental presentation of thin media images on body satisfaction: A meta-analytic review,' *International Journal of Eating Disorders*, 31: 1–16.

Grogan, S. (1999) *Body image: Understanding body dissatisfaction in men, women and children*, London: Routledge.

—— (2006) 'Body image and health: Contemporary perspectives,' *Journal of Health Psychology*, 11(4): 523–30.

Grogan, S. and Wainwright, N. (1996) 'Growing up in the culture of slenderness: Girls' experiences of body dissatisfaction,' *Women's Studies International Forum*, 19: 665–73.

Grogan, S. and Richards, H. (2002) 'Body image; focus groups with boys and men,' *Men and Masculinities*, 4: 219–133.

Grogan, S., Shepherd, S., Evans, R., Wright, S. and Hunter, G. (2006a) 'Experiences of anabolic steroid use; interviews with men and women steroid users,' *Journal of Health Psychology*, 11(6): 849–60.

Grogan, S., Williams, Z. and Conner, M. (1996) 'The effects of viewing same gender photographic models on body satisfaction,' *Women and Psychology Quarterly*, 20: 569–75.

Grogan, S., Donaldson, C., Richards, H. and Wainwright, N. (1997) 'Men's body image: Body dissatisfaction in eight- to twenty-five-year-old males,' paper presented to the European Health Psychology annual conference, Bordeaux, 3 September.

Grogan, S., Evans, R., Wright, S. and Hunter, G. (2004) 'Femininity and muscularity: Accounts of seven women bodybuilders,' *Journal of Gender Studies*, 13(1): 49–63.

Grogan, S., Conner, M. and Smithson, H. (2006b) 'Sexuality and exercise motivations: Are gay men and heterosexual women most likely to be motivated by concern about weight and appearance?,' *Sex Roles*, 55(7–8): 567–72.

Guillen, E. and Barr, S. (1994) 'Nutrition, dieting, and fitness messages in a magazine for adolescent women, 1970–1990,' *Journal of Adolescent Health*, 15: 464–72.

Guinn, B., Semper, T., Jorgensen, L. and Skaggs, S. (1997) 'Body image perception in female Mexican American adolescents,' *Journal of School Health*, 67: 112–15.

Haiken, E. (1997) *Venus envy: A history of cosmetic surgery*, Baltimore and London: Johns Hopkins University Press.

Halliwell, E. and Dittmar, H. (2004) 'Does size matter? The impact of model's body size on women's body-focused anxiety and advertising effectiveness,' *Journal of Social and Clinical Psychology*, 23(1): 104–22.

—— (2005) 'The role of self-improvement and self-evaluation motives in social comparisons with idealised female bodies in the media,' *Body Image: An International Journal of Research*, 2: 249–62.

Hanna, C.F., Loro, A.D. and Power, D.D. (1981) 'Differences in the degree of overweight: A note on its importance,' *Addictive Behaviors*, 6: 61–2.

Hargreaves, D. and Tiggemann, M. (2002) 'The effect of television commercials on mood and body dissatisfaction: The role of appearance-schema activation,' *Journal of Social and Clinical Psychology*, 21: 287–308.

—— (2006) ' "Body image is for girls": A qualitative study of boys' body image,' *Journal of Health Psychology*, 11: 567–76.

Harris, M.B., Walters, L.C. and Waschull, S. (1991) 'Gender and ethnic differences in obesity-related behaviors and attitudes in a college sample,' *Journal of Applied Social Psychology*, 21: 1545–66.

Harris, S. (1994) 'Racial differences in predictors of college women's body image attitudes,' *Women and Health*, 21: 89–104.

Harrison, K. (2000) 'Television viewing, fat stereotyping, body shape standards, and eating disorder symptomatology in grade school children,' *Communication Research*, 27: 617–40.

Hatfield, E. and Sprecher, S. (1986) *Mirror, mirror: The importance of looks in everyday life*, New York: State University of New York Press.

Health and Safety Executive (2001) *Health and safety issues related to body piercing, tattooing and scarification* [www.hse.gov.uk/lau/lacs/76-2.htm] accessed 22 May 2003.

Heinberg, L. and Thompson, J.K. (1992) 'Social comparison: Gender, target importance ratings, and relation to body image disturbance,' *Journal of Social Behavior and Personality*, 7: 335–44.

—— (1995) 'Body image and televised images of thinness and attractiveness: A controlled laboratory investigation,' *Journal of Social and Clinical Psychology*, 14: 325–38.

Heinberg, L., Thompson, J.K. and Stormer, S. (1995) 'Development and validation of the Sociocultural Attitudes Toward Appearance Questionnaire,' *International Journal of Eating Disorders*, 17(1): 81–9.

Henwood, K., Gill, R. and McLean, C. (2002) 'The changing man,' *The Psychologist*, 15: 182–6.

Higgins, E.T. (1987) 'Self-discrepancy: A theory relating self and affect,' *Psychological Review*, 94(3): 319–40.

Higgins, E.T., Klein, R. and Strauman, T. (1992) 'Self-concept discrepancy theory: A psychological model for distinguishing among different aspects of depression and anxiety,' *Social Cognition*, 3: 51–76.

Hildebrandt, T., Langenbucher, J., Carr, S., Sanjuan, P. and Park, S. (2006) 'Predicting intentions for long-term anabolic steroid use among men: A covariance structure model,' *Psychology of Addictive Behaviors*, 20: 234–40.

Hill, A., Oliver, S. and Rogers, P. (1992) 'Eating in the adult world: The rise of dieting in childhood and adolescence,' *British Journal of Clinical Psychology*, 31: 95–105.

Hodkinson, W. (1997) 'Body image stereotypes: The idealisation of slimness and perceptions of body image and occupational success,' unpublished BSc dissertation, Manchester Metropolitan University.

Hofstede, G. (1980) *Culture's consequences: International differences in work-related values*, Beverly Hills, CA: Sage.

Hogg, M.A. and Vaughan, G.M. (1995) *Social Psychology*, Hemel Hempstead, UK: Prentice-Hall Europe.

Holt, K. and Ricciardelli, L.A. (2002) 'Social comparisons and negative affect as indicators of problem eating and muscle preoccupation among children,' *Journal of Applied Developmental Psychology*, 23: 285–304.

Hopkins, V. (2006) 'Understanding pre-pubescent and post-pubescent boys' body image: An interpretative phenomenological analysis,' unpublished MSc Health Psychology dissertation, Staffordshire University.

Horm, J. and Anderson, K. (1993) 'Who in America is trying to lose weight?,' *Annals of Internal Medicine*, 119: 672–6.

Hough, D.O. (1990) 'Anabolic steroids and ergogenic aids,' *American Family Physician*, 41: 1157–64.

Huddy, D.C. and Cash, T.F. (1997) 'Body-image attitudes among male marathon runners: A controlled comparative study,' *International Journal of Sport Psychology*, 28: 227–36.

Huon, G. (1988) 'Towards the prevention of eating disorders,' in D. Hardoff and E. Chigier (eds) *Eating disorders in adolescents and young adults* (447–54), London: Freund.

—— (1994) 'Towards the prevention of dieting-induced disorders: Modifying negative food- and body-related attitudes,' *International Journal of Eating Disorders*, 16(4): 395–9.

Huon, G., Morris, S. and Brown, L. (1990) 'Differences between male and female preferences for female body size,' *Australian Psychologist*, 25: 314–17.

Huxley, C. and Grogan, S. (2005) 'Tattooing, piercing, healthy behaviours and health value,' *Journal of Health Psychology*, 10(6): 831–41.

Institute for the Study of Drug Dependence (1993) *Steroids*, London: College Hill Press.

Irving, L. (1990) 'Mirror images: Effects of the standard of beauty on the self- and body-esteem of women exhibiting varying levels of bulimic symptoms,' *Journal of Social and Clinical Psychology*, 9: 230–42.

Irving, L.M. and Beral, S.R. (2001) 'Comparison of media-literacy programs to strengthen college women's resistance to media images,' *Psychology of Women Quarterly*, 25(3): 103–11.

Iwawaki, S. and Lerner, R.M. (1974) 'Cross-cultural analyses of body–behavior relations. I. A comparison of body build stereotypes of Japanese and American males and females,' *Psychologia*, 17: 75–81.

Jarry, J.L. and Beraldi, K. (2004) 'Characteristics and effectiveness of stand-alone body image treatments: A review of the empirical literature,' *Body Image: An International Journal of Research*, 1: 319–33.

Jarry, J.L. and Ip, K. (2005) The effectiveness of stand-alone cognitive-behavioural therapy for body image: A meta-analysis', *Body Image: An International Journal of Research*, 2: 317–33.

Jones, D.C. (2004) 'Body image in adolescent girls and boys: A longitudinal study,' *Developmental Psychology*, 40(5): 823–35.

Kawamura, K. (2002) 'Asian-American body images,' in T.F. Cash and T. Pruzinsky (eds) *Body image: A handbook of theory, research, and clinical practice* (243–9), New York: Guilford Press.

Kay, R. (2004) 'Now it's size six Sophie,' *Daily Mail*, 23 August: 1.

Kennard, J. (2006) *Male cosmetic surgery* [http://menshealth.about.com/cs/surgery/a/cosmetic.htm] accessed 20 November 2006.

Kenrick, D.T. (1989) 'Bridging social psychology and socio-biology: The case of sexual attraction,' in R.W. Bell and N.J. Bell (eds) *Sociobiology and social sciences* (5–23), Lubbock, TX: Texas Tech University Press.

Kiernan, M., Rodin, J., Brownell, K.D., Wilmore, J.H. and Crandall, C. (1992) 'Relation of level of exercise, age, and weight-cycling history to weight and eating concerns in male and female runners,' *Health Psychology*, 11: 418–21.

Kim, O. and Kim, K. (2001) 'Body weight self-esteem and depression in Korean female adolescents,' *Adolescence*, 36: 315–22.

King, T.K., Matacin, M., White, K. and Marcus, B.H. (2005) 'A prospective examination of body image and smoking cessation in women,' *Body Image: An International Journal of Research*, 2: 19–28.

Kitzinger, C. (1987) *The social construction of lesbianism*, London: Sage.

Koenig, L.M. and Carnes, M. (1999) 'Body piercing: Medical concerns and cutting-edge fashion,' *Journal of General Internal Medicine*, 14: 379–85.

Koff, E. and Bauman, C. (1997) 'Effects of wellness, fitness, and sport skills programs on body image and lifestyle behaviors,' *Perceptual and Motor Skills*, 84: 555–62.

Korkia, P. (1994) 'Anabolic steroid use in Britain,' *International Journal of Drug Policy*, 5: 6–9.

Kowner, R. (2002) 'Japanese body image: Structure and esteem scores in a cross-cultural perspective,' *International Journal of Psychology*, 37: 149–59.

LaFrance, M.N. Zivian, M.T. and Myers, A.M. (2000) 'Women, weight and appearance satisfaction: An ageless pursuit of thinness,' in B. Miedema, J.M. Stoppard and V. Anderson (eds) *Women's bodies, women's lives* (227–36), Toronto: Sumach Press.

Lakoff, R.T. and Scherr, R.L. (1984) *Face value: The politics of beauty*, Boston: Routledge and Kegan Paul.

Lamb, C.S., Jackson, L., Cassiday, P. and Priest, D. (1993) 'Body figure preferences of men and women: A comparison of two generations,' *Sex Roles*, 28: 345–58.

Laure, P., Lecerf, T., Friser, A. and Binsinger, C. (2004) 'Drugs, recreational drug use and attitudes towards doping of high school athletes,' *International Journal of Sports Medicine*, 25: 133–8.

Leit, R.A., Pope, H.G. Jr. and Gray, J.J. (2001) 'Cultural expectations of muscularity in men: The evolution of *Playgirl* centerfolds,' *International Journal of Eating Disorders*, 29: 90–3.

Leit, R.A., Gray, J.J. and Pope, H.G.J. (2002) 'The media's representation of the ideal male body: A cause for muscle dysmorphia?,' *International Journal of Eating Disorders*, 31: 334–8.

Leith, W. (2006) 'We used to settle for one like this; now we all want one like this,' *Observer Woman*, February Edition: 30–5.

Lennehan, P. (2003) *Anabolic steroids*, London: Taylor & Francis.

Lerner, R.M. and Korn, S.J. (1972) 'The development of body build stereotypes in males,' *Child Development*, 43: 912–20.

Levesque, M. and Vichesky, D. (2006) 'Raising the bar on the body beautiful: An analysis of the body image concerns of homosexual men,' *Body Image: An International Journal of Research*, 3: 45–56.

Levine, M.P. and Smolak, L. (2002) 'Ecological and activism approaches to the prevention of body image problems,' in T.F. Cash and T. Pruzinsky (eds) *Body image: A handbook of theory, research, and clinical practice* (497–505), New York: Guilford Press.

Levine, M.P. and Piran, N. (2004) 'The role of body image in the prevention of eating disorders,' *Body Image: An International Journal of Research*, 1: 57–70.

Levine, M.P., Smolak, L. and Hayden, H. (1994) 'The relation of sociocultural factors to eating attitudes and behaviors among middle school girls,' *Journal of Early Adolescence*, 14(4): 471–90.

Lewis, R. (1996) *Gendering orientalism: Race, femininity and representation*, London: Routledge.

Lewis, R.J., Cash, T.F., Jacobi, L. and Bubb-Lewis, C. (1997) 'Prejudice toward fat people: The development and validation of the Antifat Attitudes Test,' *Obesity Research*, 5: 297–307.

Lewis, V., Blair, A. and Booth, D. (1992) 'Outcome of group therapy for body-image emotionality and weight-control self-efficacy,' *Behavioural Psychotherapy*, 20: 155–65.

Long, G.E. and Rickman, L.S. (1994) 'Infectious complications of tattoos,' *Clinical Infectious Diseases*, 18: 610–19.

Lorenzen, L.A., Grieve, F.G. and Thomas, A. (2004) 'Exposure to muscular male models decreases men's body satisfaction,' *Sex Roles*, 51: 743–8.

Ludwig, M.R. and Brownell, K.D. (1999) 'Lesbians, bisexual women and body image: An investigation of gender roles and social group affiliation,' *International Journal of Eating Disorders*, 25: 89–7.

Luo, Y., Parish, W.L. and Laumann, E.O. (2005) 'A population-based study of body image concerns among urban Chinese adults,' *Body Image: An International Journal of Research*, 2: 333–47.

Lynch, S.M. and Zellner, D.A. (1999) 'Figure preferences in two generations of men: The use of figure drawings illustrating differences in muscle mass,' *Sex Roles*, 40: 833–43.

McAlpine, J. (1993) 'Mr Muscle cleans up,' *The Scotsman*, 13 August: 4.

McCabe, M.P. and Ricciardelli, L.A. (2001) 'Body image and body change techniques among young adolescent boys,' *European Eating Disorders Review*, 9: 335–47.

—— (2003) 'Sociocultural influences on body image and body changes among adolescent boys and girls,' *Journal of Social Psychology*, 193: 5–26.

—— (2004) 'Body image dissatisfaction among males across the lifespan: A review of past literature,' *Journal of Psychosomatic Research*, 56: 675–85.

McCabe, M.P., Ricciardelli, L.A., Sitaram, G. and Mikhail, K. (2006) 'Accuracy of body size estimation: Role of biopsychosocial variables,' *Body Image: An International Journal of Research*, 3: 163–73.

McCreary, D.R. and Sasse, D.K. (2000) 'Exploring the drive for muscularity in adolescent boys and girls,' *Journal of American College Health*, 48: 297–304.

—— (2002) 'Gender differences in high school students' dieting behaviour and their correlates,' *International Journal of Men's Health*, 1: 195–213.

McCreary, D.R., Sasse, D.K., Saucier, D.M. and Dorsch, K.D. (2004) 'Measuring the drive for muscularity: Factorial validity of the Drive for Muscularity Scale in men and women,' *Psychology of Men and Masculinity*, 6: 83–94.

McCreary, D.R., Saucier, D. and Courtenay, W. (2005) 'The drive for muscularity and masculinity: Testing the associations among gender-role traits, behaviours, attitudes, and conflict,' *Psychology of Men and Masculinity*, 6: 83–94.

McCreary, D.R., Karvinen, K. and Davis, C. (2006) 'The relationship of drive for muscularity and anthropometric measures of muscularity and adiposity,' *Body Image: An International Journal of Research*, 3: 145–53.

Major, B., Testa, M. and Bylsma, W. (1991) 'Responses to upward and downward social comparisons: The impact of esteem relevance and perceived control,' in J. Suls and T. Wills (eds) *Social comparison: contemporary theory and research* (237–60), Hillsdale, NJ: Erlbaum.

Maloney, M., McGuire, J., Daniels, S. and Specker, B. (1989) 'Dieting behaviour and eating attitudes in children,' *Pediatrics*, 84: 482–9.

Malson, H. (2000) 'Anorexia nervosa,' in J. Ussher (ed.) *Women's Health* (363–71). Leicester, UK: BPS Books.

Mansfield, A. and McGinn, B. (1993) 'Pumping irony: The muscular and the feminine,' in S. Scott and D. Morgan (eds) *Body matters* (49–68), London: Falmer.

Marchessault, G. (2000) 'One mother and daughter approach to resisting weight preoccupation,' in B. Miedema, J.M. Stoppard and V. Anderson (eds) *Women's bodies, women's lives* (203–26), Toronto: Sumach Press.

Markus, H. (1977) 'Self-schema and processing information about the self,' *Journal of Personality and Social Psychology*, 35: 63–78.

Markus, H., Hamill, R. and Sentis, K. (1987) 'Thinking fat: Self-schemas for body-weight and the processing of weight-relevant information,' *Journal of Applied Social Psychology*, 17(1): 50–71.

Marshall, J. (1981) 'Pansies, perverts and macho men: Changing conceptions of male homosexuality,' in K. Plummer (ed.) *The making of the modern homosexual* (133–54), London: Hutchinson.

Martin, K.A. and Lichtenberger, C.M. (2002) 'Fitness enhancement and changes in body image,' in T.F. Cash and T. Pruzinsky (eds) *Body image: A handbook of theory, research, and clinical practice* (414–21), New York: Guilford Press.

Martin-Ginis, K.A., Eng, J.J., Arbour, K.P., Hartman, J.W. and Phillips, S.M. (2005) 'Mind over muscle? Sex differences in the relationship between body image change and subjective and objective physical changes following a 12-week strength training program,' *Body Image: An International Journal of Research*, 2: 363–72.

Mayers, L.B., Judelson, D.A., Moriarty, B.W. and Rundell, K.W. (2002) 'Prevalence of body art (body piercing and tattooing) in university undergraduates and incidence of medical complications,' *Mayo Clinic Proceedings*, 77: 29–34.

Mazur, A. (1986) 'U.S. trends in feminine beauty and overadaption,' *Journal of Sex Research*, 22: 281–303.

Melnick, M.J. and Mookerjee, S. (1991) 'Effects of advanced weight training on body-cathexis and self-esteem,' *Perceptual and Motor Skills*, 72: 1335–45.

Meredith, B. (1988) *A change for the better*, London: Grafton.

Metropolitan Life Assurance Company (1983) *Statistical bulletin*, New York: Metropolitan Life Assurance Company.

Meyer, R. (1991) 'Rock Hudson's body,' in D. Fuss (ed.) *Inside out: Lesbian theories, gay theories* (259–90), New York: Routledge.

Miller, C.T. (1984) 'Self schemas, gender and social comparison: A clarification of the related attributes hypothesis,' *Journal of Personality and Social Psychology*, 46: 1222–9.

Miller, K.J., Gleaves, D.H., Hirsch, T.G., Green, B.A., Snow, A.C. and Corbett, C.C. (2000) 'Comparisons of body image dimensions by race/ethnicity and gender in a university population,' *International Journal of Eating Disorders*, 27: 310–16.

Mintz, L. and Betz, N. (1986) 'Sex differences in the nature, realism, and correlates of body image,' *Sex Roles*, 15: 185–95.

Mishkind, M., Rodin, J., Silberstein, L. and Striegel-Moore, R. (1986) 'The embodiment of masculinity: Cultural, psychological, and behavioral dimensions,' *American Behavioral Scientist*, 29: 545–62.

Mitchell, J. (1989) ' "Going for the burn" and "pumping iron": What's healthy about the current fitness boom?,' in M. Lawrence (ed.) *Fed up and hungry: Women, oppression, and food* (156–74), London: Women's Press.

Monaghan, L. (1999) 'Challenging medicine? Bodybuilding, drugs and risk,' *Sociology of Health and Illness*, 21(6): 707–34.

—— (2005a) 'Discussion piece: A critical take on the obesity debate,' *Social Theory and Health*, 3: 302–14.

—— (2005b) 'Big handsome men, bears and others: Virtual constructions of "fat male embodiment," ' *Body and Society*, 11: 81–111.

Monteath, S.A. and McCabe, M.P. (2006) 'The influence of societal factors on female body image,' *Journal of Social Psychology*, 137: 708–27.

Morgan, D. (1993) 'You too can have a body like mine: Reflections on the male body and masculinities,' in S. Scott and D. Morgan (eds) *Body matters* (69–88), London: Falmer.

Morgan, K. (1991) 'Women and the knife: Cosmetic surgery and the coloniza-tion of women's bodies,' *Hypatia*, 6: 25–53.

Morris, D. (1985) *Bodywatching*, New York: Crown.

Morrison, M.A., Morrison, T.G. and Sager, C.-L. (2004) 'Does body satisfac-tion differ between gay men and lesbian women and heterosexual men and women?,' *Body Image: An International Journal of Research*, 1: 127–38.

Mort, F. (1988) 'Boys' own? Masculinity, style and popular culture,' in R. Chapman and J. Rutherford (eds) *Male order: Unwrapping masculinity*, London: Lawrence and Wishart.

Muller, M. (1998) *A part of my life – photographs*, London: Scalo.

Myers, B.S. and Copplestone, T. (1985) *Landmarks of Western art*, Feltham, UK: Newnes.

Myers, P. and Biocca, F. (1992) 'The elastic body image: The effects of television advertising and programming on body image distortions in young women,' *Journal of Communication*, 42: 108–33.

Myers, R. and Roth, D. (1997) 'Perceived benefits and barriers to exercise and stage of exercise,' *Health Psychology*, 16: 277–83.

Nagami, Y. (1997) 'Eating disorders in Japan: A review of the literature,' *Psych-iatry and Clinical Neuroscience*, 51: 339–46.

Nayak, A. (1997) 'Disclosing whiteness in Haagen-Dazs advertising,' *Body and Society*, (3): 33–51.

National Eating Disorders Association (2002) [*http://www.nationaleatingdis-orders.org/nedaDir/files/documents/handouts/stats.pdf*] accessed 10 January 2007.

Neff, L., Sargent, R., McKeown, R., Jackson, K. and Valois, R. (1997) 'Black–white differences in body size perceptions and weight management practices among adolescent females,' *Journal of Adolescent Health*, 20: 459–65.

Negrao, A.B. and Cordas, T.A. (1996) 'Clinical characteristics and course of anorexia nervosa in Latin America, a Brazilian sample,' *Psychiatry Research*, 62: 17–21.

Neumark-Sztainer, D., Croll, J., Story, M., Hanno, P.J., French, S.A. and Perry, C. (2002) 'Ethnic/race differences in weight-control concerns and behaviours among adolescent girls and boys: Findings from project EAT,' *Journal of Psychosomatic Research*, 53: 963–74.

Neumark-Sztainer, D., Paxton, S.J., Hannon, P.J., Haines, J. and Story, M. (2006) 'Does body satisfaction matter? Five-year longitudinal associations between body satisfaction and health behaviours in adolescent females and males,' *Journal of Adolescent Health*, 39: 244–51.

Nichter, M. (2000) *Fat talk: What girls and their parents say about dieting*, Cambridge, MA: Harvard University Press.

Nishina, A., Ammon, N.Y., Bellmore, A.D. and Graham, S. (2006) 'Body dis-satisfaction and physical development among ethnic minority adolescents,' *Journal of Youth and Adolescence*, 35(2): 189–201.

Nochlin, L. (1991) *The politics of vision*, London: Thames and Hudson.

O'Dea, J. (1995) *Everybody's different – A self-esteem program for young adoles-cents*, Sydney: University of Sydney.

—— (2004) 'Evidence for a self-esteem approach in the prevention of body image and eating problems among children and adolescents,' *Eating Disorders*, 12: 225–41.

O'Dea, J.A. and Abraham, S. (2000) 'Improving the body image, eating attitudes and behaviors of young male and female adolescents: A new educational approach that focuses on self-esteem,' *International Journal of Eating Disorders*, 28: 43–57.

O'Dea, J. and Caputi, P. (2001) 'Association between socioeconomic status, weight, age and gender, and the body image and weight control practices of 6- to 19-year-old children and adolescents,' *Health Education Research*, 16(5): 521–32.

Office of National Statistics (ONS) (2005) *Health related behaviour: Gender.* [*http://statistics.gov.uk/cci/nugget.asp?id=1658*] accessed 21 November 2006.

Ogden, J. (1992) *Fat chance: The myth of dieting explained*, London: Routledge.

Ogden, J. and Mundray, K. (1996) 'The effect of the media on body satisfaction: the role of gender and size,' *European Eating Disorders Review*, 4: 171–81.

O'Kelly, L. (1994) 'Body talk,' *The Guardian*, 23 October: 30–2.

Olivardia, R. (2002) 'Body image and muscularity,' in T.F. Cash and T. Pruzinsky (eds) *Body image: A handbook of theory, research, and clinical practice* (210–18), New York: Guilford Press.

Orbach, S. (1993) *Hunger strike: The anorectic's struggle as a metaphor for our age*, London: Penguin.

Paxton, S.J. (1993) 'A prevention programme for disturbed eating in adolescent girls: A one year follow up,' *Health Education Research: Theory and Practice*, 8: 43–51.

Paxton, S.J., Neumark-Sztainer, D., Hannon, P.J. and Eisenberg, M.E. (2006) 'Body dissatisfaction prospectively predicts depressive mood and low self-esteem in adolescent girls and boys,' *Journal of Clinical Child and Adolescent Psychology*, 35: 539–49.

Peterson, R.D., Tantleff-Dunn, S. and Bedwell, J.S. (2006) 'The effects of exposure to feminist ideology on women's body image,' *Body Image: An International Journal of Research*, 3: 237–46.

Petrie, T.A. (1996) 'Differences between male and female college lean sport athletes, nonlean sport athletes, and nonathletes on behavioral and psychological indices of eating disorders,' *Journal of Applied Sport Psychology*, 8: 218–30.

Piran, N. (1996) 'The reduction of preoccupation with body weight and shape in schools: A feminist approach,' *Eating Disorders: The Journal of Treatment and Prevention*, 4(4): 323–33.

Piran, N., Jasper, K. and Pinhas, L. (2004) 'Feminist therapy and eating disorders,' in J.K. Thompson (ed.) *Handbook of eating disorders and obesity*, Hoboken, NJ: Wiley.

Pitts, V.L. (2003) *In the flesh: The cultural politics of body modification*, New York: Palgrave Macmillan.

Pliner, P., Chaiken, S. and Flett, G. (1990) 'Gender differences in concern with body weight and physical appearance over the life span,' *Personality and Social Psychology Bulletin*, 16: 263–73.

Polivy, J. and Herman, C. (1983) *Breaking the diet habit*, New York: Basic Books.

Pope, H., Katz, D. and Hudson, J. (1993) 'Anorexia nervosa and "reverse anorexia" among 108 male bodybuilders,' *Comprehensive Psychiatry*, 34: 406–9.

Pope, H.G., Phillips, K.A. and Olivardia, R. (2000) *The Adonis complex: The secret crisis of male body obsession*, New York: Free Press.

Posavac, H.D., Posavac, S.S. and Weigel, R.G. (2001) 'Reducing the impact of media images on women at risk for body image disturbance: Three targeted interventions,' *Journal of Social and Clinical Psychology*, 20(3): 324–40.

Pruzinsky, T. and Cash, T. (1990) 'Integrative themes in body-image development, deviance and change,' in T. Cash and T. Pruzinsky (eds) *Body images: Development, deviance and change* (337–49), New York: Guilford Press.

Pruzinsky, T. and Edgerton, M. (1990) 'Body image change in cosmetic plastic surgery,' in T. Cash and T. Pruzinsky (eds) *Body images: Development, deviance and change* (217–36), New York: Guilford Press.

Pultz, J. (1995) *Photography and the body*, London: Orion.

Raudenbush, B. and Zellner, D. (1997) 'Nobody's satisfied: Effects of abnormal eating behaviours and actual and perceived weight status on body image satisfaction in males and females,' *Journal of Social and Clinical Psychology*, 16: 95–110.

Reid, S. (2000) 'Spot the lollipop ladies,' *The Sunday Times Style Magazine*, 7 May: 10–11.

Rhodes, E. (2004) 'Investigating body piercing: Lived experience and the theory of planned behaviour,' unpublished MSc Health Psychology thesis, Staffordshire University.

Ricciardelli, L.A. and McCabe, M.P. (2001) 'Children's body image concerns and eating disturbance: A review of the literature,' *Clinical Psychology Review*, 21: 325–44.

—— (2002) 'Psychometric evaluation of the Body Change Inventory: An assessment instrument for adolescent boys and girls,' *Eating Behaviors*, 3: 45–59.

—— (2003) 'A longitudinal analysis of the role of biopsychosocial factors in predicting body change strategies among adolescent boys,' *Sex Roles*, 48: 349–59.

—— (2004) 'A biopsychosocial model of disordered eating and the pursuit of muscularity in adolescent boys,' *Psychological Bulletin*, 130: 179–205.

Ricciardelli, L.A., McCabe, M.P. and Ridge, D. (2006) 'The construction of the adolescent male body through sport,' *Journal of Health Psychology*, 11: 577–87.

Ricciardelli, L.A., McCabe, M.P., Mussap, A.J. and Holt, K.E. (in press) 'Body image in preadolescent boys,' in L. Smolak and J.K. Thompson (eds) *Body image, eating disorders and obesity in youth* (2nd edn), Washington, DC: APA.

Ricciardelli, L.A., McCabe, M.P., Williams, R.J. and Thompson, J.K. (in press) 'The role of ethnicity and culture in body image and disordered eating among males,' *Clinical Psychology Review*.

Rich, E. (2005) 'Obesity, eating disorders, and the role of physical education,' paper presented at the British Sociological Association Sport Study Group Conference, Leicester University, 6 May 2005.

Richins, M. (1991) 'Social comparison and the idealised images of advertising,' *Journal of Consumer Research*, 18: 71–83.

Rickert, V., Pawlak-Morello, C., Sheppard, V. and Jay, S. (1992) 'Human growth hormone: A new substance of abuse among adolescents?,' *Clinical Pediatrics*, December: 723–5.

Robinson, T., Killen, J., Litt, I., Hammer, L., Wilson, D., Haydel, F., Hayward, C. and Taylor, B. (1996) 'Ethnicity and body dissatisfaction: Are Hispanic and Asian girls at increased risk for eating disorders?,' *Journal of Adolescent Health*, 19: 384–93.

Robinson, T.N., Chang, J.Y., Haydel, K.F. and Killen, J.D. (2001) 'Overweight concerns and body dissatisfaction among third grade children: The impacts of ethnicity and socioeconomic status,' *Journal of Pediatrics*, 138: 181–7.

Rodin, J., Silberstein, L.R. and Streigel-Moore, R.H. (1985) 'Women and weight: A normative discontent,' in T.B. Sonderegger (ed.) *Nebraska Symposium on Motivation*, Vol. 32, *Psychology and gender* (267–307), Lincoln, NB: University of Nebraska Press.

Rohlinger, D.A. (2002) 'Eroticising men: Cultural influences on advertising and male objectification,' *Sex Roles*, 46: 61–74.

Rosen, J. (1990) 'Body image disturbances in eating disorders,' in T. Cash and T. Pruzinsky (eds) *Body images: Development, deviance and change* (190–214), New York: Guilford Press.

Rotello, G. (1997) *Sexual ecology: AIDS and the destiny of gay men*, New York: Dutton.

Rothblum, E.D. (1990) 'Women and weight: Fad and fiction,' *Journal of Psychology*, 124: 5–24.

—— (2002) 'Gay and lesbian body images,' in T.F. Cash and T. Pruzinsky (eds) *Body image: A handbook of theory, research, and clinical practice* (257–68), New York: Guilford Press.

Rozin, P. and Fallon, A. (1988) 'Body image, attitudes to weight, and misperceptions of figure preferences of the opposite gender: A comparison of men and women in two generations,' *Journal of Abnormal Psychology*, 97: 342–5.

St Martin, L. and Gavey, N. (1996) 'Women's bodybuilding: Feminist resistance and/or femininity's recuperation,' *Body and Society*, 2: 45–57.

Sanders, T. and Bazelgette, P. (1994) *You don't have to diet*, London: Bantam.

Schilder, P. (1950) *The image and appearance of the human body*, New York: International Universities Press.

Schoemer, K. (1996) 'Rockers, models, and the new allure of heroin,' *Newsweek*, 26 August: 50–6.

Schulman, R.G., Kinder, B.N., Powers, P.S., Prange, M. and Glenhorn, A. (1986) 'The development of a scale to measure cognitive distortions in bulimia,' *Journal of Personality Assessment*, 50: 630–9.

Schur, E.A., Sanders, M. and Steiner, H. (2000) 'Body dissatisfaction and dieting in young children,' *International Journal of Eating Disorders*, 27: 74–82.

Secord, P.F. and Jourard, S.M. (1953) 'The appraisal of body cathexis: Body cathexis and the self,' *Journal of Consulting Psychology*, 17: 343–7.

Seligman, M.E.P. and Csikszentmihalyi, M. (2000) 'Positive psychology: An introduction,' *American Psychologist*, 55: 5–14.

Shapiro, H. (1992) 'Adjusting to steroid users,' *Druglink*, 7: 16.

Share, T.L. and Mintz, L.B. (2002) 'Differences between lesbians and heterosexual women in disordered eating and related attitudes,' *Journal of Homosexuality*, 42: 89–106.

Shaw, H., Ramirez, L., Trost, A., Randall, P. and Stice, E. (2004) 'Body image and eating disturbances across ethnic groups: More similarities than differences,' *Psychology of Addictive Behaviors*, 18: 12–18.

Shilling, C. (1993) *The body and social theory*, London: Sage.

Siever, M. (1994) 'Sexual orientation and gender as factors in socioculturally acquired vulnerability to body dissatisfaction and eating disorders,' *Journal of Consulting and Clinical Psychology*, 62: 252–60.

Signorile, M. (1997) *Life outside: The Signorile report on gay men*, New York: Harper.

Silverstein, B., Peterson, B. and Purdue, L. (1986) 'Some correlates of the thin standard of physical attractiveness of women,' *International Journal of Eating Disorders*, 5: 898–905.

Singh, D. (1993) 'Adaptive significance of female physical attractiveness: Role of the waist-to-hip ratio,' *Journal of Personality and Social Psychology*, 65: 293–307.

—— (1995) 'Female judgement of male attractiveness and desirability for relationships: role of the waist-to-hip ratio and financial status,' *Journal of Personality and Social Psychology*, 69: 1089–1101.

Skouteris, H., Carr, R., Wertheim, E.H., Paxton, S.J. and Duncombe, D. (2005) 'A prospective study of factors that lead to body dissatisfaction during pregnancy,' *Body Image: An International Journal of Research*, 2: 347–61.

Slade, P. (1982) 'Toward a functional analysis of anorexia nervosa and bulimia nervosa,' *British Journal of Clinical Psychology*, 21: 167–79.

Slade, P. and Russell, G. (1973) 'Awareness of body dimensions in anorexia nervosa: Cross-sectional and longitudinal studies,' *Psychological Medicine*, 3: 188–99.

Smeets, M.A.M., Smit, F., Panhuysen, G.E.M. and Ingleby, J.D. (1997) 'The influence of methodological differences on the outcome of body size estimation studies in anorexia nervosa,' *British Journal of Clinical Psychology*, 36: 263–77.

—— (1998) 'Body perception index: Benefits, pitfalls, ideas,' *Journal of Psychosomatic Research*, 44: 457–64.

Smith, D. (1990) *Texts, facts and femininity: Exploring the relations of ruling*, New York: Routledge.

Smith, M.C. and Thelen, M.T. (1984) 'Development and validation of a test for bulimia,' *Journal of Consulting and Clinical Psychology*, 52: 863–72.

Smolak, L. (2004) 'Body image in children and adolescents: Where do we go from here?,' *Body Image: An International Journal of Research*, 1: 15–28.

Smolak, L., Murnen, S.K. and Ruble, A.E. (2000) 'Female athletes and eating problems: A meta-analysis,' *International Journal of Eating Disorders*, 27: 371–80.

Snyder, E.E. and Spreitzer, E. (1974) 'Involvement in sports and psychological well-being,' *Research Quarterly*, 44: 249–55.

Snyder, E.E. and Kivlin, J.E. (1975) 'Women athletes and aspects of psychological well-being and body image,' *Research Quarterly*, 46: 191–5.

Snyder, R. and Hansbrouck, L. (1996) 'Feminist ideology, gender traits, and symptoms of disturbed eating among college women,' *Psychology of Women Quarterly*, 20: 593–8.

Sobal, J. and Stunckard, A. (1989) 'Socio-economic status and obesity: A review of the literature,' *Psychological Bulletin*, 105: 260–75.

Sonstroem, R.J. and Morgan, W.P. (1989) 'Exercise and self-esteem: Rationale and model,' *Medicine and Science in Sports and Exercise*, 21: 329–37.

Sorell, G.T. and Nowak, C.G. (1981) 'The role of physical attractiveness as a contributor to individual development,' in R.M. Lerner and N.A. Bush-Rossnagel (eds) *Individuals as producers of their development: A life-span perspective* (389–446), New York: Academic Press.

Sperry, K. (1992) 'Tattoos and tattooing. II. Gross pathology, histopathology, medical complications and applications,' *American Journal of Forensic Medicine and Pathology*, 13(1): 7–17.

Springer, E.A., Winzelberg, A.J., Perkins, R. and Taylor, C.B. (1999) 'Effects of a body image curriculum for college students on improved body image,' *International Journal of Eating Disorders*, 26: 13–20.

Staffieri, J.R. (1967) 'A study of social stereotypes of body image in children,' *Journal of Personality and Social Psychology*, 7: 101–4.

Steese, S., Dollette, M., Phillips, W., Hossfeld, E., Matthews, G. and Taormina, G. (2006) 'Understanding Girls' Circle as an intervention on perceived social support, body image, self efficacy, locus of control, and self-esteem,' *Adolescence*, 41: 55–64.

Stewart, T.M. and Williamson, D.A. (2004) 'Assessment of body image disturbances,' in J.K. Thompson (ed.) *Handbook of eating disorders and obesity* (495–541), New York: Wiley.

Stice, E. and Shaw, H. (2004) 'Eating disorder prevention programs: A meta-analytic review,' *Psychological Bulletin*, 130: 206–27.

Stirn, A. (2003) 'Body piercing: Medical consequences and psychological motivations,' *Lancet*, 361: 1205–15.

Story, M., French, S.A., Resnick, M.D. and Blum, R.W. (1995) 'Ethnic racial and socioeconomic differences in dieting behaviours and body image perceptions in adolescents,' *International Journal of Eating Disorders*, 18(2): 173–9.

Strahan, E.J., Wilson, A.E., Cressman, K.E. and Buote, V.M. (2006) 'Comparing to perfection: How cultural norms for appearance affect social comparisons and self-image,' *Body Image: An International Journal of Research*, 3: 211–28.

Strauman, T.J., Vookle, J., Berenstein, V. and Chaiken, S. (1991) 'Self-discrepancies and vulnerability to body dissatisfaction and disordered eating,' *Journal of Personality and Social Psychology*, 61(6): 946–56.

Strauss, R.H. and Yesalis, C.E. (1991) 'Anabolic steroids in the athlete,' *Annual Review of Medicine*, 42: 449–57.

Striegel-Moore, R.H., Silberstein, L.R. and Rodin, J. (1986) 'Toward an understanding of risk factors for bulimia,' *American Psychologist*, 41: 246–63.

Striegel-Moore, R.H., Tucker, N. and Hsu, J. (1990) 'Body image dissatisfaction and disordered eating in lesbian college students,' *International Journal of Eating Disorders*, 9: 493–500.

Strong, S.M., Williamson, D.A., Netemeyer, R.G. and Geer, J.H. (2000) 'Eating disorder symptoms and concerns about body differ as a function of gender and sexual orientation,' *Journal of Social and Clinical Psychology*, 19: 240–55.

Stunckard, A.J., Sorensen, T. and Schulsinger, F. (1983) 'Use of the Danish adoption register for the study of obesity and thinness,' in S. Kety (ed.) *The genetics of neurological and psychiatric disorders*, New York: Raven Press.

Stunckard, A.J., Harris, J.R., Pedersen, N.L. and McClearn, G.E. (1990) 'A separated twin study of the body mass index,' *New England Journal of Medicine*, 322: 1483–7.

Swami, V., Caprario, C., Tovee, M.J. and Furnham, A. (2006) 'Female physical attractiveness in Britain and Japan: A cross-cultural study,' *European Journal of Personality*, 20: 69–81.

Sweetman, P. (1999) 'Anchoring the (postmodern) self? Body modification, fashion and identity,' *Body and Society*, 5(2–3): 51–76.

Tantleff-Dunn, S. and Thompson, J.K. (1995) 'Romantic partners and body image disturbance: Further evidence for the role of perceived-actual disparities,' *Sex Roles*, 33: 589–605.

Taub, J. (1999) 'Bisexual women and beauty norms: A qualitative examination,' *Journal of Lesbian Studies*, 3: 27–36.

Taylor, C. (1997) 'Does my bum look big in this?,' *The Independent on Sunday*, 11 May.

Taylor, M.J. and Cooper, P.J. (1986) 'Body size overestimation and depressed mood,' *British Journal of Clinical Psychology*, 14: 134–46.

Taylor, S. (1995) *Health psychology* (3rd edn), London: McGraw-Hill.

Teachman, B.A. and Brownell, K.D. (2001) 'Implicit anti-fat bias among health professionals: Is anyone immune?,' *International Journal of Obesity*, 25: 1–7.

Thomas, T. (1993) 'Slimming eats into new man's soul,' *The European*, 12 November.

Thompson, J.K. and Spana, R.E. (1988) 'The adjustable light beam method for the assessment of size estimation accuracy: Description, psychometrics and normative data,' *International Journal of Eating Disorders*, 7: 521–6.

Thompson, J.K. and Tantleff, S. (1992) 'Female and male ratings of upper torso: Actual, ideal, and stereotypical conceptions,' *Journal of Social Behavior and Personality*, 7: 345–54.

Thompson, J.K. and Stice, E. (2001) 'Thin-ideal internalization: Mounting evidence for a new risk factor for body-image disturbance and eating pathology,' *Current Directions in Psychological Science*, 10(5): 181–3.

Thompson, J.K. and Van Den Berg, P. (2002) 'Measuring body image attitudes among adolescents and adults,' in T.F. Cash and T. Pruzinsky (eds) *Body image. A handbook of theory, research, and clinical practice* (142–254), New York: Guilford Press.

Thompson, J.K. and Cafri, G. (eds) (2007) *The muscular ideal*, Washington, DC: American Psychological Association.

Thompson, J.K., Penner, L. and Altabe, M. (1990) 'Procedures, problems, and progress in the assessment of body images,' in T. Cash and T. Pruzinsky (eds) *Body images: Development, deviance and change* (21–46), New York: Guilford Press.

Thompson, J.K., Heinberg, L., Altabe, M. and Tantleff-Dunn, S. (1999) *Exacting beauty: Theory, assessment, and treatment of body image disturbance*, Washington, DC: American Psychological Association.

Thompson, S., Corwin, S. and Sargeant, R. (1997) 'Ideal body size beliefs and weight concerns in fourth grade children,' *International Journal of Eating Disorders*, 21: 279–84.

Thornhill, R. and Gangestad, S.W. (1994) 'Human fluctuating asymmetry and sexual behavior,' *Psychological Science*, 5: 297–302.

Tiggemann, M. (1992) 'Body-size dissatisfaction: Individual differences in age and gender, and relationship with self-esteem,' *Personality and Individual Differences*, 13: 39–43.

—— (1996) ' "Thinking" versus "feeling" fat: Correlates of two indices of body image dissatisfaction,' *Australian Journal of Psychology*, 48: 21–5.

—— (2002) 'Media influences on body image development,' in T.F. Cash and T. Pruzinsky (eds) *Body image: A handbook of theory, research, and clinical practice* (91–8), New York: Guilford Press.

—— (2003) 'Media exposure, body dissatisfaction and disordered eating: Television and magazines are not the same!,' *European Eating Disorders Review*, 11: 418–30.

—— (2004) 'Body image across the adult lifespan: Stability and change,' *Body Image: An International Journal of Research*, 1: 29–41.

—— (2005) 'Body dissatisfaction and adolescent self-esteem: Prospective findings,' *Body Image: An International Journal of Research*, 2: 129–36.

—— (2006) 'The role of media exposure in adolescent girls' body dissatisfaction and drive for thinness: Prospective results,' *Journal of Social and Clinical Psychology*, 25(5): 523–41).

Tiggemann, M. and Rothblum, E. (1988) 'Gender differences and social consequences of perceived overweight in the United States and Australia,' *Sex Roles*, 18: 75–86.

Tiggemann, M. and Pennington, B. (1990) 'The development of gender differences in body-size dissatisfaction,' *Australian Psychologist*, 25: 306–13.

Tiggemann, M. and Pickering, A.S. (1996) 'The role of television in adolescent women's body dissatisfaction and drive for thinness,' *International Journal of Eating Disorders*, 20: 199–203.

Tiggemann, M. and Williamson, S. (2000) 'The effect of exercise on body satisfaction and self-esteem as a function of gender and age,' *Sex Roles*, 43: 119–27.

Tiggemann, M. and Slater, A. (2001) 'A test of objectification theory in former dancers and nondancers,' *Psychology of Women Quarterly*, 25: 57–64.

Tiggemann, M. and Golder, F. (2006) 'Tattooing: An expression of uniqueness in the appearance domain,' *Body Image: An International Journal of Research*, 3: 309–16.

Toro, J., Castro, J., Garcia, M., Perez, P. and Cuesta, L. (1989) 'Eating attitudes, sociodemographic factors, and body shape evaluation in adolescence,' *British Journal of Medical Psychology*, 62: 61–70.

Touyz, S.W., Beaumont, P.J.V. and Collins, J.K. (1984) 'Body shape perception and its disturbance in anorexia nervosa,' *British Journal of Psychiatry*, 144: 167–71.

Tovee, M.J. and Cornelissen, P.L. (2001) 'Female and male perceptions of female physical attractiveness in front-view and profile,' *British Journal of Psychology*, 92: 391–402.

Tricker, R., O'Neill, M.R. and Cook, D. (1989) 'The incidence of anabolic steroid use among competitive body-builders,' *Journal of Drug Education*, 19: 313–25.

Truby, H. and Paxton, S. (2002) 'Development of the Children's Body Image Scale,' *British Journal of Clinical Psychology*, 41: 185–203.

Turner, B.S. (1992) *Regulating bodies: Essays in medical sociology*, London: Routledge.

—— (1999) 'The possibilities of primitiveness: Towards a sociology of body marks in cool societies,' *Body and Society*, 5(2–3): 39–50.

Turtle, J., Jones, A. and Hickman, M. (1997) *Young people and health: The health behaviour of school-aged children*, London: Health Education Authority.

Tykla, T.L., Bergeron, D. and Schwartz, J.P. (2005) 'Development and psychometric evaluation of the Male Body Attitudes Scale (MBAS),' *Body Image: An International Journal of Research*, 2: 161–75.

Tyler, C.A. (1991) 'Boys will be girls: The politics of gay drag,' in D. Fuss (ed.) *Inside out: Lesbian theories, gay theories* (32–70), New York: Routledge.

Ussher, J. (ed.) (1993) *The psychology of the female body*, London: Routledge.

Ussher, J. (1997) *Body talk: The material and discursive regulation of sexuality, madness and reproduction*, London: Routledge.

Vartanian, L.R., Herman, C.P. and Polivy, J. (2005) 'Implicit and explicit attitudes toward fatness and thinness: The role of the internalisation of societal standards,' *Body Image: An International Journal of Research*, 2: 373–82.

Vernon, P. (2001) 'Lean, clean and maybe a little mean—21st century woman is kicking sand in the face of the waif,' *The Independent on Sunday: Life Etc. Supplement*, 24 June: 1.

Villeneuve, P.J., Holloway, E.J., Brisson, J., Xie, L., Ugnat, A., Latulippe, L. and Mao, Y. (2006) 'Mortality among Canadian women with cosmetic breast implants,' *American Journal of Epidemiology*, 164: 334–41.

Viner, K. (1997) 'The new plastic feminism,' *The Guardian*, 4 July: 5.

Von Soest, T., Kvalem, I.L., Skolleborg, K.C. and Roald, H.E. (2006) 'Psychosocial factors predicting the motivation to undergo cosmetic surgery,' *Plastic and Reconstructive Surgery*, 117: 51–62.

Wadden, T., Brown, G., Foster, G. and Linowitz, J. (1991) 'Salience of weight-related worries in adolescent males and females,' *International Journal of Eating Disorders*, 10: 407–14.

Wannamethee, G. and Shaper, A.G. (1990) 'Weight change in middle-aged British men: Implications for health,' *European Journal of Clinical Nutrition*, 44: 133–42.

Ward, T. (1983) *Against ageism*, Newcastle: Search Project.

Wardle, J. and Marsland, L. (1990) 'Adolescent concerns about weight and eating: A social-developmental perspective,' *Journal of Psychosomatic Research*, 34: 377–91.

Wardle, J., Bindra, R., Fairclough, B. and Westcombe, A. (1993) 'Culture and body image: Body perception and weight concern in young Asian and Caucasian British women,' *Journal of Community and Applied Social Psychology*, 3: 173–81.

Warren, C. and Cooper, P.J. (1988) 'Psychological effects of dieting,' *British Journal of Clinical Psychology*, 27: 269–70.

Welch, C., Gross, S.M., Bronner, Y., Dewberry-Moore, P. and Paige, D.M. (2004) 'Discrepancies in body image perception among fourth-grade public school children from urban, suburban, and rural Maryland,' *Journal of the American Dietetic Association*, 104: 1080–5.

Wells, W. and Siegel, B. (1961) 'Stereotyped somatotypes,' *Psychological Reports*, 8: 77–8.

Werlinger, K., King, T., Clark, M., Pera, V. and Wincze, J. (1997) 'Perceived changes in sexual functioning and body image following weight loss in an obese female population: A pilot study,' *Journal of Sex and Marital Therapy*, 23: 74–8.

Wheatley, J. (2006) 'Like mother like daughter: The young copycat dieters,' *The Times*, 11 August: 6–7.

Whitehead, M. (1988) 'The health divide,' in P. Townsend, N. Davidson and M. Whitehead (eds) *Inequalities in health* (217–357), Harmondsworth UK: Penguin.

Wiederman, M. and Pryor, T. (1997) 'Body dissatisfaction and sexuality among women with bulimia nervosa,' *International Journal of Eating Disorders*, 21: 361–5.

Wilcosky, T., Hyde, J., Anderson, J.J.B., Bangdiwula, S. and Duncan, B. (1990) 'Obesity and mortality in the Lipid Research Clinics Program Follow-up Study,' *Journal of Clinical Epidemiology*, 43: 743–52.

Williams, L.K., Ricciardelli, L.A., McCabe, M.P., Waqa, G.G. and Bavadra, K. (2006) 'Body image attitudes and concerns among indigenous Fijian and European Australian adolescent girls,' *Body Image: An International Journal of Research*, 3: 275–88.

Williamson, S. and Delin, C. (2001) 'Young children's figural selections; accuracy of reporting and body size dissatisfaction,' *International Journal of Eating Disorders*, 29(1): 80–4.

Wilson, A.E. and Ross, M. (2000) 'The frequency of temporal self and social comparisons in people's personal appraisals,' *Journal of Personality and Social Psychology*, 78: 928–42.

Wilson, E. (1997) 'Why are more men having cosmetic surgery?,' *The Express*, 18 February: 48–9.

Wolf, N. (1991) *The beauty myth: How images of beauty are used against women*, New York: William Morrow.

Wooley, O., Wooley, S. and Dyrenforth, S. (1979) 'Obesity and women,' *Women's Studies International Quarterly*, 2: 81–92.

Wright, S, Grogan, S. and Hunter, G. (2000) 'Motivations for anabolic steroid use among bodybuilders,' *Journal of Health Psychology*, 5: 566–72.

—— (2001) 'Body-builders' attitudes towards steroid use,' *Drugs: Education, Prevention and Policy*, 8: 91–5.

Wykes, M. and Gunter, B. (2005) *The media and body image*, London: Sage.

Yamamiya, Y., Cash, T.F., Melnyk, S.E., Posavak, H.D. and Posavac, S.S. (2005) 'Women's exposure to thin-and-beautiful media images: Body image effects of media-ideal internalisation and impact-reduction interventions,' *Body Image: An International Journal of Research*, 2: 74–80.

Yates, A., Edman, J. and Aruguete, M. (2004) 'Ethnic differences in BMI and body/self dissatisfaction among whites, Asian subgroups, Pacific Islanders, and African Americans,' *Journal of Adolescent Health*, 34: 300–7.

Yelland, C. and Tiggemann, M. (2003) 'Muscularity and the gay ideal: Body dissatisfaction and disordered eating in homosexual men,' *Eating Behaviors*, 4: 107–16.

Yesalis, C. and Bahrke, M. (1995) 'Anabolic-androgenic steroids,' *Sports Medicine*, 19: 326–40.

Yingling, T. (1991) 'AIDS in America: Postmodern governance, identity and experience,' in D. Fuss (ed.) *Inside out: Lesbian theories, gay theories* (291–310), New York: Routledge.

# Name index

Note: *italic* page numbers denote references to Plates/Figures.

# Subject index

Note: *italic* page numbers denote references to Plates/Figures.

CPSIA information can be obtained at www.ICGtesting.com
Printed in the USA
BVOW05s2018050116

431887BV00011B/159/P